The Hidden Roots of Critical Psychology

The Hidden Roots of Critical Psychology

Understanding the Impact of Locke, Shaftesbury and Reid

Michael Billig

SAGE Publications
Los Angeles • London • New Delhi • Singapore

SAGE Publications Ltd
1 Oliver's Yard
55 City Road
London EC1Y 1SP

SAGE Publications Inc.
2455 Teller Road
Thousand Oaks, California 91320

SAGE Publications India Pvt Ltd
B 1/I 1 Mohan Cooperative Industrial Area
Mathura Road
New Delhi 110 044

SAGE Publications Asia-Pacific Pte Ltd
33 Pekin Street #02-01
Far East Square
Singapore 048763

Library of Congress Control Number: 2007933831

British Library Cataloguing in Publication data

A catalogue record for this book is available from
the British Library

ISBN 978-1-4129-4723-7
ISBN 978-1-4129-4724-4 (pbk)

Typeset by CEPHA Imaging Pvt. Ltd., Bangalore, India
Printed in Great Britain by The Cromwell Press,
Trowbridge, Wiltshire
Printed on paper from sustainable resources

To Sheila

Contents

Foreword

This is a quite extraordinary and original book. Michael Billig has managed to seamlessly interweave the history of philosophy, history of psychology, critical psychology and a deep grasp of the social nature of language, and, moreover, has done so in very readable fashion. Ostensibly centred on the long-marginalized figure of Anthony Ashley Cooper, the 3rd Earl of Shaftesbury, John Locke's pupil and, later, philosophical opponent, what the book really does is revolutionize our understanding of modern critical psychology's roots and invent what is almost a new mode or genre of historically informed psychological writing (or perhaps that should be the other way round). Especially exciting is the freshness of viewpoint he brings to the seventeenth- and eighteenth-century material, the immersion in which he obviously relishes. To top it off, Billig periodically throws in challenging and humorous remarks and asides, making entirely novel connections and highlighting amusing ironies, as well as displaying a capacity for impressive historical detective work. Locke and Shaftesbury are soon jostling with Bakhtin, Thomas Reid, Ernst Cassirer, Kenneth Gergen, Wittgenstein, Diderot and others from widely scattered points of the intellectual compass. And yet, at heart, this remains a very astute and sometimes moving account of Shaftesbury's own brief career and a plea for acknowledging his enduring philosophical importance. But there's the rub, for to do so would, he shows, entail rethinking the nature of psychology itself. Billig is a creative thinker of the first order, and this work will become essential reading for critical psychologists, historians of psychology and philosophers. It *ought* to be essential for mainstream psychologists as well.

Graham Richards
Formerly Professor, History of Psychology, Staffordshire University
Director, British Psychological Society History of Psychology Centre,
London

1 Introduction

On September 29, 1694, a young man wrote to his old teacher and family friend about the progress of his studies. No, he had not made any new discoveries, he wrote. And if he had, he would have kept quiet about them. Mankind did not need any more so-called inventions. So, it was all the better that he had little to report. Perhaps, down the ages, young people have written in this way to teachers and parents, justifying why their youthful promise was remaining unfulfilled. Such letters hardly deserve to be preserved for posterity. But this letter was different. It symbolizes a crucial moment in the history of psychology – but it is a moment that has become forgotten, even hidden.

The teacher was John Locke, whose *Essay Concerning Human Understanding* sought to show how the human mind operated. Locke's *Essay* has been justly hailed as one of the great books in psychology's early history. It changed the way that later generations thought about the human mind and it laid the basis for today's cognitive psychology. The young man would become the third Earl of Shaftesbury. His name is no longer familiar today, particularly among psychologists. Yet, in arguing against the views of Locke, he proposed a very different way of understanding human nature. He was, it will be suggested, a great psychological thinker, whose ideas deserve far more than the general neglect that is their present fate.

To recognize the intellectual importance of Shaftesbury requires a rewriting of psychology's history. In most histories of psychology, he does not even figure as a footnote. The first volume of a recent magisterial *Handbook of Psychology* was devoted to the history of psychology (Freedheim, 2003). None of the contributors to this large volume mention Shaftesbury. He is beyond the scope of psychology's past, as seen by psychologists. Any claim to the contrary involves reversing a number of assumptions that have become entrenched within the discipline. This is why the revision is so important: more is at stake than events that occurred over three centuries ago.

Of course, the temptation is to ask why on earth psychologists should bother with Locke and the third Earl. The topic might be vaguely interesting in its own right, but surely it hardly merits great attention. Academic psychologists are extremely busy people. They have studies to design, data to analyse, papers to write. From all sides, the journals keep rolling out new research reports. One must not slip behind. International congresses must be attended, sponsored workshops organized and opportunities for funding pursued. There is simply too much to be done. It seems unreasonable to expect psychologists to attend to exchanges between long dead figures. The past will have to wait for the peaceful, future moment that never seems to arrive.

Nevertheless, there are a good number of reasons why Locke and Shaftesbury – and other figures discussed in this book, such as Thomas Reid and Pierre Gassendi – matter to the present. The past is never finished. As new intellectual challenges arise, so our views of the past change. Sometimes it is necessary to ask what the conventional views are overlooking: what is being concealed today by the histories that have been regularly told? Is there something decisive that needs to be recaptured? The works of Shaftesbury, with their wholly different psychological insights, are one such gain from a revision. They are, indeed, a treasure worth digging up.

There are particular reasons why the re-evaluation of psychology's past is so timely. At present, the orthodox ways of doing psychology are being challenged by the emergence of new forms of psychology. These new forms can be loosely bracketed under the heading of 'critical psychology'. The label is not entirely felicitous, but it will do for present purposes. Critical psychology includes such trends as social constructionism, post-modern psychology, discursive psychology and a number of forms of feminist psychology. By and large, the critical psychologists accuse conventional psychologists of having an overly narrow view of humans.

This can be seen in relation to a key, psychological question: how do we get our ideas of the world? The dominant form of psychology over the past thirty years has been cognitive psychology. In answering the question, cognitive psychologists tend to look towards the functioning of the individual brain or mind. They seek to understand how an individual receives information from their senses, computes this information and structures it into representations of the world. By and large, critical psychologists take issue with this perspective. They contend that we do not construct our ideas of the world purely from our own individual minds. We receive ideas from others. Thus, our ideas, even before they enter our minds and become ours, have a long, social history. In this way, our minds – or, rather, our ways of thinking – are constructed by the social processes of history.

In this clash, two visions of psychology can be discerned. The cognitive perspective is concerned with the processes of individual thought.

The analysis of society is left to sociologists, social historians and other social scientists. It is, as it were, put beyond the boundaries of psychology. The critical perspective, by contrast, seeks to break down these disciplinary boundaries. It claims that the analysis of the individual mind cannot be separated from understanding social processes, for the so-called 'individual mind' is always part of the wider social world. It is easy for critical psychologists to imagine that, in posing this challenge to cognitive psychology, they are breaking with established patterns of thinking and, thereby, proposing new ideas.

This is where the confrontation between Locke and Shaftesbury is so fascinating and so important. In many respects, their differences three hundred years ago mirror the debates of today. Locke was the cognitivist, shutting out history from his analysis of the mind. Shaftesbury was deeply immersed in history, stressing the social nature of humans. Their respective views of the human condition reflected their views of their own work. Locke imagined that he was doing something entirely novel, breaking with past traditions of understanding. Shaftesbury always took the historical perspective. He connected his own vision of the human condition, as well as Locke's opposing vision, with a long history that stretched back to ancient times.

One big difference between critical and cognitive perspectives lies in their respective stances towards history. According to the critical perspective, historical and social analyses are part of psychology. There is no firm boundary to demarcate exactly where the psychology stops, and where the history starts. If we are examining how history creates patterns of thinking – how social processes create the individual mind – then there cannot be a clear boundary. For this reason, the present inquiry is not purely, or even primarily, a study of history. Strictly speaking, it is not a history *of* psychology: as if history is the subject and psychology is the object. The psychology and the history are mixed together. This is as much a psychological investigation – or, at least, an investigation of psychological ideas – as it is a historical one. It is, if anything, a plea for psychological ideas to be understood historically.

This applies to the critical perspective itself. If the critical perspective is to be genuinely historical, as well as being genuinely critical, then it needs to pay critical attention to its own history. This is where the necessity for revising the history of psychology comes in. Any sustained challenge to the present ways of doing psychology should involve a challenge to the way that its past is understood. The matter can be put quite simply. Critical psychologists are arguing that the scope of psychology should be widened. Ways of thinking and doing research, which were not traditionally part of the discipline of psychology, are now being encouraged. These new forms of psychology have not come into the world without a past. They, too, have a history. As they become part of psychology, so they should be bringing with themselves a different past into the scope of psychology.

A figure such as the third Earl of Shaftesbury would scarcely have seemed a psychologist a while ago. He did not conduct experiments or write treatises that sought to systematize the inner processes of thinking. In the eyes of standard experimentalists or today's cognitive scientists he is not recognizable as a psychological thinker. However, it will be argued that many of the central themes of his writing anticipate post-modern ways of understanding the nature and practice of thinking. The parallels can, indeed, be quite striking. On so many matters, Shaftesbury's ideas resemble those of Mikhail Bakhtin, who has been so influential in recent years, especially within critical psychology. Thus, with the emergence of critical psychology, Shaftesbury becomes identifiable as a psychological thinker.

In addition, Shaftesbury's ideas about the importance of 'common sense' influenced the philosophers of the Scottish Enlightenment in the eighteenth century. Thomas Reid took up the notion of 'common sense' and developed it in an original way. In so doing, Reid anticipated the ordinary language philosophy of the twentieth century and, in particular, what has come to be known as Speech Act theory. Discursive psychologists, who criticize the theories and methodologies of cognitive psychology, have been using Speech Act theory to investigate how language, and particularly how psychological language, is used in everyday life. In doing this, they are using ideas and insights with a longer history than is often supposed.

One might ask why this history is not generally appreciated. The present book is not primarily an investigation into the forgetting of thinkers such as Shaftesbury and Reid – that would require an examination of the nineteenth century rather than the eighteenth. However, the issue cannot be avoided. It is possible to point to occasions when the historical roots have not merely been forgotten; they have also been wilfully neglected and sometimes even hidden. The story of critical psychology's hidden roots therefore, includes stories about accusations of plagiarism.

Structure of the Book

In general outline, the book will move forward in time. After a theoretical chapter, examining the relations between psychology and history, there will be two chapters on Locke. Then there will be three chapters on Shaftesbury. And finally there is a chapter on Reid. The sequence is clear, going from the late seventeenth century, when Locke published his *Essay*, through to the late eighteenth century, when Reid's final works appeared. Because this is a psychological investigation, as well as a historical one, the narrative does not simply move forward. Past psychological ideas are continually being reflected against present ones.

The narrative movement not only shuttles between past and present, but also between the early modernity and an even more distant past. Locke may be thought to be a starting-point. He may have imagined that he owed no intellectual debts to forebears. But his ideas, as Shaftesbury argued, have a history. And so, in considering Locke, the movement is not only forwards, to see how his ideas fare in terms of modern cognitive science. The movement also goes backwards to his neglected forebear, Pierre Gassendi, and from there even further back to the Epicureans of the ancient world. A chronological table is included following the last chapter, in order to help readers unfamiliar with the events and periods discussed.

The first of the Locke chapters outlines his cognitive approach, which came to be known as his 'way of ideas'. The radical nature of Locke's 'way of ideas' cannot be appreciated without some understanding of the dangerous times in which he lived and worked. Therefore Locke's life and its political context are described. In this chapter, Locke's ideas about the mind will be evaluated in terms of modern cognitive science. The second Locke chapter attempts to go further. It examines the historical roots of Locke's own ideas, questioning the cognitive account that he tried to give of his own thoughts. Locke claimed that he spun his ideas from his own mind. The record is much more ambiguous. There are much longer lines of historical continuity.

The following three chapters deal with Shaftesbury. The first of these three chapters outlines Shaftesbury's life and his relations with Locke. There we meet the young letter-writer tactlessly dismissing the 'discoveries' of thinkers such as his teacher and showing his impatience with Locke's sort of cognitive psychology. The ancient ideas of stoicism were attracting him. In the second of these three chapters, we find Shaftesbury reacting against the basis of Locke's cognitivism and particularly against his individualism. Shaftesbury emphasized the social nature of humans; we are not merely driven by individual motives but we possess moral and aesthetic natures. Locke's theories of judgement were, in Shaftesbury's view, fundamentally flawed. And so was Locke's failure to develop a full historical consciousness.

The third chapter on Shaftesbury discusses how the third Earl proposed some surprisingly post-modern views about the mind. He emphasized the importance of language, suggesting that we discover truths through dialogue, and especially through using ridicule in conversation. Thinking is not an inner, perceptual process, as Locke envisaged, but it involves dialogues with the self; and that necessitates a divided ego. Generally, Shaftesbury championed contradictions and varieties of opinion – or what Bakhtin in the twentieth century would call 'heteroglossia'. On a whole range of issues, Shaftesbury was proposing a pre-Bakhtinian psychology. This is not entirely surprising, given some hidden links.

Chapter eight traces the influence of Shaftesbury on Reid and then shows how Reid systematically challenged Locke's 'way of ideas'. In doing this, Reid was developing an approach that would become associated many years later with Wittgenstein. Reid was criticizing metaphysical speculation in the name of common sense. Most importantly, he was questioning the reality of Locke's concept of 'ideas'. Reid's criticisms could just as easily be applied to the notions of 'mental representation' or 'cognition', as used today in cognitive science. Reid's view that we do things with words – rather than use words to mirror ideas – was an argument directed against Locke. More than that, it strikingly anticipates the view of language which was seemingly created anew in the mid-nineteenth century and which is currently so influential in discursive psychology today. Again, there has been forgetting in the interests of celebrating the so-called 'new'.

Caveats

One problem with tracing the history of psychology back into the early modern period is that the word 'psychology' was not then in general use, at least not in English. Locke, when he was writing about the nature of understanding in his *Essay*, believed that he was writing philosophy, not psychology. At that time, the term 'philosophy' had a much wider significance. The natural sciences, then, were typically described as being 'natural philosophy'. The borders between 'natural philosophy' and 'philosophy' were porous. There were no guards checking documents to see which side of the boundary particular thinkers belonged to. The result is that the thinkers discussed here often used 'philosophy' in ways that today would include psychology.

Readers will not be continually warned about the undisciplinary use of the word 'philosophy'. For example, a later chapter will mention a letter Shaftesbury wrote complaining of Locke's theory. According to Shaftesbury, Locke was implying that all desires have to be learnt. Very poor philosophy, Shaftesbury commented. There will be no addition in brackets, warning readers that Shaftesbury actually meant 'Very poor psychology'.

In part, the absence of routine warnings about the word 'philosophy' reflects stylistic considerations. To avoid continually breaking up the text, it is hoped that this general warning will suffice. In part, there is a theoretical reason for the absence of continual reminders. By and large, critical psychologists regret the expulsion of philosophy (as well as other disciplines) from the disciplinary territories that psychologists have founded for themselves and that they jealously protect. Continual reminders would have the effect of suggesting that certain matters are 'really' psychological while others are 'really' philosophical. In this way, the reminders might have the effect of re-instating boundaries that merit being challenged.

A word about quotation is also necessary. Late seventeenth and early eighteenth century English does not look the same as modern English. Most obviously, there are differences in spelling and the use of capital letters. In those days, letter-writers were very free with their spellings and abbreviations. There is more than a passing resemblance between the letter-writing of that period and modern codes of text-messaging. For the sake of convenience, quotations from early English printed texts and letters have been rendered into standard, modern English formats. For this reason, Lawrence Klein's text of Shaftesbury's *Characteristicks* is used, for Klein has already undertaken this task of linguistic modernization. But, as the previous sentence indicates, there is one inconsistency. For the name of Shaftesbury's great work, the old spelling has been retained. Modernizing the title of that obstinately un-modern work seems to take away more than just the penultimate letter.

Telling the story of Locke and Shaftesbury, of course, does not mean that there are no other historical stories worth telling. The present account concentrates on the development of psychological ideas and counter-ideas in Britain, at the expense of similar developments elsewhere. Certainly, late seventeenth century Britain was a special place. The scientific spirit was in the air. The Royal Society was founded, with Locke as an early member. Newton and Boyle, both of whom were friends of Locke, were uncovering the secrets of the universe. As will be argued, Shaftesbury was reacting against the idea that the scientific spirit would transform our knowledge of ourselves, as it was transforming our knowledge of atoms, gravity and corpuscles.

Although critical psychologists have largely ignored Shaftesbury's reaction to Locke, some have sought to find other early modern roots for their ideas. They have tended to look towards Italy, rather than Britain. Some have seen Giambattista Vico as an early radical thinker, who recognized the social nature of humans (e.g., Glasersfeld, 1984; Shotter, 1986 and 1993c). There would be good reason to explore in detail the links between Shaftesbury's and Vico's ideas. The issue will be touched upon in the first chapter on Shaftesbury. But one thing can be predicted with a fair degree of confidence. If there are links between Vico's and Shaftesbury's ideas, then the links should run from Shaftesbury to Vico, rather than in the opposite direction. The remembering of Vico as an early psychological thinker makes the forgetting of Shaftesbury all the more poignant.

There is another matter. This concerns the selection of intellectual ancestors. It may be objected that the present account of the past is only being extended to encompass more males. In the case of the third earl and his views on gender, there is much to make the contemporary admirer cringe with embarrassment. It must be conceded that this search for roots predominantly uncovers male contributions. But it is not an exclusively male story. Along the way, we will also see Lady Damaris Masham make her philosophical entrance, albeit all too briefly. The present work will mention Shaftesbury's use of Epictetus and, less centrally, Condillac's debt to Locke. However, it will not explore the intellectual contribution to the times made by Elizabeth Carter, the seventeenth century blue-stocking who translated Epictetus into English; nor will it discuss Mlle Ferrand, who, as Condillac admitted in the preface to his *Traité des sensations*, was the intellectual genius behind that work and deserved to be credited as its author (Condillac, 1754/1798, pp. 12ff). It would be too much of a diversion to go into these stories. Without a doubt, these tales should be told.

Theoretical reasons can be given for recounting the history of Locke and Shaftesbury. Theory, however, has its limitations. There is an additional reason: it is a wonderful story. The personal relations between the two are probably unique within the history of ideas. Once the history of ideas becomes a dry account of concepts, removed from all considerations of personality, politics and private life, then something crucial is lost. Accordingly, the story of Locke and Shaftesbury deserves to be re-told, as a tale which mixes the personal and the philosophical. This makes the story of their disagreement all the more fascinating.

2   History and Psychology

Before getting down to the stories of Locke, Shaftesbury and Reid, some preliminary words are necessary, in order to justify why psychologists, and especially critical psychologists, should take the past seriously. The argument is not that it would be nice if psychologists were to show an interest in history. The argument is stronger. On its own terms, critical psychology demands a historical awareness – not as an optional extra but as a crucial component. Kenneth Gergen, one of the most influential and creative of critical psychologists, has for the past thirty or so years been arguing that psychology is – or rather, should be – historical. He outlined this view in a classic paper which stated that psychology does not stand outside of history but is 'primarily a historical inquiry' (1973, p. 310).

This chapter will explore the implications of Gergen's argument. If psychological ideas are to be understood historically, then this applies just as much to the ideas of critical psychology as it does to those of more mainstream psychology. This means that critical psychologists should seek to be historically self-reflexive, exploring the roots of their own ideas. Taking a longer perspective on psychological ideas may guard against the assumption that today's ideas are fundamentally new and, thus, totally modern – or, rather, given the passé nature of modernity, totally post-modern.

De-Historicized Psychology

Gergen's paper was published in one of the major journals for experimental social psychology. At the time, it provoked a great deal of fuss in social psychological circles. Established social psychologists wrote angrily to the journal's editors. They objected that Gergen was challenging the view that psychology was a natural science. In effect, Gergen was threatening the barrier that supposedly separated scientific psychology from unscientific arts subjects such as history. That was the problem. Psychologists did not want to find themselves positioned on the wrong side of this imagined border: they wanted to be on the scientific side. Years later, Gergen was to write that his professional colleagues castigated him 'for nihilism' and then proceeded to ignore his arguments completely (Gergen, 1994, p. x; see also Gergen, 1997, pp. 117f).

There are a number of reasons why mainstream, experimental psychologists would wish to distinguish their discipline from that of history. One critic of the prevailing ethos in psychology has commented that 'experimentalism reigns in the psychology produced in universities and research institutes' and that 'its status surpasses all other contenders for the production of scientific knowledge about the psyche' (Morawski, 2005, p. 78). Experimental scientists like to distinguish their methods from arts-based inquiries. Psychologists have long claimed that their study of humans is not based upon 'subjective' biases, but upon 'objective' analyses of the 'facts'. The 'facts' are the data that are produced by controlled, experimental situations.

According to this perspective, historians, in common with literary scholars or philosophers, deal with opinions rather than 'objective facts'. Historians lack complete records of the past. They have to fill in gaps as they tell stories about what happened. They cannot run experiments to test hypotheses. A historian might claim that Protestantism was vital to the development of capitalism in the early modern period. Supporting evidence might be assembled. A plausible story might be told. But the thesis can never be 'proved' to the rigorous standards demanded by an experimental scientist, such as a chemist or physicist. No controlled experiment could be conducted on past events. One cannot re-run the processes of European history, this time controlling for factors such as Henry VIII's divorce, the doctrines of Martin Luther and the failure of the Catholic Church to stop the selling of pardons, in order to assess what precise weightings these 'variables' would have on the rise of capitalism.

By contrast, experimental psychologists seek absolute control of the micro-situations that they create. They aspire to control rigidly the messiness of history and social life within their laboratory walls. One group of experimental subjects will be told to do a certain task, while another group does this same task but with one vital difference. All extra 'contaminating' variables are to be excluded. Any variations in performance between the two groups can then attributed to that single variable that differed, for everything else happened in precisely the same way. That is the logic of the well-designed experiment. For experimental psychologists, this logic provides the very rationale of their discipline, elevating it above disciplines that are methodologically undisciplined.

In the eyes of experimentalists, history belongs on the side of the undisciplined. Historians have no rigorously repeatable methods that enable them time and again to produce 'true facts'. Instead, they have to rely on judgement, guesswork and, worst of all, imagination. Gergen has recently described the relations between historians and psychologists. Orthodox psychologists, he writes, treat historians 'with little more than tolerant civility'. They claim that history lacks the proper 'controlled and systematic' research methods that characterize experimental psychology. Moreover, psychologists view historians as looking backwards, 'when the proper emphasis should be placed on building knowledge for the future' (Gergen, 2001a, p. 82).

Gergen's original argument was directed against the way that psychologists place their trust in experimentation. Psychologists, according to Gergen, hope that the laboratory will reveal basic, and therefore universal, processes of human psychology. They assume that what they observe in the controlled conditions of the laboratory can be generalized: the laboratory reveals the psychological processes of all humans, whatever the social conditions and historic times in which they live. Experimentalists accordingly tend to treat their experimental subjects as if they represented de-historicized, universal figures.

When Gergen was writing, most of the important theories of social psychology were universal theories. Such theories claim that humans are driven by basic motives – such as the desire to have consistent attitudes, to have positive identities or to compare one's fortunes with those of others. These motives were presumed to be found in all societies and in all historical epochs. It was assumed that ancient Mayans, Greeks or indigenous inhabitants of Australasia all would wish to have consistent beliefs and to reduce 'cognitive dissonance'. Under controlled laboratory conditions they would behave just as the citizens of modern America had done.

Gergen argued that this assumption of universality was mistaken, for the simple reason that our behaviour is socially and historically bounded. Mental states are socially constructed: there is no universal law of 'dissonance-reduction' or 'social comparison'. The patterns being explored in American laboratories were reflections of a particular time and place: they were not indicators of basic, trans-historical motivations. Whether people will reduce dissonance or compare themselves to others – and how they will do so – depends on historical circumstances. The results of social psychological experiments could well be different if repeated at a different point in history. Indeed, there was always the possibility of what Gergen termed the 'historical invalidation of psychological theory' (1973, p. 313). If the results of the experiments become common knowledge, then it is likely that future experimental subjects will behave differently when they find themselves in those laboratory situations that they already know about.

Gergen was making a theoretical point, rather than a methodological one. He was not arguing that social psychologists need to repeat their experiments across different time frames in order to 'control' for an ever greater number of historical factors. Gergen was saying that we need to change the way we understand the processes of psychology and, in particular, psychologists need to develop a consciousness of history. Gergen has subsequently repeated his criticisms of psychology's tendency to universalize (e.g., Gergen, 1992; 1999; and 2001a). How people think, react, feel towards others in one age is no guide to how they might experience the world in very different historical circumstances. If social actions are situated in history, then, according to Gergen, social psychology must be 'primarily the systematic study of social history' (1973, p. 319).

Around the time that Gergen was outlining his views of social psychology as history, the experimental social psychologist, Henri Tajfel, was making a very similar point. He did so in an important article entitled 'Experiments in a vacuum', which was originally published in 1972 and which Tajfel included in a revised form in his book *Human Groups and Social Categories* (see Tajfel, 1972 and 1981; for a superb appreciation of this important article, see Condor, 2003). Tajfel argued that experimental subjects take their norms, beliefs and values with them into the laboratory. In consequence, experimental results must be understood in relation to the times and contexts in which they have occurred. They do not have universal validity.

Gergen and Tajfel were writing not long after Stanley Milgram had attracted much attention with his famous obedience experiments. In these studies, Milgram demonstrated that ordinary Americans would obey an authority who told them to administer potentially lethal electric shocks to innocent victims. They would continue obeying even when they received indications that the shocks were causing dangerously high levels of pain (Milgram, 1974). Both Tajfel and Gergen denied that Milgram had uncovered a universal law of behaviour. There was no reason for supposing that humans will in all times and places obey a self-constituted authority to inflict pain on another person; or that humans have an inborn predisposition to behave in this way. Milgram's experiments were demonstrating that, in post-war United States, some, but by no means all, people were likely to behave obediently in these situations.

In the shadow of the Holocaust this was a shocking enough finding. It was suggesting that some of the psychological factors leading to the Holocaust were not peculiar to Germany or to Germans. Ordinary people in post-war America might have reacted similarly had they found themselves in analogous circumstances. Although the experiments suggested that they 'might have' so acted, the experiments could not prove definitively that they would have done so. The suggestion was particularly troubling, because Milgram's experiments coincided with the trial of the Nazi official Adolf Eichmann, and with Hannah Arendt's controversial, but well publicized, interpretation of that trial.

Arendt (1963) argued that evil did not just come in monstrous forms but there was a 'banality of evil'. Ordinary people can follow orders, closing their minds to the moral consequences of their actions and contributing in humdrum ways to awful, murderous criminality. The phrase 'the banality of evil' seemed to fit the subjects in Migram's experiments, just as it did the middle-to-upper ranking members of the Nazi bureaucracy for extermination. In fact, Milgram claimed that Arendt's ideas supported his own work.

Both Tajfel and Gergen would have thought it absurd to have tried to understand the significance of the Milgram studies without considering their historical background. These were not studies revealing basic psychological processes. These studies were telling us about the times in which they were conducted. Indeed, both Tajfel and Gergen, in their different ways, were drawn to social psychology for this very reason. Knowledge about human failings – about prejudices, about unthinking reactions, about closing the mind to the consequences of actions – could help to prevent the faults of the past being repeated in the future. That would be impossible if psychology could only produce generalizations about universal, and thereby unchangeable, facts of human nature. Instead, the psychology of today can help to change circumstances for an altered psychology of tomorrow.

Histories of Psychology

If psychology is a form of social history, then psychologists will need to develop a historical outlook that is sensitive to historical and ideological processes. This means more than recognizing that people's mental states and views of the world arise from historical circumstances (Gergen, 2001b). The sense of historical awareness must also be applied to psychology itself (Gergen, 1997). Psychology, just as much as beliefs about the mystical power of witches, alchemy and celebrities, is historically situated. Accordingly, Gergen has written that the notion of the mind itself is a form of social myth, arising in the modern period (Gergen, 1985; for histories of 'emotions' and the idea of the 'self', see Dixon, 2003, and Seigel, 2005). As we do psychological research, we should be aware that our theories and methods do not stand outside of history. Historical sensitivity means being reflexive about ourselves and, therefore, 'historical reflexivity becomes an essential component of the scientific process' (Gergen and Graumann, 1996, p. 5).

If historical reflexivity is taken seriously, then Locke and the third Earl of Shaftesbury cease to be antiquarian topics, to be considered by psychologists when they have a spare moment. Potentially at least, Locke and Shaftesbury are part of the process of doing psychology with historical reflexivity. This is particularly true since Gergen himself posits Locke, along with other British philosophers such as Hume and Mill, as creating the 'exogenic perspective'. Adherents of this perspective see the mind as passively reflecting the external world, rather than constructing its own version of the external world (Gergen, 1985 and 1994). The exogenic perspective, in which the mind mirrors reality, is according to Gergen yet another myth of the modern period in which psychology developed as a discipline.

Historical reflexivity entails a sceptical view of psychology's own history. The 'radical doubt', which Gergen (1985) sees as essential to a post-modern psychology, should be used to expose myths about psychology's own past. New critical histories of psychology are doing precisely this. They do not see the discipline's establishment as a morality story about science triumphing over ignorance, knowledge over superstition, facts over opinions. Instead, psychology is seen as a social and historical construction with its own myths, biases and disciplinary powers (e.g., Danziger, 1990 and 1997; Jones and Elcock, 2001; Richards, 2002a; Rose, 1985). As Graham Richards (2002b) has argued, the psychological study of human beings is itself a social act that must take place in particular social contexts. Experimentalism, rather than being portrayed as the method that produces scientific fact, is seen as a historical product that has narrowed the theories and scope of psychology (Gigerenzer, 1996).

This historical perspective is very different from that traditionally found in books on the history of psychology. In the main, such texts have been written by psychologists for other psychologists, and they have tended to celebrate the rise of their shared discipline. The classic celebratory work was Edwin Boring's *History of Experimental Psychology* (1929 and 1950). Boring was an experimental psychologist who had conducted laboratory research into the sensory processes. His history told about the rise of experimental (and, thereby, scientific) psychology. There was no question where Boring's sympathies lay. He was recounting the triumphant march of the discipline to which he prominently belonged.

Boring's tradition of celebratory history continues in many of today's textbooks and 'official' histories (e.g., Fuchs and Milar, 2003). Kurt Danziger has recently said that most conventional histories of psychology create two false impressions. They portray an image of psychology as being more united than it is; and they tell a story of scientific progress within psychology (Danziger, 2001). Both impressions can be found in modern textbooks that, like Boring's classic history, are written for psychology undergraduates, who are taking a course in the history of psychology as part of their degree programme. These textbooks generally aim to make students appreciate, rather than criticize, their chosen discipline. Not all histories of psychology have such intellectually narrow aims. Most notably, the books of Kurt Danziger (1990 and 1997),

Graham Richards (1992 and 2002a) and Daniel Robinson (1986) are wide-ranging, theoretically aware achievements.

Many others, however, fit the pattern that Danziger described. James Goodwin begins his textbook, A *History of Modern Psychology* (1999), by suggesting that students of psychology will benefit from taking a historical perspective. They will be unable to understand the present state of psychology unless they know how it has developed. He offers the example of the American Psychological Association (APA). Students cannot possibly appreciate the present status of the APA without knowing the history of its relations with American Psychological Society (APS). Knowledge of the past is important if young psychologists are to understand the professional world that they are about to enter (p. 4). This clearly is a history designed to assist insiders.

Goodwin recognizes that the courses of an undergraduate degree in psychology cover a bewildering range of subjects that often seem disconnected from each other. He hopes that the history course 'can serve as a synthesizing experience' (p. 6). He addresses his readers directly: 'By the time you reach the final chapter of this text, where the issue of psychology's increased diversity and specialization will again be addressed, you will have learned enough to begin to understand the interconnectedness of the different areas of psychology' (Goodwin, 1999, p. 6). In this way, the historical accounts of the past are directly serving the pedagogic and disciplinary purposes of the present. By studying history, the student can appreciate that psychology really is a more integrated discipline than it might otherwise appear. And this is presumed to be a benefit.

The bias in favour of so-called 'scientific' psychology can be seen in Hergenhahn's *Introduction to the History of Psychology* (2001). Hergenhahn states that psychology contains both scientific and non-scientific approaches and that 'psychology need not apologize for its non-scientific aspects' (p. 20). On the surface, Hergenhahn seems to be presenting psychology as broad church, welcoming both those who bend the knee at the altar of science and those who do not. However, once inside the church, it is clear that some are more favoured than others. Non-scientific elements are likely to give way to the scientific ones: 'Often the concepts developed by nonscientific psychologists are later fine-tuned by psychologists using the scientific method' (p. 20). In this way, science moves forward, diminishing the space left for the non-scientific. This is a story of progress.

The celebratory histories of psychology differentiate, in the words of Nikolas Rose (1996), the 'sanctioned' from the 'lapsed'. The sanctioned past tells of geniuses, precursors, crucial discoveries and so on. The 'lapsed history' includes the false paths, errors and so on. By telling these stories, the histories legitimate certain aspects of contemporary psychology, while de-legitimating others. In Hergenhahn's textbook, scientific psychologists definitely belong to the sanctioned, while the non-scientific ones are on the way to lapsing. Like pre-historic dinosaurs, the unscientific approaches face ultimate extinction in a Darwinian process that ensures the survival of the most scientific.

Such textbooks tend to sanction Locke as a seventeenth century precursor of the scientific psychology that was to come. According to Michael Wertheimer's *Brief History of Psychology*, Locke was 'a forerunner of twentieth century structuralism in psychology' (1987, p. 98). Similarly, Thomas Leahey, in the second edition of his *History of Psychology*, commended Locke for having an 'empirical attitude' which was 'unencumbered by metaphysics'. Of course, Locke was not perfect; he 'did not practise a scientific psychology, collecting data and designing research programmes'. But he did believe that the mind could be studied. In this way, Locke 'opened the way for a science of the mind' (1987, p. 98). According to Leahey (2003), empiricism began with Locke.

In most textbooks Shaftesbury does not even figure as part of the 'lapsed history' – not even as a pre-scientific figure who mistakenly challenged the man who opened the way for a scientific study of the mind. The textbooks on the history of psychology, that have just been quoted, do not mention the third Earl of Shaftesbury. Both Daniel Robinson (1986) and Graham Richards (1992), as befits the scope and scholarship of their respective works, do discuss Shaftesbury. Nevertheless, they do not accord him a special place in the story of psychology. Neither envisages that the discipline – or, at least, significant parts of the discipline – might be moving towards a vision of the mind that resembles key themes to be found in Shaftesbury's *Characteristicks*.

So, Shaftesbury is not generally presented as belonging to psychology's story. It is easy to see why. The orthodox textbooks project their contemporary image of scientific psychology back onto the past, and then collect historic figures, such as Locke, who can be hailed as primitive variants of this image. Not only did Shaftesbury fail to collect data or design research programmes, he did not even propose studying the mind with the sort of soundly empirical attitude that Locke displayed. To insert Shaftesbury into the story would require a fundamental change, not in the idea of the past but in the image of the present. A very different sort of psychology needs to be projected backwards if the third Earl is to emerge today with ancestral glory.

The Rise of Critical Psychology

When Kenneth Gergen published his article arguing that social psychology was a historical inquiry, he appeared somewhat as a lone voice. Certainly, in the United States, there was no identifiable counter-movement in psychology for him to associate himself with, although in Germany there was a tradition of critical psychology, associated most notably with the work of Klaus Holzkamp (Teo, 1998; Tolman and Maiers, 1991; Tolman, 1994). There were other lone voices in the States and Europe reacting against the prevailing experimentalist view of psychology and proclaiming there to be a crisis in social psychology. From the lone voices something akin to a recognizable movement has developed, establishing alternative forms of psychology in opposition to the mainstream. With the development of new types of psychology comes the possibility of new histories, claiming different ancestral heritages.

The past twenty years has seen the growth of 'critical psychology', separate from the earlier critical psychology of Holzkamp. Critical psychology draws its inspiration from a number of different theoretical traditions that have been developed outside the formal discipline of psychology. These include feminist theories, post-modern social theory, cultural studies, Marxism, psycho-analysis, discourse analysis and various micro-sociological approaches, including conversation analysis and ethnomethodology. Given this range of background theories, critical psychology is not a single approach. Just as there are different types of mainstream psychology, so there are different critical psychologies. Whatever their differences, critical psychologists are, nevertheless, united by an opposition to mainstream psychology, which they consider too narrow in its focus and too rigid in its approach.

There is a further point of agreement. They tend to share the same basic premise as Gergen's 'social constructionism': namely, psychological phenomena are constituted within social processes. Accordingly, psychologists should not be trying to study the isolated, de-historicized individual, but should be examining how social and historical forces combine to construct individuals. In this respect, critical psychologists would agree with Gergen's claim that orthodox psychology lacks a historical consciousness. Critical psychologists differ about how to remedy this deficiency. Some critical psychologists turn to feminist theory, some to reconstituted forms of Marxism and some to post-modernist theory to provide historical perspectives – and some take from all three in various mixtures. Others have tended to put history to one side and have recommended that psychology should be re-orientated towards the study of language, especially as it is used in natural, social interaction.

Although critical psychology is small when compared with the institutions of mainstream psychology, it is nevertheless showing the conventional signs of becoming established academically, at least in particular locations. There has been a spate of textbooks with variants of the term 'critical psychology' in their titles (e.g., Fox and Prilleltensky, 1997; Gough and McFadden, 2001; Hepburn, 2003;

Ibáñez and Iñinguez, 1997; Parker, 2002; Sloan, 2000; Tuffin, 2005; Walkerdine, 2000). The publishing of textbooks is always a significant sign that something is academically and economically afoot. Publishers would not be investing in such texts if they did not believe that under-graduate and postgraduate courses in psychology were featuring 'critical psychology' and were thus creating a profitable market for course texts.

Certainly some of the textbooks have their own celebratory air, presenting critical psychology as a successfully growing movement. One such book claims that critical psychology has 'flourished in the last fifteen years and has resulted in many new courses, conferences and assorted publications, not only in the UK: there are "critical" fragments developing in Australia, the USA and parts of Europe' (Gough and McFadden, 2001, p. 2). There are now journals that specialize in 'critical psychology'. In the first issue of the journal *Annual Review of Critical Psychology*, the opening editorial declared that critical psychology has 'emerged in the academic arena very fast in recent years' (Parker, 1999, p. 3).

The development of critical psychology has occurred within a broader intellectual and economic context, which has seen parallel develop-ments of other critical sub-disciplines, such as 'critical social policy', 'critical anthropology', 'critical discourse analysis' and even 'critical rhetoric'. Chouliaraki and Fairclough begin their book *Discourse in Late Modernity* with the statement: 'Critical discourse analysis ... has established itself internationally over the past twenty years or so as a field of cross-disciplinary teaching and research which has been widely drawn upon in the social sciences and the humanities ... and has inspired critical language teaching at various levels and in various domains' (1999, p. 1; see also Billig, 2003; Fairclough, 1995; van Dijk, 1993; Weiss and Wodak, 2003). Given that some critical psychologists use discourse analysis as a tool of analysis, there has inevitably been overlap between critical discourse analysis and critical psychology.

The various critical approaches within psychology and other disci-plines tend to present themselves as being critical in two related senses. First, they claim to be critical of the present social order. Van Dijk (1993) writes that the targets of critical discourse analysis are power elites sustaining social inequality and injustice. Critical discourse analysts see themselves as challenging this existing order by studying critically the discourses that sustain current patterns of privilege and discrimination. Similarly, critical psychologists claim to be critical because they are mounting a radical critique of current social relations (e.g., Parker, 1999). Hepburn (2003) writes that 'critical social psychology is critical of society or at least some basic elements of its institutions, organizations and practices' (p. 1).

The contributors to Sloan's edited book, *Critical Psychology* (2000), also make this point. Edward Sampson, who has been a major figure in the development of critical psychology, claims that critical psychology has three main principles: that social reality is socially constructed; that this social construction involves power and vested interests and that in unmasking vested interests, critical psychologists should be 'dedicated to helping provide voice' for those 'groups who have been systematically exploited and whose voice is not generally heard' (Sampson, 2000, p. 3). Giving voice to the powerless is also a central theme of critical anthropology (Kulick, 2006).

The second way that critical psychologists, linguists, anthropologists and so on are critical is that they criticize their own discipline. They often do so on the grounds that their discipline fails to explore the dynamics of social power, especially its own involvement with the practices of power. Critics contrast their own approaches with mainstream disciplines/paradigms/theories whose assumptions seem to exclude political or radical analyses. With respect to the discipline of linguistics, Fairclough (1992) writes that 'critical approaches differ from non-critical approaches in not just describing discursive practices, but also showing how discourse is shaped by relations of power and ideologies' (p. 12). By the same token, critical psychologists claim that conventional psychology, with its focus on the de-historicized individual, has failed to analyse how social inequalities have created many of the psychological phenomena that psychologists study. Feminist theorists, in particular, stress how psychology has failed to address issues of patriarchy and dominance. Psychology, when considering the issue of gender, has historically tended to produce an uncritical 'psychology of sex differences' that assumed differences between males and females to be immutable rather than being the product of unequal social conditions (Burman, 1996; Ussher, 2000; Wilkinson, 1986).

The critics not only accuse their established discipline of academic failings, they also maintain that the orthodox discipline represents an outlook that unreflexively accepts its own position within a wider hierarchy of power. Critical anthropologists claim that classic anthropology did not provide a neutral view of undeveloped societies. Instead, it had its own secrets to conceal. Anthropology was compromised by its role in colonialism; it refused to explore how colonialism might have shaped the disciplinary outlook and practices of anthropology. Similarly, critical psychologists charge psychology with modelling the image of the universal, de-historicized individual on middle-class, white, able-bodied males.

In consequence, the critical sub-disciplines refuse to accept the celebratory way that their mainstream disciplines portray themselves. They look askance at the 'official' histories, which portray the discipline triumphantly emerging from past ignorance into present knowledge. The critical movements demand that this type of history should be revised. The present and the past that has produced this present are not matters for celebration. They should be objects of critique. In consequence, the critics call for different sorts of history. Out go the Whiggish histories celebrating the onwards and upwards march of the discipline. In come darker, critical accounts challenging the image that the discipline would like to project of itself.

Critical Psychology and Historical Reflexivity

Critical histories of psychology are now being written, contesting the old onwards and upwards accounts. Nevertheless, Gergen's arguments demand a further step should be taken. Gergen called for 'historical reflexivity', not merely 'a historical consciousness'. Reflexivity demands an awareness of one's own actions, not just those of others. The call to 'historical reflexivity' requires at its minimum that psychologists trace the origins of their psychological ideas, linking them to broader historical and ideological contexts (Morawski, 2005).

It is tempting for critical psychologists to interpret the call for historical reflexivity as a requirement that the mainstream discipline should examine critically how its ideas have been historically produced. The call for historical reflexivity, however, must go further than a critique of others: it should also involve a critical awareness of the historical origins of one's own ideas. For example, reflexive historical sociologists have sought to understand how their own ways of understanding society emerged in the later modern period (Szakolczai, 1998, 2000a and 2000b). In doing this, such sociologists looked for the sociological and historical roots of their own critical, reflexive awareness. Something similar is required by critical psychologists. They need to understand historically their own ideas. This is particularly necessary as critical psychology becomes established – as it becomes an orthodox voice for students taking courses and degrees in critical psychology. To date, the depth of historical critique, which critical psychologists have directed outwards on mainstream psychology, has not generally been matched by a similar inwards depth of historical self-reflexivity, although there have been moves towards studying the history of the critique of psychology (Teo, 2005).

Kurt Danziger (1994 and 2001) has made a useful distinction between 'shallow' and 'deep' histories. Shallow histories tend to trace intellectual ideas across a short period, often in a somewhat perfunctory manner. According to Danziger, the natural sciences, in particular, tend to encourage shallow histories. Scientific papers, including those of experimental psychology, typically begin with a brief historical introduction to the problem that is being studied. Past research is presented to show how the present study has emerged from previous ones. Of course, the account will be organized rhetorically as a self-justification: its purpose is to present the present study as one that needed to be conducted. Although experimentalists might disparage historians for relying on subjective judgement, they will, nevertheless, routinely incorporate historical stories into their research reports.

Danziger has noted a difference between the histories told by natural scientists and those told by social scientists. Natural scientists, in describing the origins of their present research, will tend to concentrate on research that has been conducted in the past ten years. Research papers in physics do not typically start with Newton, just as those in chemistry will not trace their problems back to Lavoisier. Scientists will assume that knowledge is cumulative and that the earlier research has been absorbed into more recent research. The result is a shallow history that excludes work from a more distant past.

The pattern can be different in the social sciences. Writers, especially if they are presenting new interpretations or theoretical frameworks, which they do with frequency, will often confront thinkers from a more distant past. Such a confrontation will be presented as contributing to the understanding of present phenomena. For example, social scientists might write articles with titles such as 'Confronting Plato and Durkheim: exploring the problems of the internet'. Experimental psychologists, by contrast, are unlikely to write 'Plato's theory of perception: an experimental test using reactions to internet stimuli'. If knowledge is cumulative, then in the first decade of the twenty-first century, Plato's theory of perception does not need to be tested.

There is another dynamic at work. As disciplines, sub-disciplines and even particular approaches develop, so they accumulate a body of work. New studies are then justified in terms of this accumulated body. There is no need to go back to first principles, but a new study will be described as developing out of a slightly older one. In this way, the habits of shallow history will supplant those of deeper history. As critical psychology develops, this can be observed. There is a tendency for research papers, especially if they are empirical studies, to adopt the shallower format. Present research will be justified in relation to the recent past of critical psychology. The author does not have to go back to founding figures or basic principles in order to explain why the study needed to be done. It is acceptable to present a research paper as a refinement, critique, development, etc. of something that has recently been published in a specialist journal. In this regard, a critical sub-discipline may come to use rhetorical practices of citation that do not diverge dramatically from those of the criticized super-discipline.

This can be briefly illustrated with respect to the issue of language. Many critical psychologists point to the importance of language in the social construction of psychological phenomena. Accordingly, critical psychology has put language at the heart of social and psychological life. In so doing, it has tended to see language, not as a system of grammar or vocabulary, nor as a way of transmitting internal ideas from one person to another, but as something that is fundamentally social and dialogical. It is through dialogue that so-called mental states are constituted and, thus, humans in their thinking are fundamentally dialogical (see, for instance, Antaki, 1994; Billig, 1996; Edwards, 1997; Edwards and Potter, 1993; Harré, 1979; Harré and Gillett, 1994; Hermans and Dimaggio, 2007; Middleton and Brown, 2005; Potter and Wetherell, 1987; Sampson, 1993; Shotter, 1993a and 1993b).

This dialogic perspective is at variance with those mainstream models in cognitive science that depict the human thinker as an information-processor. The questions, here, are: How do critical psychologists depict the origins of their own ideas about the dialogical nature of humans? What sort of history is given for the emergence of these ideas? Although there are some notable exceptions, there is a tendency to provide somewhat shallow histories that do not lead much further back than the mid-twentieth century. By and large, the names that are routinely mentioned as founding influences are philosophers such as Ludwig Wittgenstein and J.L. Austin, the Russian linguist and critic Mikhail Bakhtin, as well as American social scientists such as Harvey Sacks, George Herbert Mead and Harold Garfinkel. These names figure routinely in the informal histories that critical psychologists cite when they are introducing their own research papers or when discussing in general terms the intellectual background of their ideas. As the research papers become increasingly technical, even these names can drop from sight.

A few examples, taken from major writers within critical psychology, can be given to illustrate the point. Jonathan Potter (2001), who has done much to create discursive psychology, has written about the intellectual origins of this perspective. He traces key elements in discursive psychology's view of language back to Wittgenstein's later works and to Austin. He writes that these thinkers provided the important insights that meaning is established through usage; that words in a public language cannot simply refer to inner psychological states and that utterances are forms of action. Potter does not ask where Wittgenstein and Austin got these ideas from. Instead, they are presented as beginning the mini-history, along with Harvey Sacks who recommended that actual language-use should be examined, rather than relying on hypothetical examples as the philosophers had done.

Gergen (2001a) in *Social Construction in Context* suggests that the nature of emotions is constituted through the ways that people talk about emotions. This view challenges the conventional perspective that there must be such 'things' as emotions – a view that has, according to Gergen, 'ornamented the Western landscape for over two thousand years' (p. 90). Gergen recommends that we need to free ourselves from this conventional belief in order to examine how emotion-words are actually used. He claims that the new discursive approach to emotions is beginning to prevail, and that Wittgenstein's

Philosophical Investigations was 'the major stimulus' for this new way of understanding (p. 91). In a similar spirit, Sampson (1993) writes in praise of the 'dialogic challenge' that is emerging as a counter-force in contemporary human sciences. He identifies Mead, Wittgenstein and Garkfinkel as being 'precursors to a more dialogic understanding of human experience' (p. 15).

In these examples, a short and, to use Danziger's term, 'shallow' history is informally invoked. Many more examples could be offered. The point is not that Potter, Gergen and Sampson are engaging in sloppy scholarship or that they have intellectually restricted visions. Quite the contrary, none is a sloppy scholar and all are intellectually wide-ranging in their outlooks. The point is not an individual one. It is that certain ways of thinking about the past are becoming routine. The challenge to mainstream views is presented as if it had a much shorter history than the mainstream views themselves. This is also true of the psycho-analytic and feminist versions of critical psychology. Mid- to late-twentieth century thinkers, such as Jacques Lacan, Judith Butler and Jacques Derrida, tend to be cited rather than thinkers from earlier times. In this way, critics tend to draw upon figures from a comparatively recent past, thereby truncating the range of their history. Why Wittgenstein or Austin or Mead should have chanced upon the views they did is left historically unexplained. They are often presented as intellectual figures without a history, without a deeper past.

Post-Modernism and Western Culture

Actually, the last paragraph oversimplifies the way that critical psychologists tend to present their past. An underlying historical narrative can be found in the writings of Gergen, Sampson and many others. It concerns the way that the turn to dialogue is part of a wider cultural movement, which, for the sake of convenience, is often called 'post-modernism'. This movement is presented as challenging the underlying assumptions of modernism and thereby is seen as a challenge to Western culture, which is presumed to be fundamentally modernist. In a curious way this narrative within critical psychology parallels mainstream psychology's informal, shallow narrative about the growth of scientific method.

The critical narrative contains several interesting features. It provides an explanation why mainstream psychology – unsatisfactory though it might be – should have enjoyed such triumphant progress. It was not because psychologists ever discovered much worth discovering. In fact, according to the critical narrative, psychologists have tended to misunderstand most of what they investigated. Psychology succeeded because it matched the dominant ideology of individualism. In his classic 'Social psychology as history' paper, Gergen wrote that 'in Western culture there seems to be a heavy value placed on uniqueness or individuality' and that psychology reflected this value (1973, p. 314). Gergen (1985) has elaborated the theme, suggesting that the new critical, or constructionist, psychology challenges deeply based, established patterns of thinking. In particular, it challenges the 'Western conception of objective, individualistic, ahistoric knowledge – a conception that has insinuated itself into virtually all aspects of modern institutional life' (p. 272). Sampson, too, has linked the rise of psychology with the dominance of individualism (Sampson, 1977 and 1981). He writes that the 'possessively individualistic view of the person' permeates 'much of Western civilization' (Sampson, 1993, p. 31). Sampson emphasizes the link between the dominance of individualism and the success of psychology: 'Without a society organized around the self-contained individual, there would be neither a field such as psychology nor a need for one' (1993, p. 42).

This narrative sets a cultural and ideological theme within a broad chronology. Western culture/civilization is built upon the ideology of modernism. Scientific methodology, knowable truth, rationality, masculinity and individualism are all modernist values. And all these values are reflected in mainstream psychology, which, as will be seen later, can claim Locke as an intellectual ancestor. Modernism, however, is in a process of collapse. The grand narratives of science and rational progress are no longer credible. In their place are multiple truths and unceasing dialogue, together with a celebration of difference, sociality, feminine emotions and irony.

Gergen has argued that the new movements in psychology belong to this post-modernist turn (Gergen, 1985, 1992, 2001a and 2001b). As Kvale (1992a) writes, psychology is part of the 'project of modernity' and it has been rendered outmoded by post-modernity (p. 31). Any such claim involves a chronology. First comes modernism, sweeping all before it in the Western world. And, then, in the mid-twentieth century the values of modernity implode, giving way to those of post-modernity. In the world of psychology, experimentalism belongs to the old, disappearing order and the new forms of psychology represent the present, and by implication, the future.

Such a narrative is superficially attractive. It seems to fulfil a basic requirement of historical self-reflexivity, in that it places its own understanding of the world within a historical time frame. However, the terms of the narrative are problematic. 'Western culture' or 'Western civilizations' are phrases that are easy to use, but harder to specify. When they form part of the chronological narrative, they imply an equation between modernism and 'Western culture'. This would imply that post-modernism is somehow non-Western, even anti-Western, maybe on a different side in the so-called clash of civilizations. When critical psychology (or critical discourse analysis/social policy/anthropology) is linked to post-modernism, then the implication is that the critique is truly radical because it stands outside of 'Western culture/civilization'. The attractions of such a narrative are obvious. It offers extra justification for the activity of critical psychology: one is not just criticizing an academic discipline; one is hastening the end of a discredited culture/civilization/system of dominance.

This aspect of the narrative implies a separation of the self from the object of critique, just as modernism's shallow narratives also have assumed the separation of experimenter from subjects. The experimentalists assume that their own scientific activities stand outside of history, inasmuch as the scientific methodology provides universal truths. The critical narrative offers the possibility for assuming that the activity of critique is separated from the continuing existence of the culture/civilization/system of dominance that is being criticized. The historical tale of Western culture being individualist serves to support this assumption of separation. The critics claim that orthodox psychology is deeply individualistic because it studies the individual removed from any social or historical context. In stressing the social creation of psychological processes, critical psychologists are being anti-individualistic. This is more than a methodological or even theoretical position. It is also an ideological one: if one is opposing individualism and if Western culture is individualist, then one cannot be a part of Western culture.

Yet, one might wish to ask how this can be possible. In a strict sense, separation is not possible. The critique is principally located in Western universities, which are generally well-funded and which under-write financially the various critical turns (albeit not as generously as they might support the non-critical super-disciplines). The narrative also contains another problematic feature. It can be accepted that mainstream psychology is historically related to the values of individualism (Jansz, 2003). It can also be accepted that individualism belongs to modernist ideology. But that does not mean that individualism is the only, or even the most dominant value, of modern times. There is something missing in the shallow accounts: the modern era was never fully individualist.

It could not have been, for the so-called era of modernism has also been the era of nationalism. Nation-states did not exist in their modern form in earlier periods, but they have dominated the political imagination of the modern age (Anderson, 1983; Billig, 1995; Gellner, 1983). Throughout modern times, young men have gone to war, sometimes under legal coercion but often voluntarily, to kill and to die on behalf of the race, nation and/or homeland. They have done so in numbers unknown in previous times. Such monumental sacrifice of life would not have been possible were rational, scientific individualism the only shared code of the modern era. Other duties, loves and hatreds have gripped the modern imagination. And it is still persisting. Nations continue to deploy armies. Scientists do not.

The critical narrative, at least in its routine, shallow forms suggests two contradictory accounts. It conveys the image of an orderly transition from one age to another – from modernism to post-modernism. It also suggests a sense of perpetuity – Western culture *is* individualist, as if it has never been otherwise and would cease to be Western if individualism could be overcome. It forgets that the 'West' was not always 'Western' in this sense. Before the modern era, it housed a patchwork of local cultures, as exotic, tightly knit and remote as any that modern, Western anthropologists came across in other continents.

This is why the early modern period is so important for understanding the present. It was a time when Western Europe was becoming 'Western' – when the processes of industrialization were beginning to uproot older patterns of life that were never wholly or principally individualist in the modern sense and that would be transformed or even disappear over the next two hundred years. It was a time of intellectual excitement, as philosophers turned their attention to the problems of knowledge. In the early modern period, we can see new ideas about the individual mind being formulated. In England, John Locke was the notable exponent of an early empirical psychology.

The new philosophy, however, never went unchallenged; it did not achieve a total conquest of the imagination. Counter-ideas were formulated from the start and these also fitted the times. As the new ideas were challenged, so the origin of these ideas became a matter of controversy. This is why Shaftesbury's reaction against Locke is so fascinating. In the modernist's imagination, the controversy might be seen to pit the modernist, who was looking to the future, against the defender of a past that would be swept away. But, as will be suggested, it was never so simple. The modernist was not entirely modern. In the eyes of his opponent, Locke's empirical psychology came into the world trailing clouds of ancient glory that it attempted to hide. And Shaftesbury was not quite as old-fashioned as his poses might suggest. No less a figure than Denis Diderot would see him as a fellow revolutionary.

All this has resonance for understanding the psychological ideas of today. The shallow critical narratives suggest that the ideas of post-modernism are new and radical. But if these ideas seem to echo the thoughts of an early eighteenth century aristocrat, then this should give pause for thought. It suggests that post-modernist psychology might be more connected with aspects of 'Western culture' than has been comfortable to admit. Similarly, the ideas of Wittgenstein did not magically emerge, when the doctrines of modernism were collapsing under the weight of their considerable contradictions. Many of them were pre-figured in the works of Thomas Reid, that religious, Scottish philosopher who was one of the finest philosophical authors ever to write in the English language.

Reid has been slightly better served than Shaftesbury in the standard histories of psychology. He is more frequently mentioned, but, even so, he has not exactly been well treated. Graham Richards (1992) has demonstrated the extent to which Reid has been neglected (pp. 236ff). According to Richards, Reid's work fails to fit the 'official' image of scientific psychology and so the histories have correspondingly downgraded his contributions. It is not just in psychological circles that the works of Shaftesbury and Reid have been forgotten. There has been a much wider neglect. In some cases, as will be seen, there has even been concealment.

The task of reviving the memory of Reid and Shaftesbury is not merely a labour of love. More is involved theoretically. The act of restitution should also involve critique, even self-critique. If psychology is intrinsically historical, then the psychological and the historical cannot be neatly separated into distinct categories. As the histories become deeper, so psychologists' understanding of their own psychological concepts should accordingly deepen. In an obvious sense, the present work concerns the origins of ideas: where do the ideas of critical psychology come from? But, as will be seen, the ideas, whose origins are being sought, are themselves psychological ideas about the origins of ideas. This is, therefore, a search for the origins of ideas about the origins of ideas. Such a search must itself be guided by notions about where origins might be found. In taking a historical stance, a step has already been made away from the sort of unhistorical, cognitive inquiry that Locke promoted.

CHAPTER

3

Locke: The Father of Cognitive Psychology

• • • • • • • • • • • • • • • • • • •

The philosopher George Santayana once described John Locke as 'the father of modern psychology' (1933, p. 1). He made the comment during a lecture celebrating the tri-centenary of Locke's birth. On such occasions the invited lecturer is expected to praise the figure in whose memory the audience has gathered. Santayana's phrase, however, indicates something interesting. It suggests a complex relation between past and present. Calling a past thinker the father (or mother) of an academic discipline implies that the story of the discipline starts with that person – and it is usually a father, rather than a mother, who is so heralded (but see Sayers, 1994). The intellectual parent is presented as someone whose ideas have broken through the bounds of history. Seldom do we hear of a historic thinker being honoured as the 'grandparent' or even 'great-grandparent' of a discipline. In the business of ancestral honouring, the grandparent is always a rival, ready to usurp the position of the parent. The genealogist can easily collapse the generations to proclaim the grandparent to be the true parent, the original genius. In consequence, the parent of an academic discipline is typically presented as parentless, as if they were an autochthonous, self-created figure.

The idea of Locke as the founder of modern psychology suggests that Locke is simultaneously modern and non-modern. The intellectual parent must be distinct from the children. Had Locke been totally modern, he would have been 'a proper psychologist', rather than 'the father of psychology'. Present psychologists will supposedly recognize parts of their own activities in the distant parent's work. But other parts ensure that the parent belongs to a pre-disciplinary generation. Locke remains an ancestor – a framed portrait gazing from the wall – rather than a distinguished colleague. Thus, the paternal label suggests a complex pattern of recognizable similarities and differences, points of identification and points of difference.

This chapter will examine the relationship between Locke's *Essay Concerning Human Understanding* and present day cognitive psychology. The aim is neither to praise nor to bury Locke. Instead, Locke's importance to psychology needs to be re-examined in the light of changing developments. He is not merely to be seen as the father of cognitive psychology – although, as a later chapter will suggest, he was a father who to a certain extent concealed his own ancestry. Locke was also the step-father to a rebellious son, who reacted against those very parts of his work that today seem modern. As such, Locke is a step-grandfather of critical psychology, occupying an interesting place in the story of critical psychology's hidden roots.

Ancestral Figures

Santayana's comment contained one obvious over-simplification. He implied that 'modern psychology' was a discipline united by a common ancestry. When Santayana delivered his lecture, psychology was certainly not unified – and it is probably even less so today. Locke is not the obvious ancestor for many of psychology's various strands. Evolutionary psychologists would not trace their ideas back to such a pre-Darwinian thinker. Locke's *Essay* hardly dealt with the range of human emotions or with individual differences. So specialists in those two areas will scarcely feel themselves to be Locke's intellectual descendants. As for Freudians, they have their own father-figure to venerate.

Yet, some, but not all, histories of psychology continue to accord Locke a special place. A recent textbook has described Locke's *Essay* as 'one of the most important books in the history of psychology' (Benjamin, 2007, p. 14). According to the author, Locke in the late seventeenth century initiated an empirical approach to the study of the mind; and nearly two hundred years later Wilhelm Wundt would develop Locke's approach into an experimental science. Certainly Wundt, who is often credited with bringing psychology into the experimental laboratory, felt an intellectual debt to Locke, crediting him with establishing the psychology of the inner sense (Wundt, 1907). Wundt's comment echoes the thoughts of another nineteenth century giant of psychology's history. Hermann Helmholtz claimed that Locke 'had correctly laid down the most important principles on which the right interpretation of sensible qualities depends' (quoted in Bennett and Hacker, 2003, p. 135).

Locke might better be thought to be the father of cognitive psychology, rather than of the whole of psychology. That is still a big claim, given that cognitive psychology has been the dominant movement within psychology for the past thirty years. In the words of Ulrich Neisser, whose book *Cognitive Psychology* did much to ignite the so-called cognitive revolution, cognitive psychology embraces such topics as 'sensation, perception, imagery, retention, recall, problem-solving, and thinking' (Neisser, 1967, p. 4). A standard current textbook claims that cognitive scientists study 'the cognitive or mental functions of perception, attention, memory, language, and thinking' (Kellogg, 2003, p. 1). This is certainly the territory of Locke's *Essay*. To quote a prominent scholar of Locke, the *Essay* represents a piece of 'descriptive cognitive psychology' (Yolton, 1985, p. 120). Some historically minded cognitive scientists agree (see, for instance, the comments of Harnish, 2001, p. 20).

Locke explored the same basic topics that cognitive psychology does today. He examined processes of perception and thinking. But it is not just the similarity of topics that connects Locke with modern cognitive science. It was also his style of examining the mind. Today's scientists can recognize in Locke an empirical spirit that they hope characterizes their own work. Locke is generally recognized to be the founder of British empiricism, which believed that knowledge was advanced by careful, systematic observation of the natural world. He belonged to the great scientific movement that swept through Britain and Europe in the seventeenth century. Consequently, in recognizing Locke as an ancestor, cognitive scientists would be affirming their own connection with empiricism.

Of course, there are large differences between Locke and contemporary cognitive psychologists. Locke did not have expensively equipped computer-driven laboratories at his disposal. He thought about the mind and he wrote down what he thought. And what he wrote was not destined to be published in specialized journals, read by professional academics. His *Essay* is a long, somewhat rambling book addressed to educated, general readers. It is written in non-technical language. Locke did not have the vocabulary of modern psychology at his disposal: one does not find references to 'stimuli', 'dependent variables' or 'information-processing' in his prose.

Nor does the word 'psychology' make an appearance in Locke's writing – and for good reason. The word was not yet commonly used in English. *Psychologia* had from the end of the sixteenth century been used in Latin to denote the study of the soul (Kristic, 1964). 'Psychology' was starting to be used in English in the first years of the eighteenth century. Henry Curzon, over twenty years after the publication of Locke's *Essay*, surveyed the various sciences and stated that 'psychology examines the constitution of the mind of man, its faculties and passions' (1712, p. 27). When the word 'psychology' finally passed into common English usage, there was to be a connection with Locke. The second book in English, containing 'psychology' in its title, was an American translation of Victor Cousin's lectures on Locke, published in 1834 under the title of *Elements of Psychology* (according to the British Library catalogue, the first book was an anonymous tract, published two years earlier, discussing whether animals had souls).

Another difference between Locke and his cognitive descendants lies in their respective conditions of life. Locke was not a professional academic, who enjoyed the comforts and irritations of working in a university. In fact, for a large part of his working life he was linked to the political life of England. Much of his writing, too, was political. His *Essay* appeared in the same year as two of his other books, *A Letter Concerning Toleration* and *Two Treatises of Government*, both of which were explicitly political and, for that reason, were published anonymously. The *Essay*, by contrast, appeared under Locke's name, but he knew that it would embroil him in controversy, especially on religious grounds. In late seventeenth century England, religion was not a matter of private belief, as it is today in most democracies. It was very much a matter of public policy, and subject to strict laws of censorship. Today, cognitive scientists, at least those in Western democracies, publish their technical papers, secure that the state and religious authorities will not be policing their words about the cognitive processes of perception and memory. It was not so in Locke's day. The *Essay* – and thus early cognitive psychology – was a highly political matter.

The political and intellectual background is important for understanding Locke's *Essay*. It throws light on Locke's congeniality as a chosen ancestor – why, for example, it is Locke who is seen as cognitive psychology's forerunner, not Thomas Hobbes, the gloomy pessimist who analysed processes of mind a generation earlier. Compared with Locke, Hobbes tends to be written out of the picture, as if he were a shameful family secret. It is necessary to set Locke's *Essay* in its times. This means combining the psychological with the social, political and, most importantly, the personal, otherwise the counter-story – the story how the reaction to Locke produced a very different set of psychological ideas – becomes harder to appreciate.

Locke and the First Earl of Shaftesbury

Locke was born in 1632 in an insignificant village near Bristol. His father was a small land-owner and lawyer, who supplemented his income by performing administrative tasks for the local government. Yet, by the time the *Essay* was published in 1690, Locke was mixing in some of the highest circles in the land. The title page of the *Essay's* early editions testifies to the pride Locke took in his status: the book is described as 'Written by John Locke, Gent'. Describing his early life, Locke said that 'I no sooner perceived myself in the world but I found myself in a storm which has lasted hitherto' (quoted by Cranston, 1985, p. 3, in his invaluable biography of Locke). The Civil War broke out when he was a boy. He lived through the persecutions of the Commonwealth and the uncertainties of the Restoration of the monarchy. Indeed, Locke's life coincided with the most troubled and dangerous period of English politics.

Locke's family was deeply Protestant and his father fought on the Parliamentary side in the Civil War, serving under the local Member of Parliament, Alexander Popham. As a reward, Popham sponsored the education of the young Locke, who first attended Westminster School and then Oxford University. During Oliver Cromwell's Protectorate, Oxford became known for its science, especially at Wadham College where John Wilkins, Cromwell's brother-in-law, was appointed. Locke was drawn to the sciences, being repelled by the sort of metaphysics that was being taught at Oxford. Despite the growth of the sciences at Oxford, the university, in common with the rest of society, was not a haven for free-thinking. Students and teachers had to take care lest they were suspected of associating with elements that were either too subversive or too reactionary. These were suspicious times.

Although Locke studied medicine at Oxford, he never actually obtained the formal qualification of a medical doctor. That did not prevent him from acting as a physician in those less regulated days. Locke associated himself with the new empirical movement in medicine. Instead of following theories proposed by Aristotle and other classical figures, this new generation of doctors was carefully recording the effects of medicines and applying the new knowledge of physiology. A suspicious public, with more faith in folk-remedies than new-fangled ideas, often derided the new practitioners as 'empirics'.

Locke stayed on at Oxford after graduation, holding a succession of short-term teaching posts. He was beginning to mix in scientific circles, associating with others who were drawn to the new spirit of observation. He became an early member of the new Royal Society, which had developed out of Wilkins's circle at Wadham. Locke might have remained at Oxford, becoming a moderately successful academic, were it not for a chance meeting that transformed his life.

In 1666 Anthony Ashley Cooper, an ambitious and powerful politician, who was later to become the first Earl of Shaftesbury, was travelling near Oxford, seeking to take spa waters for his indifferent health. His preferred doctor was indisposed and Locke was recommended as a substitute. Cooper was so impressed by the young doctor that he immediately recruited him to his staff. Over the years Locke became Cooper's trusted personal and political advisor. In such a capacity, Locke mixed in circles far beyond the social reach of his forebears, and he even held official positions of state in his own right.

Cooper was one of the most important and least trusted politicians of his generation. He came from old landed gentry and had a strongly Protestant background. His inherited estate might have been in severe decline, but his social position was still several notches above that of Locke. Cooper acquired substantial estates through smart business deals, relentless politicking and three advantageous marriages.

Politics was not an easy trade in those troubled times. A wrong move, an incautious opinion and the executioner beckoned.

Cooper had the precious gift of anticipating political trends. He changed sides during the Civil War, ending up with the victorious Parliamentarians. Commercially he also prospered, buying plantations in Barbados and a part share in a profitable slaving ship. Cooper was a senior figure in Cromwell's administration. In that position, he was able to appreciate the extent to which the Republican government was weakened by the death of Cromwell. Sensing that power was slipping from the Protectorate, he made overtures to the exiled royalists. By the time that the Republic finally collapsed in 1660 and the monarchy was restored, Cooper was well in favour with the new king, Charles II.

Consequently, when he met Locke in 1666, Cooper's fortunes were in the ascendant. He had been granted a Royal Pardon for his behaviour during the Protectorate and he was soon to be appointed Chancellor of the Exchequer. Within a few years there was to be further advance. In 1672 he became High Chancellor and was ennobled, taking the title of Earl of Shaftesbury. The new High Chancellor ensured that his trusted advisor secured an official position in government. So Locke became Secretary for the Clergy and also Secretary to the Board of Trade and Plantations. Both Locke and his patron were strong advocates of parliamentary power, siding with the liberal Whigs against the Tories.

The liberal Whigs seem to have had a curious blindness with regard to slavery. In their speeches and writings they liberally used the rhetoric of freedom. Locke would start his *Two Treatises of Government* with the stirring declaration that slavery was a 'vile and miserable' estate of man (1690/1977, p. 3). That did not prevent him, as secretary to the Board of Trade, working for the prosperity of the slave plantations in the colonies. Shaftesbury delivered speeches warning against the evils of slavery. When he did so, he was referring to the slavery that he imagined Catholics – especially French Catholics – to be plotting for English Protestants. He was not speaking of the practices in the West Indies that were contributing so substantially to his family fortunes.

During the early years of the Restoration, it must have seemed to Shaftesbury that the dangerous years were over. Nothing, however, was constant in the political life of the first Earl, except his opposition to Catholicism and his distrust of monarchical power. He was an inveterate, closed-door plotter. Along with many Protestants, Shaftesbury feared that the King was a closet Catholic and was deeply worried because James, the King's brother and heir to the throne, was a practising Catholic. The King seemed unwilling to take measures to ensure a Protestant succession. So Shaftesbury allied himself with the Whig opposition that was scheming to undermine the authority of the King.

In 1676 Shaftesbury found himself imprisoned in the Tower of London for a year. Rumours of Catholic conspiracies encouraged the Protestant opposition to foment their own conspiratorial cabals. Shaftesbury, on his release, was back in the thick of the plotting. He was widely suspected of being implicated in a plan to overthrow Charles II and replace him with his illegitimate son, the Duke of Monmouth. In 1681 Shaftesbury was back in the Tower, having been arrested for treason. The following year, he came to trial but was fortuitously acquitted. He wisely left England for the safety of Holland, realizing that, were he to be arrested again, he might not find such a pliable court. Shaftesbury, now old and tired, was to die the following year in exile.

Locke had always been prudent in his judgement and secretive in his actions. He was aware that his links with Shaftesbury put him in danger of arrest. Therefore, Locke followed his patron into exile, on the way giving royalist spies the slip. Locke was now cut off from his friends in England. Instead of obtaining a post at Oxford University – something he desired greatly – he seemed destined to live out his latter years in exiled discomfort. But Shaftesbury, even in his final days, had not lost his political touch, although he personally did not live long enough to benefit.

In 1688 fortune was to swing back Locke's way. Parliament, now dominated by Shaftesbury's old Whig friends, overthrew Charles's successor, James II. This was the Glorious Revolution. It lacked the bloodiness of Cromwell's Revolution but it had enduring consequences for the development of parliamentary power in Britain. William of Orange and his wife Anne, both suitably Protestant, were formally invited to become the new monarchs of the kingdoms of England, Scotland and Ireland (Wales being constitutionally integrated with England). With a Protestant monarchy established and a parliament powerful enough to depose and appoint monarchs, Locke felt that he could now safely return from Holland.

It was also time to start publishing. In the year before the Revolution, Locke was taking steps to publish the *Essay* that he had been working on for many years. A lengthy summary appeared in the French journal *Bibliothèque Universelle* in 1688. The *Essay* was to appear properly in 1690. In the same year, Locke was to publish anonymously his *Two Treatises of Government* and *Letter Concerning Toleration*. He never lost his lifetime habits of caution and concealment. Even to good friends Locke would not admit to being the author of the *Two Treatises* or the *Letter*. Few friends, however, were fooled by his denials.

At the time, the *Two Treatises* was reckoned to have provided a philosophical justification for Parliament's *coup d'état*. Locke was arguing against the divine right of kings. Society did not owe its origins to the divinely ordained powers of kings. Instead, social authority derived from the decisions of the individual members of society. The *Two Treatises* suggested that society originated when individuals had come together to make the reasonable decision, or 'compact', to appoint an authority to protect their own interests. If society (and monarchy) originated in this way, then authority was not based upon the king being put above other mortals by divine decision. It was based on the decisions of individuals, who are rationally acting in their own interests. This thesis contained political implications of revolutionary importance.

The *Letter Concerning Toleration* discussed religious and political matters directly. Locke was generally in favour of extending tolerance to Protestant dissenters, so long as their dissent was not too radical. Locke wanted a broad Church of England that embraced as many nonconformist sects as possible. In the language of the time, he was a 'latitudinarian' and his personal library contained over a hundred works by latitudinarians (Spellman, 1997). Locke, ever cautious, did not advertise his latitudinarian sympathies openly. In common with most latitudinarians, his tolerance was strictly bounded: it did not extend to Catholics.

Locke's *Essay* did not emerge into a world of free intellectual inquiry, where ideas could be enjoyed for their own sake. Legal censorship protected the interests of the monarchy and the established church. Publicly, Locke's *Essay Concerning Human Understanding* may not have been linked to the *Letter Concerning Toleration*. Nevertheless, critics and supporters considered the *Essay* to contain controversial religious and political messages. Much of the early criticism was theologically based. While Locke ignored most of his theological critics, he did respond to the attacks on the *Essay* mounted by Edward Stillingfleet, Bishop of Worcester. To counter his critics, Locke revised and added sections for further editions that were published during his lifetime. When he died in 1704, Locke had just finished revising the text for a fifth edition that would appear posthumously two years later.

Outline of Locke's 'Essay'

Locke's *Essay* is a big book. To be precise, it comprises four 'books', which, in the early editions, were published in two large, separate volumes. It took Locke many years to write the *Essay*, having to find the time in between his various services to Shaftesbury. Locke may have been encouraged by his patron to pursue his intellectual interests but the practical duties came first. In the preface, Locke apologized to readers that the book was somewhat rambling and repetitive. The problem, he said, arose because the work was written with 'many long intervals of interruption'. Locke admitted the whole book needed re-writing but, with engaging frankness, he confessed 'I am now too lazy, or too busy to make it shorter' (1690/1768: quotations are taken from the sixteenth edition of the *Essay*, which does not give page numbers for Locke's prefatory 'Epistle to the Reader').

Actually, the *Essay* has a clear construction. The first two books, which comprised the first volume, discussed the psychological origins of our knowledge of the world. Locke asked where our ideas come from and how do we form concepts, etc. Locke argued that our knowledge of the world is based upon perceptual experience. Complex, abstract ideas are ultimately based on simpler perceptions. In the third and fourth parts of the *Essay*, Locke uses this psychological theory of knowledge as a guide for evaluating our beliefs, in order to prevent our ideas of the world becoming too detached from the simple, perceptual ideas on which they should be based. His message was that we should particularly be suspicious of abstract concepts that have become remote from experience.

The *Essay* therefore, is part psychology and part philosophy. It is, in the words of one commentator, a 'hybrid' work (Jolly, 1999). This hybridity contributes to the intellectual force of the work. Victor Cousin, who was to introduce the work of Reid and Locke's other Scottish critics to a French audience, pointed out that Locke had changed the basis of philosophy by turning metaphysical questions into psychological ones (Cousin, 1834, pp. 88ff). Locke had not sought to define the nature of truth and then use such a definition to distinguish between knowledge and error. He had begun with psychology, seeking to discover how we come by the ideas that we take to be true. According to Cousin, Locke was arguing that the study of human nature, whether it be called 'psychology or by any other name', should provide philosophy's 'foundation and its starting-point' (1834/1871, p. 98).

In tracing the connections between Locke and today's cognitive psychology, more attention will be paid to the psychological aspects of the *Essay*. However, the psychological issues cannot be neatly detached from the philosophical ones. Locke's *Essay* is integrally 'hybrid', rather than a compendium of two separate types of inquiry. This is apparent in Locke's basic question. He is asking about the nature of understanding. By proposing to answer the question through examining how we understand in practice, Locke is already implying that understanding is possible: his psychological method depends upon his understanding how people understand. Thus, he must practise understanding in order to examine how understanding takes place.

Locke's professed method is empirical. He does not want to base himself on abstract speculation. Like any modern empirically minded psychologist, he wants to observe how people actually think, how they actually understand the world, where their ideas come from, etc. He uses what he calls his 'historical, plain method' (I.i.2, p. 2), although, as will be seen, his method is neither plain nor historical.

Locke's method of understanding (or, at least the method that Locke claimed to be using) complements his psychological theory of understanding. He suggests that understanding is based on sensation, and thereby on observation. His psychological theory about the nature of understanding reflects his idealized image of what he himself is doing: he is observing how observation leads to knowledge. In making such a self-applicable claim, Locke was doing something that would be repeated by many later psychologists, including cognitive psychologists.

Bertrand Russell joked about the way that psychological theories of thinking reflect the characteristics of the psychologists rather than their subjects. Russell noted that the animals studied by American psychologists 'rush about frantically, with an incredible display of hustle and pep', solving their problems by chance; on the other hand 'the animals observed by Germans sit still and think, and at last evolve the solution out of their inner consciousness' (1927/1999, p. 23). There is a serious historical point behind Russell's joke. Psychologists have often projected their own ways of doing psychology onto their general views about the nature of human thinking. For example, statistically minded theorists have tended to see the human thinker as a lay statistician, while those who use computer modelling see thinking primarily as a means of computing information (Gigerenzer, 1996). Generally, cognitive scientists have created their own subjects in their own idealized image, imagining the ordinary thinker as some sort of lay cognitive scientist (Cohen-Cole, 2005).

Locke, the empiricist, was imagining thinking as an empirical activity. It was a more attractive image of thinking than that offered a generation earlier by Thomas Hobbes. In *Human Nature*, Hobbes had presented a very different psychology. The individual, according to Hobbes, was driven by selfish emotions, which were concealed by self-deceiving protestations of moral virtue. For Hobbes, human nature was fundamentally dangerous: people could not be trusted either in their emotions or in their thoughts. Locke, by contrast, was formulating a much more attractive picture – the human thinker as an empirical scientist. Certainly it is a picture that would appeal to later cognitive psychologists. Few psychologists would rush to hail the gloomy sage of Malmesbury as the father of their discipline, although, just like Locke, he examined the nature of thinking. On the other hand, later cognitive scientists could happily recognize themselves and their science in Locke's accounts of thinking.

Ideas and Cognitions

In psychology's big, continuing debate on the relative contributions of nature versus nurture, Locke was firmly on the side of nurture. The *Essay* became famous for its attack on the theory that we are born with innate ideas. Whenever Locke is mentioned in textbooks on the history of psychology, there usually follows a reference to his belief that the child comes into the world with an empty mind – a *tabula rasa*, or clear tablet, to use the Latin phrase. Locke's rejection of innate ideas was not a discrete hypothesis existing on its own. It was part of a wider view of the mind.

The first thing to note about the *Essay* is its subject matter. Locke was attempting to outline the workings of the mind; he was not interested in the brain. He wrote on the very first page, 'I shall not at present meddle with the physical consideration of the mind' (I.i.2, p. 1). He was concerned with what is in the mind and how it got there. Locke called his method of inquiry 'historical', because his central problem was to account for the history of the ideas that individuals entertain in their minds.

In the Introduction, Locke explained his key term – 'idea'. He was using the word to stand for 'whatsoever is the object of the understanding when a man thinks' (I.i.8, p. 5). Whatever the mind is thinking about is an 'idea', whether it be phantasms, notions or species or 'whatsoever it is which the mind can be employed about in thinking' (p. 5). 'Idea' was Locke's catch-all term to describe the contents of the mind. It was not, perhaps, a fortuitous choice of term. Normally the word 'idea' denotes views or opinions that can be expressed in propositions, such as 'political ideas', 'common sense ideas', etc. Locke was using the word in a wider sense: perceptions, feelings and sensations were also 'ideas' in that they too were in the mind.

Today's cognitive psychologists also have similar catch-all terms to describe the contents of the mind. Many have used 'cognition' in ways that are analogous to Locke's 'ideas'. Neisser (1967) claimed that the term 'cognition' refers 'to all the processes by which the sensory input is transformed, reduced, elaborated, stored, recovered, and used' (p. 4). These in Locke's *Essay* were all 'ideas' – ranging from simple perceptions to complex thoughts. More recently, cognitive scientists have been using 'mental representation' as a catch-all description, especially in relation to those mental elements that are derived from the senses. For example, Sperber writes that 'cognitive systems are characterized by their ability to construct and process mental representations' (2000, p. 3). Some analysts have specifically claimed that the concept of 'mental representation' can be traced back to Locke's notion of ideas (Downes, 2005, p. 48; Markova, 2003, p. 8).

Just as modern cognitive psychologists take it for granted that the mind contains such things as 'cognitions' or 'mental representations', so Locke also assumed the existence of ideas: 'I presume it will be easily granted me that there are such *ideas* in men's minds' (I.i.8, p. 5, emphasis in original). This seemed obvious to Locke. So did the existence of 'the mind', which was something that could be studied empirically. Similarly, today's cognitive scientists define their discipline as 'the scientific study of the mind', thereby assuming both the mind's existence and its examinable nature (Branquinho, 2001, p. xii).

It is easy to slip into the assumption that the mind and its contents exist as things like other physical objects. Often cognitive scientists treat them in this way. One notable cognitive scientist asserts that the mind 'is packed with high-tech systems' (Pinker, 1997, p. 4) and another has claimed that cognitive psychology explores 'the structure and function of mind' (Mandler, 1985, p. 27). In such comments, there is, as Rom Harré (2002) has pointed out, an element of metaphysics: the mind and its contents are being talked about as if they were objects on a par with familiar physical objects. The assumption that the subject matter of psychology consists of these mental objects is sometimes described as *cognitivism*.

Certainly, Locke's *Essay* proceeds from cognitivist assumptions. As will be seen, Thomas Reid in the mid-seventeenth century questioned Locke's assumption that 'ideas' exist as objects of the mind. Reid's anti-cognitivist challenge was to be repeated in the twentieth century by Wittgenstein, Austin and others. Anti-cognitivism has become an important theme in today's critical psychology, especially in the work of discursive psychologists. Such critics contend that cognitivism has led psychology to take a wrong turning.

For Locke, however, it would have seemed absurd to deny the existence of 'ideas' – or even to consider that there was anything metaphysical about assuming their existence. It was plain common sense that they existed. Having justified his use of the term 'ideas' in the *Essay's* introduction, Locke then asserted 'our first inquiry then shall be, how they came into the mind' (I.i.8, p. 5). In this way, he set up his inquiry as being plain and historical.

Against Innate Ideas

Locke states unambiguously that the mind does not have any innate ideas. It has been said with justice that Locke, in the early parts of the *Essay*, writes like a developmental psychologist (Macnamara, 1999). Locke's argument against innate ideas is basically an appeal to the so-called facts of child psychology. In effect, he is saying: if you look and see what a young child is capable of doing, you will find no evidence of inborn ideas. The child is not born with truths imprinted on the mind but there are various 'steps by which the mind attains several truths' (I.ii.15, p. 19). For example, mathematical knowledge depends on the acquisition of prior abilities: 'A child knows not that three and four are equal to seven, till he comes to be able to count to seven, and has got the name and idea of equality' (I.ii. 16, p. 20). In this way, complex skills depend on the prior acquisition of simpler ones. In arguing thus, Locke was anticipating the notion of developmental stages, which

James Mark Baldwin introduced into psychological theorizing at the end of the nineteenth century and which was subsequently to prove so influential within developmental psychology (Baldwin, 1897).

Locke supported his case by appealing to observation. He described the state of the newborn child: 'If we will attentively consider new-born children, we shall have little reason to think that they bring many ideas into the world with them', except for 'some faint ideas of hunger and thirst, and warmth, and some pains' (I.iv.2, p. 48). These faint notions are certainly not what others have thought to be 'those universal propositions that are esteemed innate principles' (I.iv.2, p. 48). So Locke advances to his famous conclusion about the nature of the mind at birth. Given that we cannot find any innate ideas worthy of the name, then we should 'suppose the mind to be ... white paper void of all characters' at the time of birth (II.i.2, p. 67). The mind of the newborn child is an 'empty cabinet' (I.ii.15, p. 19).

In presenting his arguments against innate ideas in the *Essay*, Locke did not draw attention to the underlying political implications. He did not, for example, make a link to his anonymous *Treatises of Government*. He must have realized that readers would not be slow to make connections of their own. The thesis of the mind as an empty cabinet indicates a form of radical egalitarianism. Whatever their social rank, all children are similar at birth. The minds of royal babies are as blank as those of commoners. No sign of divine anointment can be detected in their mewling – not that Locke put the point directly. He had no need to.

Locke writes confidently about the state of the child's mind. He cites the principles of observation: if we observe attentively the condition of newborn children, we will see that they come into the world without pre-formed ideas. He does not detail the evidence for his observations, but he implies that, if anyone had observed children as he had done, they would come to the same conclusion. There is an interesting little mystery here. When, in the late nineteenth century, psychologists started charting the course of infant development, they tended to base their observations on their own children. Darwin (1877) had set the pattern. He was followed by the German psychologist Preyer (1889) and also by Sully (1895) in his *Studies of Childhood*. All had watched their own children closely, using them to come to conclusions about what children could and could not do at particular ages. Milicent Shinn, however, had no children of her own but she closely watched her brother's daughter from birth. Her classic book *The Biography of a Baby* was based on these observations (Shinn, 1900).

Locke, by contrast, was a childless bachelor, who lacked access to a handy niece or nephew. Yet, he was writing confidently about the cognitive abilities of infants. When he was writing the first draft of the *Essay* between 1670 and 1671, he was closely familiar with one particular infant. He had been entrusted to supervise the welfare of the future third Earl of Shaftesbury. Everything we know about Locke suggests he would have discharged his duties carefully and attentively. The fascinating possibility is that the confidence with which Locke wrote about infant capabilities stemmed from his observation of a young child who would grow up to reject Locke's empty cabinet theory and, indeed, Locke's whole cognitivist perspective. Seldom in the history of psychology can the child have been father to both the thesis and the anti-thesis.

Sensation and Reflection

Having dismissed the possibility of innate ideas, Locke started the second book of the *Essay* by asking where our knowledge of the world comes from. He gave a simple reply to his own question: 'I answer, in one word, from experience; in that all our knowledge is founded' (II.i.2, p. 67). This simple answer expresses the hybrid nature of the *Essay*. In what follows Locke outlines a psychological theory, which traces human knowledge back to experiences. There is also a prescriptive element. Whatever belief is not based on experience has little right to be considered as knowledge.

Locke may have declared that the origins of knowledge can be described by the single word – 'experience', but, almost immediately, this single source bifurcates. We have two ways of knowing about things: experience consists of sensation and reflection. First, there is sensation, informing us about the external world, and also internal bodily states. Our senses tell us whether something is yellow, hot, cold, soft, bitter, sweet, etc. The experience of the senses must come first. We can formulate general categories of heat, coldness, bitterness, sweetness, etc. only after we have experienced the requisite sensations. This means that sensation is the 'great source of most of the ideas we have' (II.i.3, p. 68).

On its own perception would not provide us with the complex understanding of things. In order to form complex thoughts, we must also have the ability to 'reflect on and consider' what the mind receives by means of perception (II.i.4, p. 68). Consequently, we possess an 'internal sense' that permits the mind to reflect 'on its operations within itself', distinguishing, for example, present sensations from memories (II.i.4, p. 68). All ideas are derived from sensation and reflection, but, in the matter of origins, sensations have priority. Without the senses providing ideas (or cognitions), the mind would not have any material on which it could reflect.

Much of the *Essay's* second book describes how we form complex ideas out of simple ones. There is no need here to go into the details of Locke's arguments, except to note that for the fourth edition he added a final chapter to the second book, 'Of the association of ideas'. One commentator has called this 'the single most productive chapter in the *Essay*', on account of its influence on later philosophy and psychology (Aarsleff, 1994, p. 268). In this chapter Locke discussed the different ways that ideas can be combined with each other. In essentials, the chapter brought together arguments that he had outlined earlier. But what Locke added in this chapter was the term 'association' and this addition was to prove historically decisive.

The term 'association' became central in the history and vocabulary of psychology. In the nineteenth century, 'associationism' was the name of those psychologies that claimed association to be the key process by which habits, thoughts and beliefs are formed. Prominent among the associationists were Mill and other thinkers taking their inspiration from Locke. William James, who was critical of associationism as a general approach to psychology, nevertheless admitted that 'few principles of analysis, in any science, have been more fertile' than that of association (1890, vol. 1, p. 604). Locke had been concerned with the association of ideas, or cognitions. However, the principle of association was to become transferred from ideas to behaviour in the early twentieth century. It was the cornerstone of behaviourism, which attempted to demonstrate how behavioural responses become associated with stimuli. In this way, as Thomas Leahey has pointed out, the concept of association remained 'the dominant force' in much of psychology until the last part of the twentieth century (2003, p. 117).

Two features of Locke's psychology can be mentioned here: its *atomism* and its *historical individualism*. Both these characteristics will be discussed in more detail in chapter four. Both characteristics provoked reactions from contemporary critics. Locke's psychological theory and his method of procedure were atomistic. He was concerned to break down complex ideas into their simple components. He claimed that, at root, our complex thoughts derived from simple, clear and distinct ideas. Simple perceptual ideas were like psychological atoms. The complex structures of thought were – and, indeed, should be – built out of these basic units.

The second characteristic was the individualism of Locke's historical method. He asked about the origins of ideas and he traced these origins to the perceptual experiences of the individual. To substantiate the point, he went back to the earliest history of each individual – to the time at birth when the mind was supposedly an empty cabinet. In this respect, Locke's plain, historical method produces a history of each individual mind, which is taken as a self-contained unit. This history always has the same story to tell. Each mind comes into the world empty. It is then filled with sensations and from these the individual constructs its own ideas. There is no sense that the mind itself may be a socio-historical creation, as individuals grow up to be members of continuing, cultural traditions. It is as if this mysterious object – the mind – is an autochthonous creation.

Locke's psychology, then, is very much a psychology of the individual, conceived as an isolated receiver of sights and sounds. Significantly, his descriptions of the newborn child exclude the actions of parents. In the search for the origins of ideas, this psychology does not look across generations; it does not see the infant as inheriting ideas from the wider historical context in which it is born; nor does it see the wider context as constructing the mind of the child. Locke might have called his method 'historical' but, in truth, this type of history excludes all history except that of the isolated individual. As will be seen in the next chapter, this sort of unhistorical, psychological history was to clash with a cross-generational history in a matter very close to Locke himself: in the controversy about the origins of his own ideas.

The Foundations of Knowledge

In the *Essay*, Locke used his observations about the origins of ideas as a justification for claiming that observation is the criterion for truth. In Locke's view, clear perceptions of the world are possible. Sometimes our perceptions can be unclear and misleading, but generally they are not. The mind is capable of receiving accurate images of the external world directly. Locke conceived the basic perceptual process to be 'merely passive', for the objects of our sense 'obtrude their particular ideas upon our minds, whether we will or no'. In this way, we obtain simple ideas from the world: 'As the bodies that surround us do diversely affect our organs, the mind is forced to receive the impressions' (II.i.25, p. 80).

Philosophically, the idea of perception as a passive process was important for Locke. It enabled him to claim that perception provides the foundation for objective knowledge. We can see the world as it really is. Our minds are not involved in a systematic distortion of external reality. Locke stated that '*our simple* ideas *are all real*, all agree to the reality of things' (II.xxx.2, p. 345, emphasis in original). He went on to underline the point: our simple ideas 'are all real and true, because they answer and agree to those powers of things which produce them in our minds' (p. 346). Thus, our senses receive true images of the world, whether we will it or not. In this way, Locke's position is *foundationalist*: knowledge has clear foundations, namely in our simple ideas.

If the simple ideas of perception provide the foundation for knowledge, then we need to ensure that our complex ideas are derived accurately from clear and distinct, simple ideas. That way our complex ideas will themselves be clear: 'Complex ideas, as they are made up of simple ones, so they are clear, when the ideas that go into their conception are clear' (II.xxix.2, p. 337). Errors of thinking occur when complex ideas are not based upon simple, clear and distinct ideas, or when we are at fault with the way that we combine simple ideas together.

In the third book, Locke discussed how the abuses of language can produce erroneous thoughts. His basic point was that the categories of language must be matched to ideas. If words become detached from clear and distinct ideas, then they can mislead. Using words without clear and distinct ideas was, according to Locke, 'the first and most palpable abuse' of language (III.x.2, p. 90). Abstract and metaphysical thinkers all too often invent complex words that are not allied to clear ideas. To remedy such abuses it was necessary to use words clearly and carefully. A man should take care to '*use no word without a signification*, no name without an idea for which he makes it stand'; the ideas that are annexed to words 'must be clear and distinct' (III.xi.9–10, p. 110, emphasis in original). This is, of course, the goal of scientific language. Each concept is to be clearly and distinctly defined, with extraneous meanings removed, just as extraneous variables are to be controlled within the laboratory.

All too often, people use words that are not linked to clear ideas. Philosophers are particularly guilty of this abuse. For instance, 'the several sects of philosophy and religion' coin new words to cover weakness in their arguments and these words fail to 'stand for any clear and distinct ideas' (III.x.2, p. 90). Worse still, these sects appropriate ordinary terms and use them loosely. In consequence, Locke aimed to make language clearer. He was as distrustful of flamboyant language as he was of jargon. He denounced fancy rhetoric: 'All the artificial and figurative applications of words eloquence has invented, are for nothing else but to insinuate wrong ideas, move the passions, and thereby mislead the judgement, and so indeed are perfect cheats' (III.x.34, p. 106). He did not justify the rhetorical eloquence of his own denunciation of rhetoric.

Locke's views about the proper and improper uses of language stem from a very restricted view of language. The basic units of his psychology were the simple ideas of experience. Because ideas belong to the mind of the person who experiences them, there needs to be a way of transmitting ideas from mind to mind. This, for Locke, was the prime function of language. He wrote: '*Words, in their primary or immediate signification, stand for nothing but the ideas in the mind of him that uses them*' (III.ii.2, p. 4, emphasis in original). Therefore, it was important to use words so that they clearly denote the ideas that are in the mind of the individual speaker.

This is a very individualist (and implausible) view of language. Many years later, Wittgenstein and others would show why the meanings of public language cannot rest on internal, subjective states. Language is a social activity and the use of words must rest on publicly available, social conventions – otherwise there could be no shared language. Besides, we do much more with language than try to name inner sensations or experienced ideas. The linguist Roy Harris has called the sort of view that Locke proposed 'telementation': it sees language as the conduit permitting 'the conveyance of ideas from the mind of one individual to another' (Harris, 1997, p. 128; see also Harris, 2002, and Toolen, 1998). Harris claims that telementation had been the prevailing view of language within Western philosophy since the ancient Greeks, but Locke gave it an extra boost, by providing it with a philosophical and psychological grounding.

Today, the critique of telementation has become a central theme in the critique of cognitivism. Anti-cognitivists claim that public language does not, and cannot, function primarily as a means of labelling private inner experiences, which then are transferred by the artificial medium of words from one mind to another (e.g., Harris, 2004; Harré, 2002; Harré and Gillett, 1994; Potter and Wetherell, 1987; Shotter, 1993a and 1993b). If this were the case, how could there ever be agreement about what words mean? And how would we understand the words of others? The critique of Locke's view of language did not have to wait until the twentieth century. As will be seen, the reaction against Locke in the eighteenth century by Shaftesbury and Reid involved a social view of language that is opposed to the theory of telementation.

Locke's distrust of language would be shared by later experimental psychologists. Experimentalists also would decry the use of rhetoric and would attempt to purge their vocabulary of terms that were not clearly and distinctly defined. Key concepts would be operationally defined in terms of experimental procedures, so that psychological terms would be linked to observable phenomena. That, at least, was the hope and the official line. There was a certain paradox relating to cognitive science – a paradox also to be found in Locke's *Essay*. A determinedly empirical approach, that rooted knowledge in observation, was being used for the study of things that were, by their very nature, unobservable. This was true of Locke's 'ideas'. It is also true of cognitive science's quest to study 'mental representations' or 'cognitions'. One cannot see or touch such entities. In Locke's sense, it is impossible to have a clear and distinct idea of an idea – or of a mental representation.

Evaluating Locke's Cognitive Psychology

If Locke is to be seen as the father of cognitive psychology, then some sort of evaluation of his theory is required. This evaluation should not initially proceed from the perspective of a critical psychologist or anti-cognitivist. Fundamental criticisms of Locke's perspective will emerge as Shaftesbury and Reid are discussed in later chapters. A very brief evaluation on cognitive psychology's own terms is first required, in order to see how Locke's ideas broadly stand in relation to recent research in cognitive science.

Locke has made some non-obvious, enduring contributions to today's cognitive science. When discussing how the mind remembers things, Locke used the metaphor that memory was 'the storehouse of our ideas' (II.x.2, p. 111). It has been suggested that later psychologists adopted Locke's metaphor which eventually became established in modern psychology as the concept of 'long-term memory store' (Draaisma, 2000, p. 44). No doubt, this is not the only conceptual link that could be found between the *Essay* and the language of today's cognitive science.

In any evaluation of Locke as a cognitive scientist, one obvious point must be made, but not over-laboured. The analyses produced by today's cognitive scientists are much more complicated and technical than those made by Locke. From the perspective of cognitive science, Locke wrote imprecisely. He tended to talk of the ways ideas become associated with each other – how for example a present thought can evoke a past memory. He did not even use the concept of 'association' with the precision that David Hume tried to in the eighteenth century. And Hume's attempts at precision are nothing compared with those of today's cognitive scientists, who will draw complex diagrams to illustrate the interconnections between the various cognitive processes that are presumed to be involved in mental operations. Nevertheless, some cognitive scientists have taken seriously the accounts offered by Locke (and by Hume) about the way that we form general categories (e.g., Collier, 2005; Fodor, 2003; Rosch, 2000).

Whereas Locke ignored the physiological basis of mental functions, most cognitive scientists today do not. The trend has been to produce models of mental connections that, it is hoped, parallel underlying physiological processes. In this regard, today's connectionist models are 'neurally inspired' (Plunkett et al., 1998, p. 10). However, this modern emphasis on neurophysiology should not itself be sufficient reason to dismiss Locke's approach as hopelessly old-fashioned. Direct evidence to link the cognitive models with their presumed neurophysiological basis is often lacking. In fact, one leading cognitive scientist, Jerry Fodor, has written scathingly about the trend to describe mental operations in terms of assumed neural connections: it may be a good tactic for getting grants 'but it does cause a lot of confusion' (Fodor and Lepore, 2002, p. 192n).

Even so, a grandfatherly link between Locke and connectionist models might still be retained. David Hartley's *Observations on Man*, published in 1748, could be considered to be the first systematic attempt to provide a speculative neurophysiological model of thinking. Hartley suggested that mental operations depended on the transmission of vibrations though the nervous system. Large vibrations had large psychological effects, while 'vibratiuncles', or 'diminutive vibrations', had lesser effects (1748/1834, p. 37). Although Hartley's physiology was entirely speculative – and would be ridiculed by Thomas Reid on that account – some historians of psychology have fulsomely praised his contributions. Hergenhahn claims that Hartley's notions about the way the brain records the association of ideas is 'remarkably modern', anticipating the conclusions of physiologists 200 years later (2001, p. 129). Wertheimer suggests that 'the spirit of Hartley is still very much alive in contemporary associationism, in the conditioning approach, in the research field of verbal learning, and in psychophysiology' (1981, p. 42). If Hartley is the ancestral father of today's connectionism, then, as he made clear in *Observations*, his description of mental processes owed everything to Locke. According to Hartley, Locke and his followers had shown 'in an accurate and precise way' the power of association over 'our opinions and affections' (Hartley, 1748/1834, p. 5).

The big question regarding Locke's psychology is the one which he poses in the opening book of the *Essay*: is the mind devoid of ideas at birth? All psychologists today (and probably nearly all philosophers in Locke's day) would accept that the young child is not born with fully fledged ideas in the ordinary sense of the term 'idea'. However, that does not mean that the mind (or brain) at birth is an empty cabinet. It might possess particular structures that determine its mode of operation. To use a term from today's cognitive science, the child might be born with an identifiable 'cognitive architecture'.

Locke's theory throws up two related, but fundamental, problems. Is perception the passive process that he presumed? And where does our ability to reflect upon perception come from? It cannot come from perception itself, especially if perception is a passive process. Locke assumed that reflection is set in motion by perception. That would imply that the ability to reflect is some sort of innate capacity – or part of the cognitive architecture of the mind.

Most cognitive psychologists today would agree that one cannot understand cognitive processing if the mind (or brain) is conceived to be merely an empty cabinet. It is necessary to assume some sort of innate, or biologically determined, predisposition. Most famously, Noam Chomsky (1957 and 1964) argued that we cannot explain children's facility with language without positing innate predispositions or what one follower has termed a 'language instinct' (Pinker, 1994). According to Chomsky, 'the child, endowed with certain innate capacities, acquires knowledge of a language – automatically, and with little if any choice in the matter' (Chomsky, 2000, p. 54). Controversially, Chomsky (1966) called these linguistic predispositions innate ideas, thereby distancing his work from Locke's cognitive analyses of language. There has been controversy amongst cognitive linguists about identifying exactly which language capacities might be innate. Chomsky has argued for the innateness of recursive thinking and the ability to use syntax. Others have claimed that Chomsky places too much emphasis on syntactical skills, while ignoring the possible innateness of representational, computational and communicative skills (see, for instance, Carey, 2001; Fitch et al., 2005; Hauser et al., 2002; Jackendoff and Pinker, 2005). In this debate, both sides agree that there must be innate language capacities that are biologically determined; neither side, however, can agree what precisely these capacities might be or identify what is their biological basis.

Certainly Locke's account of perception as an essentially passive process would not satisfy cognitive scientists today. External stimuli do not simply flood into the perceptual apparatus that records them faithfully. Attention is directed and stimuli are selected, organized and grouped. One cognitive scientist has written that perception possesses an 'essentially active character', making it distinct from the 'passive, receptive view of that faculty that Locke held' (Fuster, 2003, p. 85). The Gestalt psychologists, whose work will be later discussed in relation to Shaftesbury's ideas, argued for an innate capacity to group patterns of stimuli into perceived wholes. Thus, we are predisposed to organize incoming perceptual information in particular ways. In this sense, the perceptual system constructs its image of the world, rather than passively receiving it.

Evidence for the innate, constructive nature of perception comes from studies of facial recognition by infants. Young infants will attend to and follow the human face from birth, as well as responding likewise to patterns resembling the face (Johnson, 2000; Nelson, 2000). As such, facial patterns are treated differently from other patterns. This gives rise to the possibility that there might be specialized cortical structures for the recognition of faces, as compared with other objects. Among cognitive neuroscientists this is a matter of dispute (see Farah, 2000, and Farah et al., 2000, for arguments in favour of specialized cortical structures for face-recognition; for opposing arguments, see Gauthier et al., 1999; Hayward and Tarr, 2005). Again, the precise skills involved and their possible biological basis may be contested, but there is broad agreement that human infants possess an innate, unlearnt predisposition to select faces for attention.

One aspect of Locke's account finds a *prima facie* resonance in the work of some cognitive theorists. Locke implied that some sort of pure perception occurred prior to the work of the understanding. Zenon Pylyshyn (2001 and 2004) distinguishes between the perception of objects and the cognitive interpretation of these perceptions. According to Pylyshyn, there is an early visual system that picks out, or indexes, objects as objects before recognizing the properties of those objects. He claims that this early visual system is 'cognitively impenetrable'. Pylyshyn's concept of an early visual system was designed to apply to adult perception. The bulk of his supporting evidence comes from complex experiments involving adults tracking objects that become masked or hidden. Not all the experimental results neatly fit the theory (Keane and Pylyshyn, 2005). The basic idea has also been applied to infant perception, to suggest that infants also have an early visual system (Scholl and Leslie, 1999; Xu et al., 2004).

At first sight, Pylyshyn's notion of 'cognitively impenetrable' perceptions seems to fit Locke's account: our perceptions come first and then we reflect on them. However, Pylyshyn's work does not fully support Locke's theory. Broadly speaking, it suggests that we recognize objects as objects, before we ascribe properties to them. But this means that the idea of 'objecthood' is primary: it is what Pylyshyn terms a 'primitive visible'. 'Objecthood', thus, functions psychologically rather like the Kantian *a priori*. The perceiver automatically locates the visual display in space and time before ascribing particular properties to the display. This means that infants are innately predisposed to see objects as objects: they are not just receiving stimuli in a purely passive manner. The human infant, when perceiving a face, will spatially connect the eyes and mouth as part of the same object. When tracking the movement of the face, the infant will be assuming that the same object is being viewed across space and time. This is not something that an empty cabinet or a white sheet of paper can do.

This all suggests that humans possess innate predispositions to understand and make sense of the world in particular ways. We do not passively receive external stimuli, but from birth we are organizing and constructing our views of the outside world. Moreover, we possess linguistic predispositions that further organize our thinking and permit us to enter into the world of conversation and dialogue. On these matters, Locke's *Essay*, with its primary emphasis on demolishing the notion of innate ideas and stressing the role of clear perception, has little to offer.

We might then conclude that Locke posed many of the key questions which continue to be asked by cognitive scientists. His own answers to the questions were too simple, especially in relation to the issue of innate cognitive predispositions. Later cognitive scientists, by virtue of carefully observing the reactions of infants in controlled situations, have been able to show that the mind/brain is not best understood as an empty cabinet at birth. Such a conclusion would fit an ordered historical story. First comes Locke with a simple theory and then there is progressively increasing knowledge about the complexities of cognition.

But that itself would be far too simple a history. It omits too much. It suggests that Locke may have been overstating things with his condemnation of innate ideas but that he was on the right track. It does not question where Locke's ideas came from – whether they have a longer history. Nor, most crucially, does it examine exactly what views Locke was opposing when he argued against innate ideas. It is too easy to presume that he was just opposing out-dated religious prejudices – rather than opposing ideas that also prefigure today's thinking about cognitive skills and innate predispositions. In short, there are further stories to be told about the history of Locke's ideas about ideas – a history that the *Essay,* with its plain historical method, does not reveal.

4 Locke's New Way of Ideas

● ● ● ● ● ● ● ● ● ● ● ● ● ● ● ● ● ● ●

Claims about originality in the history of ideas are by no means simple. It is not just a matter of praising the supposed innovator. To claim that Locke is a precursor of modern cognitive psychology is to suggest a similarity between his way of thinking and that of today's cognitive psychologists. As was seen in the previous chapter, there are reasonable grounds for making such a claim. But that is only part of being heralded as the parent of an academic discipline. The other part concerns the relations between the parent and their forebears. The parent must be seen to have accomplished a rupture of intellectual history. They have to appear to be stepping out from their own past and towards a future that is familiar to us.

In the case of cognitive psychology, the claim of historical parentage involves a double rupturing of history. The parent, like any disciplinary ancestor, must be seen to disrupt intellectual history by the power of original thinking. In this way, the parent separates the start of 'our' enlightenment from the darkness of earlier times. The insights of cognitive psychology also involve a further rupturing of history. It has been argued that cognitive psychology, like much modern psychology, tends to treat individuals as self-contained units that stand outside of the processes of history. Locke's historical method involved tracing the origins of ideas back to the birth of the individual and no further. The continuity of history is theoretically ruptured. There is no movement across generations. Instead, the subjects of psychology are presented as if they were universal, self-created, cognitive beings.

One can ask how Locke might have accomplished this double rupture. The rhetorical presentation of his work was crucial. As will be seen, Locke introduced his work as if he were starting anew, sweeping aside the rubbish of past ages. In doing this, Locke suggested a discontinuity of reasonableness: the reasonableness of now is contrasted with the unreasonableness of the past. It is one thing to claim historical discontinuity; it is another to substantiate it. It will be suggested that Locke's self-presentation hides as much as it reveals.

Contrary to what Locke was implying, there was a double continuity of reasonableness. Some of the thinkers, whom Locke was sweeping aside, were actually saying things that were not totally marked by pre-scientific prejudice. In fact, some of the ideas, which Locke dismissively lumped under the heading of 'innate ideas', prefigure thinking in today's cognitive psychology. There is another line in the continuity of reasonableness. This is the continuity that connects Locke, and thereby cognitive psychology, with earlier philosophers. Locke followed his own psychological method to present himself as the self-creator of his own thoughts. But this self-presentation downplayed, and even concealed, his intellectual continuities with the past. Locke's seemingly open style – his straightforward, down-to-earth rhetoric – contains its own secrets and omissions.

To substantiate these claims of continuity, it will be necessary to remember thinkers, who are omitted in Locke's texts and in most of psychology's disciplinary histories. The story, here, will include figures such as Epicurus, Pierre Gassendi, Ralph Cudworth and Damaris Masham – names that will mean little to most psychologists today. But that is the point. The critical evaluation of a discipline's own self-history must involve remembering the forgotten, in order to suggest different lines of continuity and discontinuity.

The Scientific Under-Labourer

The short, prefatory 'Epistle to the Reader' is the place to start, in order to see how Locke presented his *Essay* to the world. There is a famous passage that has been much quoted over the years. Locke introduced his work with great modesty, saying he was not proposing a grand system. He was merely the under-labourer, clearing the ground for the great builders of the day:

> The commonwealth of learning is not at this time without master-builders, whose mighty designs, in advancing the sciences, will leave lasting monuments to the admiration of posterity; but everyone must not hope to be a Boyle or a Sydenham; and in an age that produces such masters as the great Huygenius and the incomparable Mr. Newton, with some others of that strain; it is ambition enough to be employed as an under-labourer, clearing the ground a little, and removing some of the rubbish that lies in the way to knowledge. ('Epistle': the early editions of the *Essay* do not number the pages of the Epistle)

Locke's choice of master-builders is interesting. None of them was a metaphysician or an ancient authority. All were modern scientists, well established in the world of science. Each of the four advocated a 'natural philosophy', which was based on close observation of the world and which rejected subservience to traditional Aristotelian theories. Locke knew each personally. Huygens, Boyle and Newton were, in common with Locke, early members of the Royal Society, which was explicitly established to examine the natural world through observation and experimentation (Gribbin, 2006; Hall, 2002; Woolhouse, 1994).

Robert Boyle (1627–1691) is known for his discoveries in chemistry. The eponymous Boyle's Law states that the pressure of gas, under a constant temperature, varies inversely according to its volume. Together with Robert Hooke, Boyle built an air pump, to disprove the ancient adage that 'nature abhors a vacuum'. Boyle dedicated his *Memoirs for the Natural History of the Human Blood* to Locke. Christiaan Huygens (1629–1695) was a Dutch mathematician and physicist who made notable contributions to the development of calculus and probability theory, as well as inventing the pendulum clock. Locke was one of the English intellectuals to whom Huygens gave a presentation copy of his *Traité de Lumière* (Axtell, 1991). For many years Locke maintained friendly correspondence with the incomparable Mr Newton who, in his dealings with people, could be incomparably difficult. Locke, ever tactful and considerate, experienced none of the fallings-out that befell so many of Newton's other friends. Their association was not just personal. When Locke was Secretary to the Board of Trade and Newton was Warden of the Mint, they met regularly to discuss monetary policies for the colonies (Laslett, 1990).

Sydenham is a less familiar name, but in his time he was known as the most notable physician in England. Sydenham was eight years older than Locke and the two met in 1677. This was the start of close friendship that lasted until Sydenham's death in 1689 (Cranston, 1985; Osler, 1990). In the early years, Locke frequently accompanied Sydenham on his rounds in London (Milton, 1994). For many years Locke was to seek Sydenham's advice about treatments for his occasional patients (see, for instance, letters in Beer, 1978, pp. 496 and 500). Both men were highly sceptical of traditional theories of illness. They shared an empirical approach, based on the close observation of what effects medicines had upon the body. Naturally, both closely followed the physiological discoveries that men like Boyle were making.

By picking out these four figures, Locke was indicating to his readers that the great system-builders of the day were scientists committed to empirical observation. Each, like Locke, believed that scientific knowledge was 'a process beginning with sense data, collected by observation or by experiment' (Harris, 1998, p. 84). The under-labourer's job was humbler than the system-builder's: it was merely to show how knowledge of the world had to proceed by way of experience. To do this, the under-labourer had some rubble to remove.

Locke does not specify who is responsible for dumping the rubbish. He is too tactful and too cautious to name his opponents. He writes in general terms. The established metaphysicians, he complains, have failed in their tasks because they have insisted on using language that is disconnected from the realities of the world:

> Vague and insignificant forms of speech, and abuse of language, have so long passed for mysteries of science; and hard and misapplied words, with little or no meaning, have, by prescription, such a right to be mistaken for deep learning and height of speculation, that it will not be easy to persuade either those who speak or those who hear them that they are but the covers of ignorance, and hindrance of true knowledge. ('Epistle')

Locke depicts himself as breaking with established, but unnamed, authorities in the name of truth, knowledge and plain language. There is an implicit sense of historical rupture. The 'Epistle' does not mention any master-builder of the past – no ancient figure is compared with the incomparable Mr Newton. It is as if the present has no need of ancestral buildings.

Locke described how the *Essay* originated. Five or six friends met in his chamber to discuss a very different (but unspecified) topic. The small group found themselves perplexed about the nature of knowledge. Locke offered to write down some thoughts on this issue for their next meeting. He originally set down 'some hasty and undigested thoughts', in the belief that 'all I should have to say on this matter would have been contained in one sheet of paper' ('Epistle'). Instead, the labour continued over many years. New discoveries led him on and so the book 'grew insensibly to the bulk it now appears in'. Locke apologized for the book's imperfections. These arose because the work was intermittent but prolonged; and it was also 'spun out of my own coarse thoughts'. This was a phrase to figure in later controversies.

The modesty is appealing: my thoughts are coarse; I am just the under-labourer, shifting rubble away. Beyond the modesty is modern confidence. We are now discarding the errors of previous ages. The ancient books can be put aside. There is no need to look backwards; we can observe the present carefully. The future holds the promise of truth. No wonder later experimental psychologists would find Locke to be an agreeable father-figure. They too imagine themselves to be replacing the metaphysical speculations of the past with the careful, systematic observation of the present.

The Epistle mentions no intellectual debts. Locke does not describe sitting down to study the works of others who might have considered similar issues. He does not thank Hobbes for his insights into the nature of human motives and into the operations of the human mind. Nor does he pay tribute to Descartes and his attempt to found human knowledge on certain reason. These modern figures are ignored both in the prefatory Epistle and, largely speaking, in the main body of the *Essay*.

Instead, Locke presents his philosophy as if it were an autochthonous creation. His analysis of the mind has come from his own thoughts and from nowhere else. There is no reason why that small meeting should not have happened at any point in history; or why anyone else might not have looked into their own mind and reported the discoveries that Locke was now making. The whole business is presented as if it did not depend on the completion of prior philosophical or scientific work. In this sense, Locke's history of his *Essay* removes the *Essay* from history. It was a self-made inquiry by a self-made man.

Ralph Cudworth and Innate Ideas

Foremost among the rubbish to be swept away was the doctrine of innate ideas. Locke presented the doctrine as if it were commonly held by philosophers and ordinary people. He began the section on innate ideas with the assertion that 'it is an established opinion amongst some men that there are in the understanding, certain innate principles, some primary notions ... as it were stamped on the mind of man, which the soul receives in its very first being and brings into the world with it' (I.ii.1, p. 13). He goes on to state that 'there is nothing more commonly taken for granted' that there are certain 'principles, both speculative and practical', which are universally accepted by all mankind (I.ii.2, p. 13). This opinion was 'the common road' from which he was going to depart (p. 13).

His argument, then, is to show the absurdity of this belief. Young children do not come into the world able to articulate maxims such as 'whatever is, is' or to make mathematical calculations. If we would only observe what infants can actually do, we would see the implausibility of innate ideas. Even if there are some beliefs which are universally accepted by all people, this does not make them innate. Locke applied these arguments to the belief in God. The belief, he wrote, is by no means universal (I.iv.8). And even if it were – which it is not – that would not prove that the idea is innate (I.iv.10). Locke saw himself to be challenging common prejudices, including the belief of religious people that God had seen fit 'to imprint, upon the minds of men, characters and notions of himself' (I.iv.12, p. 15). He foresaw that some would be offended but that was no reason for him to desist. In this way, Locke depicted himself as a battler against common orthodoxy.

At no point does Locke quote from, or even identify, a philosopher, who held the doctrine of innate ideas either in the present or the past. Locke writes as if he expected his readers to know who these orthodox thinkers were, just as he expected them to recognize the near universality of the belief in innate ideas. However, with the distance of time – and with the decline of the belief in the 'naturalness' of religion – it is now necessary to fill in some of the gaps.

Educated readers in England would have been aware of the Cambridge Platonists, who were reviving the ideas of Plato in order to combat, as they saw it, the philosophical trends towards materialism and atheism (Cassirer, 1953; Hutton, 1996 and 2002). Plato had suggested that we come into the world with memories of a life before birth, and that learning often was a process of remembering this past, rather than acquiring new memories. Foremost among the Platonists was Ralph Cudworth (1617–1688), whose immensely scholarly and densely argued *The True Intellectual System of the World* had appeared in 1678. In that book, Cudworth sought to trace the intellectual roots of atheism and materialism so that those evils could be repelled all the better. Cudworth died a couple of years before Locke's *Essay* appeared, but while Locke was drafting and re-drafting his great work, Cudworth was the dominant figure in English academic philosophy.

Locke's *Essay* could not be more different in style from Cudworth's *True Intellectual System*. Locke's work barely contains any quotations from previous writers. He was discarding the old traditions of metaphysics in order to describe the operations of the mind as he saw them. Cudworth was steeped in ancient and theological learning. He was spinning out thoughts from the library. Quotations, footnotes, references to obscure texts were his warp and woof. Locke's *Essay* may at times be repetitious; Cudworth is virtually unreadable.

The difference between Cudworth and Locke was more than stylistic. They were proposing very different psychologies of thinking. Whereas Locke claimed that the mind passively received sensations from outside, Cudworth stressed that the mind was an active producer of thought. He argued that our abstract ideas could not merely come through the senses. Nor are they simply acquired from other people. Learning is not to be compared with pouring liquid into an empty vessel. Nor is it a process of remembrance as Plato suggested. It is an active process, in which the mind is excited to 'awaken, compare and compound its own notions' (1678, p. 693).

Cudworth discussed at length the concept of God, which he believed to be an almost universal idea amongst humanity. He suggested that if there were no God, then it is inconceivable 'how the forementioned idea should have entered into the minds of men' (p. 693). Atheists might claim that humans pick up the idea of God from what others tell them. But that would imply, so Cudworth argued, that we passively receive the words of others. His whole theory of the mind was designed to counter such a notion of passivity. Even if the idea of God were passed on by others, that would not explain the force of the idea and how it excites the imagination when it is received from others. The idea of God, Cudworth suggested, must possess a special force, which appeals to the inborn nature of the mind.

If that is the case, then the mind must already possess its own potential powers before learning can take place. It cannot be an empty vessel but it is primed to be excited by certain ideas. Therefore, from the moment of birth the mind is equipped with its own active power or what Cudworth, in his *Treatise Concerning Eternal and Immutable Morality*, called its 'innate cognoscitive power'. Knowledge derives from within the soul as much as from the external world. According to Cudworth, 'this innate cognoscitive power in the soul can be nothing else but a power of raising intelligible ideas and conceptions of things from within itself' (1731/1996, p. 77). Cudworth did not believe that this innate power equips the infant with particular ideas at birth, but it predisposes the developing child to think in certain ways and, most crucially, to take up particular ideas. In so arguing, Cudworth was able to produce a theory of mind that suited his theology.

Cudworth's theory of innate powers is more sophisticated than the doctrines that Locke dismissed in the opening book of the *Essay*. Cudworth was not supposing that infants could understand complex, abstract concepts; he was suggesting that we are predisposed to make active sense of the world. In this regard, Cudworth was prefiguring important themes of today's cognitive science. The mind is not an empty vessel which will democratically receive each stimulus in the same way; it has a cognitive architecture or possesses innate 'cognoscitive powers'; perception and learning, therefore, do not occur passively but are the means by which we actively create our views of the world.

Cudworth's account of language resonates with the ideas of Chomsky, although, of course, the latter did not suggest that there was an innate predisposition to accept the concept of God. Nevertheless, in broad terms Chomsky would be able to agree with Cudworth's comments. They both claim that children do not passively accept the words of adults. The language of adults sets off the child's powers to combine words and create new meanings. As Chomsky argued, a theory of passive acceptance cannot explain how children, from a very early age, create new sentences that they have never heard. To do this, children must possess, to adapt Cudworth's heavy handed vocabulary, innate cogno-linguistic powers.

Today Cudworth attracts very few readers and even fewer admirers. As a philosopher he is a minor, easily overlooked figure. His brand of Protestant Platonism certainly does not figure in the histories of academic psychology. However tortuous his theological exegesis might be, his psychological ideas about the nature of the mind are by no means ridiculous. Locke might have wished to create the impression of a decisive rupture between his own empirical view of the mind and the metaphysical speculations that preceded him. Nevertheless, in the intellectual relations between Locke and Cudworth, the rupture between present reasonableness and past unreasonableness is not quite as clearcut as Locke might have hoped. In the light of today's work in the cognitive sciences, it is possible to see a continuity of reasonableness between present psychology and the approach that Locke wished to sweep aside.

Plain Rhetoric and a Secret

In seeking to refute the doctrine of innate ideas, Locke chose not to address the specific arguments of the Cambridge Platonists. He could easily have mentioned the Reverend Cudworth and other learned gentlemen, who had of late entertained the theory of innate ideas. He was, of course, no stranger to polemical argument. *The Treatises of Government* (1690/1977) was a refutation of Robert Filmer, about whose work Locke was not exactly complimentary. We cannot know exactly why Locke chose to ignore the work of opposing philosophers in the *Essay*. But we can judge the rhetorical benefits of his choosing to do so.

The absence of opponents lifts the *Essay* out of the context of controversy. Had Locke addressed the work of the Cambridge Platonists, he would have positioned his work as an intervention in a debate. Readers might then have expected the followers of Cudworth to offer counter-arguments against the book that they were reading. And so a continuing debate might be expected. Instead, Locke's rhetoric suggests a closing of debate: prejudice is being finally exposed. Locke's metaphor of clearing away rubble conveys the final removal of opposing ideas, not a persisting engagement with them.

Locke also had private reasons for not referring to Cudworth. In the narrow world of English metaphysics, the philosophical was often personal. There is evidence that during his life Locke had one great love – Lady Damaris Masham, who was several years younger than him. The story is told in Maurice Cranston's biography of Locke. She was a philosopher in her own right, publishing several books and corresponding with European thinkers such as Leibnitz. Locke had met her in 1682, when she was a young single woman. They exchanged loving letters, writing to each other using the pseudonyms Philander and Philoclea. Locke conducted correspondences with a series of women, using a flirtatious tone with just sufficient irony to suggest an escape route should the relationship start becoming serious. With Damaris things might have actually developed. However, Locke suddenly fled to Holland in 1683. Much to Darmaris's consternation, he gave her no warning, nor sent a forwarding address.

When they resumed their correspondence after a period of several years, she had married Sir Francis Masham, a widower with eight children. Sir Francis seems to have been a good-natured, country squire with few intellectual interests. When Locke discovered Damaris's change in status, it was his turn to be distraught. Damaris hinted that had Locke indicated the seriousness of his feelings in their earlier correspondence, things might well have turned out differently. But when the opportunity existed, Locke either did not want to commit himself, or, more likely, was unwilling to expose himself to the possibility of rejection.

When Locke returned to England, the Mashams became his new patrons. Locke went to live at their home at Oates in Essex. It was a comfortable arrangement for Locke, whose health was no longer good. There were to be no more loving letters to Damaris, a respectably married lady, who continued to publish books about virtue and Christian duty. Locke would occasionally write ambiguously flirtatious letters to her step-daughter Esther.

Locke's influence on Damaris Masham's writings is clear. In her book *Occasional Thoughts in Reference to a Virtuous or Christian Life* (1705) she wrote about education and used Lockean notions about our knowledge being 'immediately derived to us from sensation or reflection' (p. 26). As might be predicted, her account of the infant's tender years accords a greater role to the mother and nurse than Locke's did. She was also sensitive to the deficiencies in the sort of education that was conventionally provided for girls. She advocated that girls should receive as good an education as boys.

Damaris Masham's philosophical views about the nature of mind were not purely Lockean. The influence of Cudworth is also discernible. She argued that our knowledge does not just come from 'sensation or reflection', but it is also 'enlarged by the perception of remote or distant truths'. If we could only know things by sensation or reflection, then 'our knowledge and enjoyment would be very short of what they now are' (1705, p. 26). It is hardly surprising that Damaris Masham should have been influenced by Cudworth. She was the great metaphysician's daughter.

Damaris Cudworth always respected her father and his circle. She even sought to soften Locke's views on the Cambridge Platonists. In 1682, she wrote to Locke: 'That I have no ill opinion of the Platonists, I confess'. She went on to say that Locke should not be surprised since she had passed most of her life 'among philosophers of that sect in whom I have always found the most virtue and friendship' (Beer, 1976, p. 493).

She also retained her friendship for Locke. In later years he was by no means an easy house-guest, not least because his presence must have been a constant reminder of old, unfulfilled love. After Locke's death

Damaris Masham sent a tribute to Locke's old friend Jean Le Clerc. She wrote of Locke's greatness as a philosopher and the integrity of his character. His conversation was 'very agreeable to all sorts of persons' and he always 'faithfully kept a secret' (Masham, 1990, p. 351). He was polite and considerate and 'if he was subject to any passion, it was anger' (p. 351). It does not take a Freudian to suspect a hint of regret – not to say, reproach – in that last phrase. But Lady Masham, like her great friend, knew how to maintain polite relations, follow duty and faithfully keep secrets.

Certainly, Locke, after years of political service with the first Earl of Shaftesbury, could handle delicate situations. To have criticized Cudworth in the *Essay* would not have been gracious to his very dear friend, Damaris. On the other hand, Locke could hardly have altered his philosophical position. The modest pose of the empirical philosopher avoids the difficulty. He is just spinning forth his own ideas, setting matters down: he is not engaging in controversy. Locke's style, in contrast to that of Ralph Cudworth, is clear and down-to-earth. Yet a rhetoric that advertises its own openness can also contain its own secrets.

The Charge of Unoriginality

Locke's story of spinning out his own thoughts does more than disavow any wish to engage in personal controversy. It also suggests that Locke was not following the lead of anyone else. The fact that Locke does not mention other philosophers, who might have criticized the notion of innate ideas, strengthens the impression of originality. The question is whether there were other such philosophers – not remote figures, who would be known only to someone of Cudworth's prodigious learning – but familiar figures in the world of late seventeenth century thought. There was, it will be suggested, one such philosopher, who was held in great standing by Locke's colleagues and whose absence from the pages of the *Essay* is notable.

The issue of Locke's originality is not a new issue. The charge of plagiarism – or taking the ideas of earlier thinkers without due attribution – has been made against him down the ages. Perhaps the most ill-tempered version was to come from the poet Coleridge, who suggested that if one subtracted from the *Essay* Locke's borrowings from other thinkers, then all that would be left would be several errors of Locke's own making (Coleridge, 1990).

The issue of originality surfaced during Locke's own lifetime in his controversy with the theologian and prolific writer Edward Stillingfleet, Bishop of Worcester. Stillingfleet first criticized Locke's *Essay* in his book *A Discourse in Vindication of the Doctrine of the Trinity* (1697a). Locke published a reply in the same year (Locke, 1697a).

Stillingfleet came back with his *Answer to Mr Locke's Letter* (1697b). Locke did not let the matter rest, but published his *Reply to the Bishop of Worcester's Answer to his Letter* (1697b). There was to be yet a further round of answer and response. As the exchanges continued, on both sides they became increasingly repetitive and tetchy.

The Bishop's main concerns were theological. He feared that what he called Locke's 'new way of ideas' was encouraging scepticism and heresy. Stillingfleet was prompted by the success of John Toland's book *Christianity Not Mysterious* (1696). Toland was an ex-Catholic who had zealously embraced Unitarianism and who seldom missed an opportunity for public controversy and self-promotion. In his book, Toland claimed that Locke's *Essay* justified a rational form of Christianity, shorn of superstitious mysteries. One of the superstitious mysteries, whose abandonment Toland was advocating, was belief in the divine Trinity – namely the belief that God, God's son and the Holy Spirit all shared the same substance. Toland argued, not without justification, that, according to Locke's theory of ideas, the general notion of 'substance' could not be derived from a clear and distinct idea of substance; and, therefore, Locke's arguments could be used against the theological notion of substance.

Stillingfleet, like most orthodox English Protestants, believed that the Trinity was essential to Christianity. He charged Locke with complicity in spreading heresy. In his answer to Locke's first letter, Stillingfleet declared that the 'world has been strangely amused with ideas of late'. He accused Locke of enabling 'the enemies of our faith to take up your new way of ideas, as an effectual battery (as they imagined) against the *Mysteries of the Christian Faith*' (1697b, p. 93). For his part, Locke argued, not altogether convincingly, that Toland had misquoted him. Locke also complained that he could not be held responsible for the use (or mis-use) that others – notably, Toland – made of his work. Stillingfleet might have charged Locke with advocating 'a new way of ideas', but Locke riposted that Stillingfleet, in attacking him for what others might have written, was using 'a new way of writing' (1699, p. 26). And so it went on, page after page, charge after peevish counter-charge.

Amongst Stillingfleet's many charges against Locke was the accusation that the 'new way of ideas' was not entirely new. Stillingfleet suggested that Locke may have taken 'the way of ideas' from a 'modern philosopher', who, though not named, clearly was Descartes (1697b, p. 81). Stillingfleet made this accusation, although in his *Discourse in Vindication* he had clearly distinguished between Locke's and Descartes' theories of knowledge (1697a, p. 246). Stillingfleet might just as well have cited Hobbes as Descartes, as the originator of the way of ideas. In the opening pages of *Leviathan*, Hobbes had written: 'There is no conception in a man's mind, which has not at first, totally or by parts, been begotten upon the organs of the sense' (1651, p. 3). In any event, Locke (1697a) denied having derived his thoughts from Descartes. He stressed that his ideas were 'spun barely out of my own thoughts' (p. 103). He was to use the phrase again, as the charge of unoriginality was repeated.

Stillingfleet was not impressed by Locke's claim that he had spun the ideas from his own thoughts. In Stillingfleet's opinion, that was beside the point: 'Many things may seem new to one that converses only with his own thoughts, which really are not so; as he may find when he looks into the thoughts of other men which appear in their books' (1697a, p. 81). Locke called this a 'gentle reprimand' (1697b, p. 73). In truth it was more than gentle: Stillingfleet was accusing Locke either of bad faith or poor scholarship. It would serve the world better, Stillingfleet had written, if people, who claimed to have had original thoughts, would 'examine what thoughts others have had before them' (1697a, p. 81).

Locke stuck to his guns. He had produced original thoughts because he had worked them out for himself, regardless of what anyone else had done in the past. What matters is not being the first to think something, but whether a thinker had invented their own thoughts without assistance: 'If in the spinning of them out of his own thoughts, they seem new to him, he is certainly the inventor of them' (1697b, p. 75). Clearly neither Locke nor Stillingfleet was going to convince the other. Locke, however, appears to have been stung by the so-called gentle reprimand. In the next revised edition of the *Essay*, he added a lengthy footnote, several pages long, dealing with the dispute with Stillingfleet (1690/1768, pp. 5–13). The exchange with Stillingfleet had stretched to well over a thousand printed pages, with the issue of originality being confined to just a handful of pages. Significantly, Locke devoted a disproportionate part of his new footnote for the *Essay* to countering the charge of unoriginality.

In their argument, Locke and Stillingfleet were producing different accounts of what it means to produce original ideas. Locke's account, as befitted the theory of the *Essay*, was psychological. The history of the individual's thought processes was all that mattered. Any individual, who had not encountered anyone else formulating such thoughts, could justly claim to have invented them: 'He that spins anything out of his own thoughts, that *seems new to him*, cannot cease to think it his own invention' (Locke, 1697b, pp. 75–6, emphasis in original). In this way, issues about the origins of ideas were reduced to questions of individual psychology.

For Stillingfleet this was unsatisfactory. No-one can truly invent something if someone else has already done so. The sense of history should stretch beyond the individual's life-story. Indeed, scholarly obligation demands that it does so: it is the duty of the thinker to search out and to study what others have done previously. In the controversy with Stillingfleet, Locke's reduction of history to individual psychology was clashing with the notion of history as a broader story. And if one sympathizes with Stillingfleet on this matter, then one is recognizing the limitations of Locke's plain, historical method.

Gassendi: Atomist and Epicurean

Rather than attempting to link the origins of Locke's ideas with Descartes, Stillingfleet would have had a stronger case had he connected Locke with another French philosopher of the previous generation. Pierre Gassendi (1592–1655) was a contemporary of Descartes and had an enormous reputation in his own day. One recent commentator has described Gassendi as one of the most important creators of modern philosophy, although modern philosophy was to obliterate his memory (Osler, 2002). Locke, whose reputation continues to far outstrip that of Gassendi, did little to prevent that obliteration.

Gassendi was both an ordained Catholic priest and a supporter of the empirical movement in the natural sciences. In common with Locke, he rejected the Aristotelianism that had formed the basis of his own education. Gassendi also criticized Descartes's rationalist approach to knowledge, arguing that knowledge should not be based on indubitable propositions derived from pure reasoning, but on the evidence of the senses. He was in close contact with astronomers, such as Gallileo and Kepler, and, in fact, Gassendi made some notable astronomical observations that confirmed some of Kepler's predictions.

Gassendi's philosophy was based upon similar empirical presuppositions to Locke's. Gassendi, like Locke – and, indeed, like Hobbes with whom he corresponded – believed that human knowledge rested on the evidence of the senses. In his *Syntagma Philosophicum* Gassendi used the maxim that 'every idea which is held in the mind takes its origin from the senses' (quoted in Joy, 2000, p. 173). Just as Locke was to do in his *Essay*, Gassendi discussed the various ways that the mind conjoins, enlarges, diminishes, adapts, compares, etc. the sensations that it receives from the senses (Osler, 1994). Gassendi was more interested in the physical processes of perception than Locke was. Bernier, in the volume of his *Abrégé* that was devoted to sensation, reproduced Gassendi's diagrams on the optical system and the way that light strikes the retina. If Locke was not interested in this aspect of perception in his *Essay*, then there was another matter on which both were agreed – the rejection of innate ideas. Gassendi wrote that at birth the 'intellect or mind is a *tabula rasa* in which nothing is engraved' (quoted, Osler, 1994, p. 107; see also Joy, 2000).

The metaphor of the mind as an empty tablet can be traced back to Aristotle. In *De Anima*, Aristotle had suggested that the mind, before it has received ideas, is vacant like a writing tablet before it has been written upon (Book III, 4). There is an interesting, but minor, curiosity in the history of ideas. Locke, today, is often credited with formulating the notion of the newborn mind as a *tabula rasa*. Commentators from various backgrounds associate Locke with the Latin phrase (e.g., Sacks, 2000, p. 10; Walker, 1994, p. 4; Wolin, 2003, p. 41). Nevertheless, Locke did not actually use the expression *tabula rasa* in the *Essay*. One might ask why commentators should attribute the phrase to Locke. The question can be turned around. If the phrase *tabula rasa* is such an apt description of Locke's ideas, then why did not Locke use it?

Locke certainly used the phrase in early drafts of the *Essay*. In what has come to be known as Draft A, he called the mind at birth a *rasa tabula* (Locke, 1990, p. 8). In Draft B he wrote that it was 'probable to me that there is no notion, idea of knowledge of any thing in the soul, but that at first it is perfectly *rasa tabula*, quite void' (p. 128). In the final version of the *Essay*, Locke substituted 'white paper' for *rasa tabula* (Goldie, 1997, p. 96n). The English phrase was more fitted for the times. Locke's readers would write with inky pens on white paper: they did not scratch written characters into a hard writing tablet as the ancients did. It is symptomatic of the rising and falling of philosophical reputations that today Locke should be remembered for a phrase that Gassendi had used.

Gassendi's life work was devoted to reviving the philosophy of Epicurus, whose work, he believed, provided the basis for a modern philosophy of empiricism. Epicurus (341–270 BCE) was the founder of the school of philosophy that bore his name. The Epicurean school was located in a garden just beyond the city wall of Athens. In post-Platonic Athens, the Epicureans competed with the rival school of stoics for students, prestige and philosophical victory. The Epicureans asserted that the good life consisted in the cultivation of sensory taste. This was no simple recommendation for hedonism, but it was an argument for an aesthetic way of life. Epicurus advised his followers to devote themselves to leading a philosophical life to the exclusion of all other distractions. This entailed cutting themselves off from the rest of society, and above all refraining from marriage and parenthood. The stoics, as was the way with these two great rival schools, argued precisely the opposite, recommending a life of disciplined rationality, public service and family duty.

What really caught the imagination of seventeenth century thinkers were not so much Epicurus's ethical and aesthetic teachings. It was his atomism. Epicurus had taken from Democritus the notion that the world was comprised of small, indivisible units of matter that were in perpetual motion. Epicurus disagreed with Democritus about the trajectories on which atoms moved. Nevertheless, both agreed that these units, or atoms, constituted the basic matter of the universe.

Familiar, recognizable objects were to be seen as comprising various combinations of atoms. In his *Letter to Herodotus*, Epicurus wrote:

> ... of bodies some are compounds, others the constituents of these compounds. The latter must be atomic and unalterable ...The primary entities, then, must be atomic kinds of bodies. (Long and Sedley, 1987, pp. 37–8)

During the Middle Ages, Epicurus's atomic theory did not attract much attention. There were few discussions of Epicureanism in the sixteenth and early seventeenth centuries (Osler, 2000). However, matters changed dramatically in the course of the seventeenth century. Suddenly the ideas of Epicurus and Democritus no longer seemed speculative oddities with pagan overtones.

With the development of microscopes, scientists were capable of examining ever-smaller units of physical reality. The basic stuff that comprised the world must have suddenly seemed knowable. Newton appeared to be reaching out towards uncovering the basic atoms of the universe. Boyle's corpuscular theory was promising to do the same for organic matter. Atomism – the belief that the universe comprised basic, discoverable units of matter – was, so to speak, in the air. One historian has claimed that the atomism of the early modern era 'reached an apotheosis at the turn of the eighteenth century in Robert Boyle's chemistry, Isaac Newton's physics and John Locke's philosophy' (Fisher, 2000).

Putting Locke's name alongside those other two scientific atomists is significant. The under-labourer was not merely clearing the ground for the scientists who would build castles from atoms, or, rather, deconstruct castles into their atomic constituents. He was attempting something similar with his chosen topic. Locke was breaking down the large complex objects of the mind into their basic, indivisible units. Out of simple ideas the mind builds up its complex ideas, just as the complex objects of the world are constructed out of basic atoms. In Locke's theory of mind, simple sensations are psychological atoms.

It has been suggested that the parallel between the composition of ideas and the composition of physical particles is, in Locke's *Essay*, 'little more than a decorative conceit', and that it reflects the 'literary style or tone of the *Essay*' rather than its philosophical argument (Ayers, 1991, p. 23). However, tone and style are more than decoration, although Locke did not see language as operating in this way. Locke's search for the basic, psychological units of thought – his psychological atomism – was neither coincidental nor decorative. Like Boyle, Newton and other natural philosophers, he was advocating a systematic approach that broke complex things down into their basic components.

But there was a curious difference. Locke, the philosophical under-labourer, expressed little interest in the history of atomism as a philosophy. His ear was deaf to the ancient traditions of understanding. The natural scientists, by contrast, were showing increasing interest in the old philosophy of atoms (Rogers, 1996). They had Gassendi to thank for this. He was making the teachings of Epicurus and the ancient atomic philosophy relevant to the new empirical spirit.

The Influence of Gassendi on the Empiricists

Gassendi had to overcome two obstacles that stood in the way of any attempt to popularize Epicurus's philosophy in the seventeenth century. First, Epicurus was, in the eyes of faithful Christians, a pagan philosopher, who believed in the existence of the ancient Greek gods. Second, Epicureanism had gained a reputation for being an immoral philosophy that encouraged hedonism and sinful excess. Christians, who might wish to limit the pleasures of the flesh, had for centuries looked askance upon this heathen doctrine. Gassendi, in his voluminous writings on Epicurus, wanted to reverse the received view. He stressed that Epicurus was a moral writer, whose teachings should not be confused with selfish hedonism. Moreover, he suggested that Epicurus's views were compatible with Christianity in general, and, in particular, they could be combined with the teachings of Rome. For Gassendi, Epicurus was Christian in spirit.

Gassendi's message was spread widely. He may not have been the easiest of writers himself, but his follower, François Bernier, boiled down Gassendi's thinking into a series of handy volumes, translating Gassendi's Latin into clear French. In those days, there was a greater potential readership for philosophical works written in French than in English. Bernier's multi-volume *Abrégé de la philosophie de Gassendi* sold widely throughout Europe (Bernier, 1784). Gassendi's ideas and his revival of Epicurus were introduced to English readers, most notably by Walter Charleton and by Thomas Stanley.

Charleton was a physician of some note. Before the Civil War he had been the personal physician of Charles I. After the Restoration he held the same post under Charles II. Charleton's pompously entitled *Physiologia Epicuro-Gassendo-Charltonia* was published in 1654. He claimed to be basing scientific knowledge upon atomic theory, which according to the book's subtitle was 'founded by Epicurus, repaired by Petrus Gassendus and augmented by Walter Charleton'. Another of Charleton's books was *Epicurus's Morals* (1670), which 'faithfully Englished' the main surviving texts of Epicurus concerning morality. Charleton's preface was full of praise for the ancient Greek philosopher. Like Gassendi, Charleton wanted to revise common prejudices against the ancient philosopher, so he praised 'the temperate, good and pious

Epicurus' (p. C1). In this work, Charleton also stressed Epicurus's contribution to the study of matter, writing that we may 'file up this first discovery of this noble principle, atoms ... among those many benefits, which the commonwealth of philosophy owes to the bounteous wit of Epicurus' (Charleton, 1670, p. 88).

In the late seventeenth century Thomas Stanley published a huge and immensely popular history of philosophy (Stanley, 1687/1743). Stanley's aim was to provide a synopsis of Western philosophy, giving special weight to ancient philosophy. In his preface he claimed that 'the learned Gassendus was my precedent'. In the thirteenth section of the book, Stanley presented the ideas of Epicurus and his followers, including their theory that matter is comprised of basic, indivisible atoms.

Stanley's whole section on Epicurus was, in fact, a direct crib from Gassendi's *Philosophiae Epicuri Syntagma* (Ayers, 1994; Osler, 1994). Stanley offered a hint of his borrowing. The third paragraph from the end of the section finishes with the words: 'Hitherto *Gassendus*' (1687/1743, p. 714). Only an astute reader, with a knowledge of Gassendi's Latin works, would appreciate that the 'hitherto' referred to the previous one hundred and twelve pages. In those days, the law did not provide penalties for such gross plagiarism.

Locke's master-builders – Newton, Boyle, Huygens and Sydenham – would certainly have been aware of Gassendi's work and his project to re-create Epicureanism. Walter Charleton was a member of the Royal Society and, in common with Sydenham, he was a Fellow of the Royal College of Surgeons. Newton certainly was familiar with Charleton's *Physiologia*. His notebooks contain substantial quotations from *Physiologia*, particularly Charleton's chapter on 'Atoms, the first and universal matter' (McGuire and Tamny, 2003).

Boyle, too, seems to have been greatly interested in the ideas of Gassendi, either reading him directly or through the works of Stanley and Charleton (Rogers, 1996). Boyle's notebooks also show many references to Epicurus. Boyle seems to have been worried about the Greek philosopher's reputation for atheism and for that reason he avoided linking his own corpuscular theory to Epicurus's theory of atoms in too direct a manner (Macintosh, 2005). However, Boyle did not refrain from openly praising Gassendi. In his *Free Inquiry into the Vulgarly Received Notion of Nature*, Boyle discussed Copernicus's idea that the earth moved around the sun. He mentioned that this theory was now embraced by 'not only those great men, Keplerus, Galileo and Gassendus, but most of the best modern astronomers' (Boyle, 1686, p. 112). Thus, Boyle placed Gassendi in the most elevated, scientific company.

Of course, not all English thinkers found Gassendi's neo-Epicureanism to their liking. Ralph Cudworth and other Platonists warned against the dangers of Epicurean philosophy in both its original and revived versions. The Platonists saw atomism as encouraging materialism and atheism. Cudworth's *True System of the Universe*, as he made clear in the preface, was written against Epicurus, the old Greek 'atomic atheist' who claimed that 'all cogitation is really nothing else but local motion'. Cudworth condemned the 'fraud and juggling of Gassendus' for extolling Epicurus 'as one who approached nearer to Christianity than all the other philosophers' (1678, p. 462). According to the Cudworth view, Epicurus was neither Christian nor correct, the two faults being connected in the mind of the great Platonist.

It is clear that at the time Locke was writing his *Essay*, Epicureanism was enjoying a revival. Locke's philosophical friends were taking Epicureanism seriously, while his philosophical adversaries were mounting attacks. The neo-Epicureans were not reactionary classicists, trying to stand in the way of the new empirical outlook and looking back to ancient glories. They were the new, modern empiricists. As they were discovering the secrets of the natural world, so they were recreating the long history of their modern science.

Locke and Gassendi

There has been much debate whether Locke was or was not directly influenced by Gassendi's thinking. The similarity between Locke's ideas and those of Gassendi, not to mention those of Epicurus, does not stop with the theory that the mind is a *tabula rasa* at birth. There is also the atomism, which Locke assumed as a methodological principle for his psychological analysis and which was basic to Gassendi's revival of Epicureanism. Earlier, four characterizing features of Locke's approach were identified. In addition to atomism, the other characteristics were: perceptual foundationalism; individualism and a theory of language that is anti-rhetorical. All four features can be found in Epicurean philosophy.

It is not difficult to find passages in Epicurean philosophy that seem to anticipate Locke's perceptual foundationalism – or the view that the senses provide a firm basis for knowledge. Lucretius, in his version of Epicurus's philosophy, wrote 'you will find that the preconception of true has its origins in the senses, and that the senses cannot be refuted'. He went on to argue that reason 'is in its entirety the property of the senses, so that if the senses are not true all reason becomes false as well' (Long and Sedley, 1987, pp. 78–9). This aspect comes over strongly in the portrayal of Epicureanism given by Gassendi/Stanley. For example, Gassendi/Stanley quoted extensively from Lucretius to suggest that sense 'is never deceived' (Stanley, 1687/1743, p. 620). The assumption was crucial, continued the French philosopher and his English plagiarist, because if we take away 'the certainty of the senses' we take away the possibility of 'the genuine knowledge of things' (p. 621). In this way, the senses provide 'the security and foundations whereon the constancy and security of life is so grounded' (p. 621).

Similarly, there are clear parallels between Epicurean texts and Locke's atomistic, or individualist, view of society. Epicurus, in the text known as *Key Doctrines*, proposed something akin to an early version of the compact theory of society that Locke proposed in his *Treatises of Civil Government*. According to Epicurus, justice 'is a guarantee of utility with a view to not harming one another and not being harmed'. Those creatures 'which were unable to make contracts over not harming one another and not being harmed' possess no sense of justice or injustice. This is because 'justice was never anything per se, but a contract, regularly arising at some place or other in people's dealings with one another, over not harming or being harmed' (Long and Sedley, 1987, p. 125). In short, justice boiled down to a contract about individual interests.

Locke allied his psychological theory to the project of reforming language. The rhetorical uses of language would be restricted. Out would go imprecise concepts and flowery language. In would come the precise linking of concepts with ideas. Epicurus, too, advocated reigning in the uses of language. He said that we should be careful to attach words to sensations, lest our vocabulary sneak in extra meanings. As Diogenes Laertius recounted, Epicurus in his lost book on rhetoric suggested that the only requirement of language was clarity. Consequently it was important to match words to objects and 'natural philosophers should proceed in accordance with the words belonging to things' (Long and Sedley, 1987, p. 100).

Critics countered by saying that the Epicureans were unreasonably attempting to reduce what could be said with language, and thereby were failing to acknowledge the central role of language in human life. In this spirit, Plutarch addressed the Epicureans: 'You completely abolish the class of sayables, to which discourse owes its existence, leaving only words and name-bearers, and denying the very existence of the intermediate states of affairs signified, by means of which learning, teaching, preconceptions, thoughts, impulses and assents come about' (Long and Sedley, 1987, p. 100). Again, it is not difficult to draw a parallel with Locke, who also wanted to limit concepts to being clear, distinct name-bearers. Later critics such as Thomas Reid would, in effect, repeat Plutarch's criticism of Epicurus, when they criticized Locke's view of language: you want to restrict language to naming, they would say, but that would make all the varied social tasks, for which we use language, impossible.

That leaves the question: How much did Locke know of Gassendi's philosophy? It is inconceivable that he knew nothing. After all, Gassendi was being hailed as a great thinker within the scientific circles in which Locke mixed. Certainly, during his period of exile, Locke became friendly with Bernier, visiting him regularly (Joy, 2000). However, it is possible that Locke may not have discussed metaphysics with Bernier. He might have preferred to talk about travellers' tales to distant lands, a topic in which Bernier had great expertise and on which he published some popular volumes (Milton, 2000). Locke's knowledge of such tales left its imprint on the *Essay*. In the section on innate ideas, Locke quoted evidence from the published accounts of European travellers to suggest that religious ideas were not to be found in all societies (I.iv.8).

Locke seems to have possessed few of Gassendi's works, although he did own a copy of Bernier's *Abrégé* (Ashcraft, 1990). Even if Locke had not studied Gassendi's own rambling works, he should, at least, have been aware of Epicurus's ideas through Stanley's *History of Philosophy*, of which he certainly owned a copy (Kroll, 1991). Lisa Sarasohn has suggested that Locke would have had a fair idea about Gassendi's ideas from Charleton, Boyle or Stanley. She comments that Locke's notebooks of 1660–1661 testify 'to Locke's long and sympathetic acquaintance with the doctrines of the French neo-Epicurean' (Sarasohn, 1996, p. 175). On the other hand, Locke may have been more interested in Gassendi's scientific, especially astronomical, interests to such an extent that he may have had only a passing knowledge of Gassendi's Epicureanism (Milton, 2000). Indeed, Locke throughout his life seems to have preferred reading scientific books to philosophical ones (Cranston, 1985; Milton, 1994).

The scholars will continue to debate exactly how much Locke knew about Gassendi's work and whether he played down this knowledge in order to make his own ideas appear all the more original. Certainly, he never publicly acknowledged that his ideas may have been similar to those of Gassendi. In the Epistle of the *Essay* and in the controversy with Stillingfleet, he portrayed himself as creating his own ideas independently, being unaware of the ideas of others. But, if his closest intellectual colleagues all knew of Gassendi's ideas, then, one might ask, how could Locke have preserved his unawareness. He must have worked hard to protect his intellectual innocence.

There is enough *prima facie* evidence to suggest that Locke may have been in what Freud, many years later, was to call that 'strange state of mind in which one knows and does not know a thing at the same time' (Freud and Breuer, 1895/1991, p. 181n). In that strange state, one has to know what one wishes not to know, in order to avoid successfully coming into contact with that thought. Locke must have known the general outlines of Gassendi's position. How could Boyle or Bernier or any of Locke's intellectual friends not have mentioned the subject, given Locke's own interests and his love of intellectual conversation? But Locke may also have taken steps to avoid knowing anything more.

He may have displayed the habits and failings of what might be termed 'scholarly avoidance'.

We can imagine Locke in conversation showing a preference for any topic other than metaphysics. Perhaps, when conversing with Bernier, he would habitually cut off any discussion of Gassendi, Epicurus or *rasae tabulae*, with a quick intervention that turned the conversation to other matters. Perhaps he would ask Bernier about further tales of the Far East. Locke had an interest in maintaining his ignorance, refusing to read philosophical speculations that were uncomfortably close to his own. How else can one explain the fact that Locke's extensive library, of which he was so proud, contained few works by a thinker who was considered by his friend Boyle to be one of the great intellects of the age?

It would be a mistake to attribute any such avoidance wholly to personal vanity, although, as is evident in the dispute with Stillingfleet, Locke was not as far removed from that failing as he might like to think himself. There were tactical reasons for not wishing to be intellectually associated with a Catholic priest, such as Gassendi, or with a heathen hedonist, such as Epicurus. It was bad enough being thought to belong to the company of protestant dissenters. It would have been a gift to an opponent such as Stillingfleet, if he could have tied Locke to far worse doctrinal company.

Tactical factors alone cannot wholly explain why Locke may not have read Gassendi's works, certainly not with the attention that one might expect of a fellow philosopher. There is an intellectual explanation that ties in with the psychological account of originality that Locke used to defend himself against Stillingfleet. It did not matter whether others might have thought similar things previously. What mattered was whether he had succeeded in creating his own thoughts. Locke was proud to be philosophically what he was socially – an independent, self-made man who had inherited no ancestral privileges.

Locke's psychological account of knowledge was removing the issue of knowledge from history. Anyone could be knowledgeable if they paid attention to the psychological origins of their own ideas and used words carefully to describe those ideas. This insight, too, was presented as if it stood outside history, as if it were heralding a rupture with the prejudices of the past. Had Locke traced the historical, rather than psychological, origins of his ideas, then there could be no sense of freedom from the hold of the past. His own ideas would then be tied to the past. In fact, a connection with Gassendi offered a double continuity and a duplicated debt. First, Locke would be tied to the previous generation, and would be perhaps identifiable as a Gassendist. But, then, through Gassendi he would be linked all the way back to Epicurus and the ancient Greeks – to a world of pre-scientific prejudices and old writing tablets. He would be entangled in the traditions of metaphysics from which he sought escape. One solution would be to stop his ears and close his eyes to the ideas of Gassendi that were so popular among his scientific contemporaries.

This offers a clue how Locke's way of ideas might be criticized. Particular hypotheses can be evaluated and found failing. His notion of ideas and their relations with words can be found implausible, as Reid was to suggest and as anti-cognitivists do today. So can his conception of the mind as an empty vessel at birth. However, Stillingfleet's phrase 'the new way of ideas' suggests that Locke was doing more than proposing a series of hypotheses. He was proposing a new way of thinking. The under-labourer had the grand ambition of releasing understanding from its ties with the past. The ambition would appear rhetorically compromised were Locke to be seen, not as a self-made, independently minded modern thinker, but as a follower of Epicurus. To be accused of Epicureanism would be doubly wounding: it would undermine his personal originality and his anti-historical theory of mind. The accusation of Epicureanism would be made by his noble patron's grandson, who would know better than anyone how to deflate the great John Locke, Gent.

5

Shaftesbury: The Rebellious Foster-Son

●●●●●●●●●●●●●●●●●●●

L ocke may be said to be the father of cognitive psychology but, in a more direct way, he also fathered a type of psychology that rejected his own approach. This does not mean that there was a contradiction between different parts of Locke's work; it was not as if his *Essay* gave rise to the traditions of cognitive science, while another book inspired a very different approach. The contradiction, if there is one, is between Locke's philosophical life and his active life in the service of the first Earl of Shaftesbury. Locke's parental link to cognitive psychology is metaphorical: cognitive psychology has no actual father or mother. However, he was much more than a metaphorical parent to his greatest critic in early eighteenth century England – the grandson of his patron.

The third Earl of Shaftesbury (1671–1713) is known for one great pot-pourri of a book: the three volume *Characteristicks of Men, Manners, Opinions, Times*, which first appeared in 1711 and which, like Locke's *Essay*, was republished many times during the eighteenth century. Although *Characteristicks* was later to fall from philosophical fashion, there is no doubting its reputation during the first hundred years of its life. Some Enlightenment thinkers considered Shaftesbury to be more than the equal of Locke. Diderot's *Encyclopédie* compared the two Englishmen: Locke 'was only a man of vast intellect, penetrating and exact', while Shaftesbury was 'a genius of the first order'. According to the encyclopaedist, Locke produced 'some great truths coldly perceived, methodically developed, and dryly presented', but Shaftesbury gave the world 'some brilliant schemes often poorly grounded, though full of sublime truths' (quoted in Grean, 1967, p. x).

Such comments suggest a profound difference of philosophical temperament between Locke and Shaftesbury – the one careful and empirically minded, the other filled with the passions of imagination. One conventional view is that Locke and Shaftesbury addressed completely different topics. Locke methodically investigated how the mind collects and organizes information. The flamboyant Shaftesbury addressed issues of beauty and morality. Certainly, Shaftesbury's defenders can point to his influence on later moral and aesthetic philosophy. A recent admirer has written that Shaftesbury's *Characteristicks* 'had tremendous influence on the development of British moral philosophy in the eighteenth century, influenced British tastes in literature and the arts, and played a role in the development of the Continental Enlightenment' (Yaffe, 2002, p. 425).

Shaftesbury should not be pigeon-holed as a moral or aesthetic philosopher, for his *Characteristicks* ranges across diverse topics. At its core, there is an account of human nature – a psychological vision – that differed fundamentally from Locke's. Shaftesbury took issue with the four features that were previously said to characterize Locke's psychology: atomism, individualism, perceptual foundationalism and an opposition to rhetoric. Shaftesbury's psychology, by contrast, was holistic, social, sceptical and intrinsically rhetorical. Locke may have been unhistorical, even anti-historical, in his analysis of the mind. Shaftesbury, by contrast, was immersed in a historical consciousness.

In practically every respect, Shaftesbury was struggling against the influence of Locke. Nevertheless, *Characteristicks* does not appear as an attack on Locke's way of understanding. Locke is hardly mentioned, either directly or indirectly. To appreciate the force of Shaftesbury's reaction against Locke, one has to go beyond the outward text of *Characteristicks* to consider his personal relations with Locke. In Shaftesbury's case, the philosophical was deeply personal, filled with tensions which could not be published openly.

This is why the story of Locke and Shaftesbury is so fascinating. It is always interesting to hear about the personal lives of notable thinkers. The history of ideas can become a dreary business when all personality is subtracted and concepts are shuffled across time. In this story there is an extra dimension – or, rather, an extra, troubling question. If two intellectual visions are so diametrically opposed, then how is it possible for their authors to be so personally close? There is an ideological version of this puzzle. How can two thinkers, who hold such different views about the human condition, share common political views? The story of Locke and Shaftesbury is more than an interesting tale; it represents a case history about the relations between ideology and psychological theory.

An Awkward Ancestor

First, there is an awkward matter. Shaftesbury is hardly the sort ancestor that most critical psychologists would willingly pick. His writing exudes a sense of superiority, even at times priggishness, especially when he writes about the importance of good manners and good breeding. Most critical psychologists generally see themselves as combating the privileges of power. The ideal intellectual forebear would not be an aristocratic male, who inherited a title, landed estates and a sense of social superiority. Even the self-made Locke, rising from obscure origins to fame rather than fortune, seems a more agreeable choice of ancestor. However, we are not entirely free to select our own intellectual genealogy, unless we give way to the temptations of collective amnesia and uncritical self-celebration.

Certainly it is easy to find quotations from Shaftesbury that cannot but embarrass admirers today. Sexism runs through much of his writing. This is not the casual, unthinking sort of sexism that was current in the late seventeenth century and that led Locke to assume that the education of girls was less important than that of boys. Shaftesbury's frequent comments on masculinity and effeminacy have a pointed force, suggesting something more than the repetition of common sense stereotypes.

At times Shaftesbury blamed the defects of contemporary manners on the influence of women and the failure of men to be genuinely masculine. In *Characteristicks*, he complained that 'our modern conversations' suffer because men pander to women, adopting 'effeminate' manners and losing their masculine sense of reason. To remedy such faults 'our sense, language and style, as well as our voice and person, should have something of that male feature and natural roughness by which our sex is distinguished' (1711/1999, p. 233). In another passage, Shaftesbury deplored the tendency to disparage critics in polite company. He attributed this habit to males using an 'effeminate plaintive tone of invective against critics'; males only do this, he suggested, when women are present in conversations and they do so in order to impress 'the tender sex' (p. 409).

In private correspondence Shaftsbury could be even more forthright. To his friend Lord Somers, he wrote that 'effeminacy and superstition' were the foes of philosophy; indeed, philosophy had 'gone to wreck' since the ladies had left their chambers and the priests their temples (Rand, 1900, pp. 337–8). In writing thus, Shaftesbury was going beyond the prejudices of his day. He was reacting against a growing tendency for women to enter into, even organize, intellectual conversations in the dining-rooms and salons of Britain and Europe. Not all males of Shaftesbury's generation deplored this trend. Jonathan Swift in his 'Hints towards an essay on conversation' wrote that the 'degeneracy of conversation' stemmed from the exclusion of women whose conversation had a civilizing effect on male manners (1709/1909, pp. 233–4).

Shaftesbury may not have entirely practised what he preached. There is no evidence that he held back from intellectually conversing with Lady Damaris Masham, who was his friend as well as Locke's. On the other hand, there can be no doubting Shaftesbury's preference for male company. He does not seem to have particularly sought the company of women, whether for intellectual or other sorts of conversations – at least before his late thirties when he began a serious search for a wife to continue the family line (Voitle, 1984). A letter written in his early thirties provides strong suggestion that Shaftesbury may have been struggling with homo-erotic desires (Voitle, 1984, pp. 242ff; Klein, 2005).

It is conceivable that his warnings against effeminate conduct and his admiration for the 'natural roughness' of men may have derived from their force of expression, if not their content, from psycho-sexual conflicts, rather than just reflecting the conventional sexism of his times and class. Whatever the reasons, there is little to make Shaftesbury's worries about the dangers of effeminacy appear congenial today.

Then there is his class snobbery. Again it is easy to find quotations that will, in the estimation of most readers today, condemn him in his own words. Shaftesbury's important defence of ridicule will be discussed later. At one point in *Characteristicks*, Shaftesbury assured his readers that he was not encouraging the uneducated to ridicule their intellectual and social betters. That was not the sort of ridicule that he was promoting: 'I am writing to you in defence only of the liberty of the Club and of that sort of freedom which is taken among gentlemen and friends who know one another perfectly well' (1711/1999, p. 36). The single sentence simultaneously displays snobbery and sexism. The present writer, in a previous work, was unable to resist quoting that sentence (Billig, 2005, pp. 75–6). Even in the eighteenth century, critics were able to amuse their readers at Shaftesbury's expense. John Brown, who was not of noble birth, had fun in his book, *Essays on the Characteristics*, mocking the third Earl's defence of well-bred, gentlemanly ridicule (Brown, 1752, particularly pp. 52f and 67ff).

Today Shaftesbury's ideas about a 'gentleman's club' convey a partic-ular, fusty image. We can imagine an oak-panelled room, in which men of a certain age and class read newspapers, offer reactionary opinions and doze in their armchairs. The only women permitted entry are those that serve or clean. In the eighteenth century, the gentleman's club was very different. Often it was a gathering of friends, who arranged to meet for conversation and intellectual discussion. Locke formed many such clubs for like-minded friends and acquaintances. The gathering, from which his *Essay* originated, would have been such a 'club'. As the example of Locke shows, the gentlemanly behaviour that was required in these clubs was not a matter of inherited position; it was a code of conduct that should be followed by any member regardless of birth – or gender, as a blue-stocking like Damaris Masham could have added.

Shaftesbury may have been using elitist language, but he was doing something important. He was identifying a topic that is as significant today as it was in the eighteenth century; but that was almost totally lacking in Locke's writing. In the *Essay* Locke wrote about the way that the individual mind gathers information from its senses. In his political works, he wrote about the institutions of government. But between individual cognition and the organization of the state, there is a huge gap about which Locke was largely silent. He did not write about the ways that people relate to one another in the conduct of ordinary life. Social manners were not Locke's topic. Nor have they featured centrally in cognitive science. Yet, this was precisely the level at which Shaftesbury directed so much of his philosophy (Klein, 1994 and 1999). Just to dismiss Shaftesbury for his views about gentlemanly behaviour or for his agonizing about effeminacy would be to miss a wider point. He was putting the conduct of social life and the dilemmas of interpersonal conduct right at the heart of his vision of human nature.

Looking Back to the Past

There is something else in Shaftesbury's style that is liable to discourage the modern reader. He was backward looking, celebrating ancient, so-called manly virtues, as he stood against the currents of his times. His stance was the antithesis of Locke's. Whereas Locke wished to rid himself of the past and its superstitions, Shaftesbury sought to understand the present in terms of the past. Today, Locke can appear as the modern figure, belonging to the age of science and reason. By contrast, Shaftesbury can easily be made to appear as a reactionary aristocrat. But we should be careful not to equate the rejection of the past with modern reasonableness. Nor should we assume that it is hopelessly reactionary to use the past to criticize the present.

Shaftesbury's image as a reactionary seems to be confirmed by the engraved portrait to be found in the editions of *Characteristicks* that were published after his death. There the noble author stands, opposite the title page. Clad in a shiny toga, he clasps a small volume to his breast, while his other arm rests on three larger volumes. The spines indicate that two of these books are written by Plato and Xenophon in classical Greek. The engraving by Simon Gribelin was based on a portrait that Shaftesbury had commissioned from the Dutch artist John Closterman.

In a satirical essay, Jonathan Swift described the battle of the books, fought in a library by competing armies of ancient and modern volumes (1704/1909). He was commenting upon a debate that was fashionable in the early years of the seventeenth century: which was the better, ancient or modern learning? Locke, with his aim of sweeping aside the rubble of the past, clearly was on the side of the moderns. It does not take an expert in iconography to see that the Earl was presenting himself as a supporter of the ancients.

However, Shaftesbury should not be dismissed merely as a voice of old aristocracy, blocking the path of progress and glancing back to a glorious, distant past (Eagleton, 1990). Shaftesbury was not generally seen as a reactionary in the eighteenth century. Like his grandfather, he was politically a Whig, benefiting from modern commerce, including the slave trade, and supporting the curtailment of ancient, monarchical privilege. The *Characteristicks* contained sufficient comments to indicate that he believed the politics and manners of England to be in a state of advance, rather than decline. Certainly Shaftesbury caught the spirit of the Enlightenment when, in 1705, he wrote to his friend Jean Le Clerc, the theologian and Hebrew scholar, that 'there is a mighty light which spreads itself over the world, especially in those two free nations of England and Holland' (Rand, 1900, p. 353).

These are not the words of a reactionary, opposing the idea of progress. Diderot was to see Shaftesbury as a radical who rejected the dogmas of traditional religion and who stressed the culture of rational learning. Diderot's first book was an approximate translation, with elaborations, of Shaftesbury's 'Inquiry concerning virtue or merit', which formed part of the second volume of *Characteristicks*. Diderot, in his preface, explained his method of translation: 'I read him and re-read him; I filled myself with his spirit; and I, so to speak, closed his book when I took up my pen' (Diderot, 1745/1876, p. 16). The young revolutionary thinker would hardly have filled himself with Shaftesbury's spirit had he imagined the latter to be an incorrigible conservative.

The Gribelin/Closterman portrait, which seems so off-putting today, needs to be understood in its context. We cannot capture the iconography of the past if we only look with eyes informed by the present. Today we would view a toga-wearer as either being ironical or pretentious. And Shaftesbury, as he poses in the portrait, scarcely looks ironic. His classicism seems today like a badge of privilege. Latin and Greek belong to the curricula of fee-paying schools that educate the elite. So, the third Earl appears to be parading his privilege somewhat ludicrously.

The image is altered with the addition of one historical consideration. The portrait was painted at the close of a century that had seen unprecedented religious violence in England. Puritan dogmatists had demanded absolute doctrinal obedience. Men and women had been burnt alive for being insufficiently Christian in their beliefs. In the portrait, Shaftesbury wears pre-Christian apparel. Worse still in the eyes of Christian dogmatists is his choice of reading matter. He is not clasping a Bible to his breast, with eyes uplifted to heaven. Instead, he looks outwards across the world, visually displaying his love for books written by pagans. In this context, the image indicates an opposition to those powerful theologians who had insisted that only impeccably Christian writers could provide truths.

The image, thus, links Shaftesbury to a stance of toleration. Other cultures, other religions, possess wisdom. Non-Christians are not to be condemned as heathens destined for hell. This is the context in which the comments about ridicule and the gentleman's club should be understood. Shaftesbury was not advocating the ridiculing of social inferiors and their manners. Nor was it a smug ridicule of new trends. His target was the sort of fierce, religious bigotry that demands unthinking obedience. In a world where religious dogmatism still retains its capacity for physical and spiritual violence, this is neither a reactionary nor an outdated position.

Locke opposed dogmatism in a different way. In his view, scientific truth, clearly and distinctly demonstrated, should replace superstition. Shaftesbury was to remain sceptical of this solution. One set of truths would be replaced by another, both sharing the characteristic of demanding absolute acceptance. We, the readers of today, will be unable to understand Shaftesbury's anti-dogmatism if we only see the tones and values that separate his world from ours, rather than those that reach across time to us.

Shaftesbury: the Early Years

To appreciate Shaftesbury's message more fully, it is necessary to switch from the philosophical to the personal. Locke's services to Ashley Cooper, the first Earl of Shaftesbury, were not confined to acting as his political advisor. He advised on family matters too. For aristocrats the personal and the political were intertwined, especially in matters of marriage. This was also true of would-be aristocrats, as Cooper was in the early years of Locke's service. By late 1660s, with his political fortunes in the ascendant once again, Cooper could hope to be rewarded by a noble title and, thereby, to establish a noble lineage through which he hoped to leave his mark for posterity.

However, there was one problem of a deeply personal nature that troubled this ambition. Despite three marriages, Cooper only had one son, who was born to his second wife. The son, born in 1651, was also called Anthony Ashley, as would be the first born sons of his descendants. From an early age the boy seems to have suffered from mental and physical disabilities, whose nature is hard to gauge today. John Dryden, the Tory poet who fiercely criticized Cooper in his poem 'Absalom and Achitophel', referred to the young boy as a 'shapeless lump'.

The family suspected that the boy would not live long. Cooper wanted to secure the family's future by ensuring that his son married young and began breeding immediately. Cooper, always ambitious in his aspirations, desired that the boy should marry upwards into an old aristocratic family. To find a suitably noble and potentially fecund bride for the unpromising lump would be a task as difficult as it was delicate. Cooper entrusted it to Locke.

Locke discharged his obligations with customary good judgement and discretion. It is unclear just how many noble families were considered. But it is known that Locke travelled to Belvoir Castle in Rutland. There he secured an agreement from the eighth Earl of Rutland that his third daughter, Dorothy, would marry the young Cooper. The wedding soon followed in September 1669. Locke's medical judgement proved sound: the young bride rapidly became pregnant. In fact, she was to produce a total of three sons and four daughters, before she tired of her husband's odd ways and decided to live separately (for details, see Voitle, 1984; see also Klein, 2005).

Shaftesbury asked Locke, as a medical man, to supervise Dorothy's first pregnancy and make arrangements for the delivery. All went well and in February 1771 Dorothy gave birth to a son, who, like his father and grandfather, received the names Anthony Ashley Cooper. When the old politician was ennobled the following year, becoming the first Earl of Shaftesbury, the future of the newly created line seemed secure, thanks in no small measure to Locke.

Socrates used to call himself a midwife of philosophy, because his style of questioning drew out philosophical replies from his fellow conversationalists. Metaphorically, he was overseeing the birth of his friends' new ideas, as it were, delivering them of philosophical opinions. But, even more literally than Socrates, Locke deserves the title of being a midwife of philosophy. He had selected the future philosopher's mother. He had watched over the mother's confinement. Without Locke's understanding, tact and medical care, there would have been no third Earl, no author of *Characteristicks*.

Locke's duties to the future third Earl were only just starting. The grandfather had no confidence in the parental abilities of his odd, lumpy son. Consequently, the first Earl officially became the child's guardian in 1674. The young boy was dispatched to live at the old family home at Wimborne St Giles in Dorset, where Locke was also living. Cooper asked Locke to supervise the child's early education. Locke laid down the basic principles of the child's upbringing and appointed the tutors. Locke was later to outline his educational philosophy in *Some Thoughts Concerning Education* (1721). Encouragement, not punishment, was to be the basic principle, although Locke stressed the importance of discipline and obedience in the early years. For young children, Locke recommended plain food, hard beds and thin shoes that let the water in. From an early age, the young Cooper was given a practical lesson in stoicism, the philosophical tradition that would eventually lead him to reject his teacher's way of thinking.

Locke ensured that the young Anthony Ashley learnt to speak Latin and Greek as living languages. This was not quite as radical as it might appear today. In the Oxford of Locke's day, students were expected to converse with their tutors in Latin. However, the movement towards the use of vernacular languages was well in train. Locke, unlike Hobbes, was to write all his philosophical works in English. The young Shaftesbury, in common with most other writers of his generation, would publish in his native language. Yet, Shaftesbury's education in the classics had an enduring effect. It began a lifetime's admiration for the ancient civilizations of Athens and Rome.

When the old Earl died in 1683, Anthony's parents took back the guardianship of the boy. Almost immediately, they sent him to school at Winchester. It was a poor choice. The boy had a miserable time in that environment of high Toryism and royalism. Delicate and scholarly, he was constantly picked on because of his grandfather's infamous politics. As the fourth Earl would write many years later in a biographical sketch of his father, the boy's 'ill-usage' at Winchester was so unpleasant that he begged his father to withdraw him from school and permit him to travel abroad in the company of a tutor (Shaftesbury, 1900b, p. xix).

So, the young boy, still only sixteen, embarked on a grand tour of Europe, accompanied by his tutor and by Sir John Cropley, who was to remain a lifelong friend. The party was to visit the great art collections of Europe. Anthony's noble, Whiggish connections enabled him to make contact with some of the outstanding free-thinking, continental intellectuals of the time. One intellectual needed no introduction. The party travelled to Holland to visit Locke, who was still living there in exile.

Locke's formal connections with the Shaftesbury household had ended when the first Earl died in 1683. However, the old philosopher continued to watch over the progress of his patron's grandson, who became Lord Ashley when his father succeeded to the Earldom. Locke and the young Lord corresponded regularly. The young man informed his mentor of his travels and studies. In return, Locke offered Anthony helpful advice. Like many a young man writing to an old family friend, Anthony was not as quick in his replies as he could have been. Many of his letters to Locke begin with an apology for not having replied sooner. The tone of their correspondence was unmistakably warm.

Unfortunately, few of Locke's letters to Ashley survive, so it is difficult to know exactly what advice he was giving the young man. Whatever it was, it was bound to have been carefully considered and generously offered. It was also gratefully received. In December 1687, the sixteen year old Ashley wrote to Locke from Paris: 'To thank you for the advice I have received in your letters, as well as from your mouth, would be a subject too big for this paper, or indeed for my tongue' (Rand, 1900, p. 275).

Locke, the Foster-Father

Ashley returned from his first grand tour in the spring of 1689. He was still in his late teens. Politically things were much changed. The Glorious Revolution had taken place and Locke was preparing to return to Britain now that it was a safer place for Whigs. The tour had been intended to take the place of a university education. Locke certainly would not have pressed the young man to go to his old university, Oxford, in order to further his philosophical studies.

Ashley had not yet achieved the legal age of majority, but in those days it was possible for a minor to enter parliament. Friends and former colleagues of his late grandfather were planning for the grandson to stand as parliamentary candidate for a Dorset constituency. Given the power of the family name, and the ease with which small constituencies could be controlled by local land owners, Ashley would almost certainly have been elected to the House of Commons. However, he did not think he was ready to enter public life. He wanted more time for studying.

On his twenty-first birthday, Ashley was delighted to receive a letter from Locke that was full of praise. In reply, Ashley expressed gratitude for the way that Locke had treated him: 'You ... dealt with me so like a friend in very strictest relation, seemed to seek my company for my company's sake, and conferred with me upon subjects as though you were really better for not being alone' (Rand, 1900, p. 289). Ashley was beginning to set his philosophical ideas down on paper and to show them privately to acquaintances, but not, as we will see, to his teacher. Locke had always combined philosophical thinking with a life of public service. Ashley wanted to follow this example. It was a sense of duty, rather than any natural inclination inherited from his paternal grandfather, that was pushing Ashley towards politics.

Accordingly, Ashley agreed to stand for the Parliamentary seat of Poole and was duly elected to the Commons in 1695. He identified with the 'country' Whigs, but he was independently minded, voting according to what he saw as the merits of the issue. On one matter, he followed class allegiance rather than liberal principles. He supported measures to raise the property qualifications for members of Parliament. He argued that those of independent means were more likely to display the sort of independent judgement that the country required and that he believed himself to possess.

Ashley's most noteworthy Parliamentary moment came when the Commons was debating whether those accused of treason should be permitted to hire a lawyer to speak on their behalf. Family history suggested a liberal stance on the matter: the first Earl, who was well able to defend himself rhetorically, had been tried for treason. Others might find themselves in the same position but lack his oratorical gifts. The third Earl's son described what happened when his father rose to address the Commons: 'The great audience so intimidated him that he lost all memory, and could not utter a syllable'. There was an embarrassing silence. Then Ashley composed himself: 'If I, sir, who rise only to speak my opinion on the Bill ... am so confounded that I am unable to express the least of what I proposed to say, what must the condition of that man be who is pleading for his life without any assistance?' (Shaftesbury, 1900b, p. xxi).

It was a brilliant oratorical move. Many believed that it was totally unplanned. Ashley, a scholar of the classics, would have been aware that Quintillian, Cicero and other rhetoricians advised speakers to hide their rhetorical tricks. In *Characteristicks*, he was to write in relation to political oratory that 'the natural and simple manner which conceals ... art is the most truly artful, truest and best studied taste' (Shattesbury, 1711/1999, p. 399). Good taste would have prevented him from drawing attention to his own moment of rhetorical triumph. Ashley's period in the Commons did not last long. He never enjoyed robust health; his asthma was badly affected by the smoke and dirt of London. Consequently, he did not stand for re-election after Parliament was dissolved in 1698.

The same year saw Ashley's first publication. He edited a collection of sermons given by the theologian Benjamin Whichcote, who had died a few years previously. Though famed for his sermons, Whichcote had not prepared them for publication. The theologian was latitudinarian in his sympathies, resisting attempts to reduce Anglican theology to a single doctrine and calling for a broad range of theological interpretations to be accepted within the church (Cassirer, 1953; Hutton, 2002). Ashley, in gathering together some of his sermons, was doing more than paying tribute to someone whom he admired. As one commentator has suggested, it is reasonable to suppose that Shaftesbury selected those sermons that were in most agreement with his own opinions (Rivers, 1991, p. 42).

In his introduction, Ashley paid tribute to the intellectual and personal qualities of Whichcote. He was, according to Ashley, respected by all parties. Whichcote had shown great tolerance and generosity of spirit, 'even in the worst of times, when feuds, and animosities, on the account of religion, were highest (during the time of the late great troubles)' (Shaftesbury, 1698, no page number in original). Ashley's preface and the sermons that he chose to include in the collection emphasized an important political and theological point: non-Christians could be as morally good as Christians. Indeed many non-Christians possessed a nature that was morally superior to those mean-spirited, doctrinaire Christians whose religious sense was based on spreading fear rather than love. As Ashley wrote in the preface, all people, whatever their religion, possessed the power for goodness, and many Christians could be said to be morally inferior 'to the civilized people, whether pagan or Mahometan, lying round them'.

This, of course, conflicted with the strict Calvinist doctrine of original sin. According to Puritans, the inborn capacity for evil could only be countered by accepting the truths of the Gospel. Thus, non-Christians, as well as Christians of the wrong denomination, lived in a state of sin. By contrast, Whichcote and the young Ashley were claiming that goodness did not depend upon accepting a particular Christian doctrine.

Whichcote spoke of there being a 'deeper foundation' for goodness than the Bible: 'the first inscription in the heart of man by God' was a sense of love, goodness and sociability (Whichcote, 1698, p. 8).The emphasis on natural goodness also suggested that Whichcote and his young editor were allying themselves with the Cambridge Platonists.

Such opinions not only contradicted Puritanism, but they flew in the face of Locke's (and Gassendi's) position. The mind of the newborn infant was not a *tabula rasa*. Its character was already inscribed by God to take a particular form. Humans come into the world, not with an empty nature, but naturally equipped with the capacity for goodness. Ashley, in his preface, pointedly mentioned a philosopher, who in describing human nature 'forgot to mention kindness, friendship, sociableness, love of company and converse, natural affection, or any thing of this kind'. The writer in question was, of course, Hobbes, who, like the Puritans, had envisaged the state of nature to be characterized by brutishness, immorality and self-interest.

By contrast, Whichcote and Ashley were proposing a different, more optimistic vision of the human nature. Whichcote was using such ideas to make a theological point: God had created humans with the capacity for goodness. Ashley, in his preface, was taking the decisive step of translating these ideas from a theological context into a philosophical one (and thereby to a psychological one). He was setting down a social and benevolent view of human nature that he was to develop in *Characteristicks*. His preface to the Whichcote collection may have contained criticisms of Hobbes, but there was no mention of Locke. However, as we shall see, he was privately thinking that Locke's views of human nature were not that far removed from those of Hobbes.

Ashley published his Whichcote volume anonymously, leaving his preface and editorial work unsigned. This was the only thing that Ashley knowingly published during Locke's lifetime. A first publication is normally a matter of happiness. However, the publication of Whichcote's sermons seems to have coincided with a low period in Ashley's life. He came close to what nowadays would be recognized as a nervous breakdown. On leaving Parliament in 1698, he travelled to Holland to recuperate, study and to meet up with old acquaintances. His friends tended to be older than himself. Most of them were also friends of Locke (Voitle, 1984, p. 201).

But not all their mutual friends were equally to be trusted. John Toland had embarrassed Locke by citing the *Essay Concerning Human Understanding* as an argument for Unitarianism. In so doing, Toland had embroiled Locke in the controversy with Stillingfleet. Next it was Ashley's turn to be upset by Toland. When Ashley was out of the country, Toland took it upon himself to publish a version of 'An Inquiry Concerning Virtue' that Ashley had been privately circulating to close friends. Ashley was appalled when he heard about this unauthorized publication. He returned to England and tried to buy up and destroy all remaining copies of the book. Ultimately he was to re-write the 'Inquiry' and include it in *Characteristicks*.

While in Holland, Ashley was working hard on his own philosophy. His notebooks show him to be drawn to the moral philosophy of the stoics, especially Marcus Aurelius and Epictetus. Many years after Shaftesbury's death, these notebooks were published under the title of 'The Philosophical Regimen' (Shaftesbury, 1900a). They provide an insight into the direction of his thoughts and, more personally, into his somewhat troubled state of mind. The notebooks portray a young man constantly questioning himself, doubting whether his own motives and actions met the high ethical standards demanded by the stoics. They reveal his quest to find a balance between the pursuit of philosophical truths and the demands of social obligations. But the quest for balance just seems to bring more self-questioning. In contrast to Locke's approach, there were no clear and distinct ideas that the young stoic could use as a foundation for knowledge in order to settle doubt, dilemma and self-critique.

Ashley's life changed shortly after his return to England in 1699. His father died and he succeeded to the Earldom. Social duties immediately faced him: he had the family estates in Dorset to manage and a seat to take in the House of Lords. Inevitably, his relationship with Locke shifted. The young boy was now the noble Lord, with responsibilities for Locke's continuing financial ties with the Shaftesbury family. In fact, Locke petitioned the new Earl to sort out a financial arrangement that the first Earl had made many years earlier. It concerned some property that Locke had rented from the Shaftesbury estate on highly advantageous terms. Locke, who was always conscious of his financial entitlements, felt that the original agreement was not being respected. The new Earl acted promptly to sort out matters. No longer was he the youthful pupil, who needed supervision and encouragement. He was now the head of a noble family with a duty to protect the material welfare of his grandfather's old advisor.

Shaftesbury took his political obligations seriously. He started attending the House of Lords regularly. The new monarchical regime favoured the Whigs, to whom they owed their power. In 1701 King William offered Shaftesbury a formal governmental position as Secretary of State. However, Shaftesbury's health was causing serious problems. He could no longer take the polluted air of London. Consequently he declined the offer and retired to his country seat in Dorset. It was his last opportunity for a political career. After Queen Anne ascended the throne, the Whigs were no longer in favour.

During this period, Shaftesbury seldom saw Locke, who was by now living with the Mashams in Essex. Like Shaftesbury, Locke was suffering badly from asthma. Shaftesbury, in his letters to Locke, regularly promised to visit the Mashams. But, just as regularly, Shaftesbury apologized that a projected visit would have to be delayed because of his ill health. Locke understood the difficulties. He felt that the younger man's body was poorly equipped to deal with the energy of his intellect. In Locke's words, 'the sword was too sharp for the scabbard' (quoted Shaftesbury, 1900b, p. xxix).

Locke's health finally gave out in late October 1704. Shortly before Locke died, Shaftesbury had written to him for a final favour. He asked Locke to compose an inscription in Latin and English for a monument which was to be erected at St Giles in memory of the first Earl (Rand, 1900, p. 323). The dying Locke obliged. It was a last act of homage to the man whom he had served so loyally. Whatever their philosophical differences, Locke and the third Earl remained united in their admiration for the first Earl. Both saw themselves as upholding his political vision.

A few months after Locke's death, Shaftesbury received a request from their mutual friend, Jean le Clerc, who was intending to write a tribute to the late philosopher. Could Shaftesbury provide some details about Locke's life? Shaftesbury was only too happy to oblige. Accordingly, he told the story how his grandfather had met the young Locke and how that chance meeting had begun their long association. Shaftesbury recounted that Locke was entrusted with the statesman's 'secretest negotiations', and had shared the dangers as well as the honours of the first Earl's career (letter included in Rand, 1900, p. 332).

Shaftesbury told Le Clerc the story how Locke had found his father's bride and then supervised the education of all the children. As the oldest son, he personally received greatest attention and Locke had 'the absolute direction of my education' (Rand, 1900, p. 332). Shaftesbury went on to say that, next to his own parents, he owed Locke the greatest obligation and gratitude. He concluded the memoir by hoping that time and health would permit him to write a longer tribute in praise of 'my friend and foster-father, Mr Locke'.

An Early Disagreement

Locke would not have needed to read the preface to Whichcote's sermons to know that his pupil was developing a very different philosophical outlook from his own. He would have been aware of this from a remarkably frank letter that Ashley had sent him a few years earlier. In 1694, Locke wrote to Ashley inquiring about the progress of his studies. Locke's letter has not survived, but Ashley's reply has. Ashley was in his early twenties and for the rest of his life he was to maintain the basic philosophical position that he outlined in that letter.

Ashley began with an apology for not keeping Locke better informed. If he had felt that his studies had contained anything of interest, then, of course, he would have told Locke 'without any need of being pressed'. After all, the whole purpose of his studies was to learn 'how to communicate every thing freely; how to be more sociable and more a friend' (Beer, 1979, p. 150). Perhaps a warning bell might have sounded as Locke read this opening paragraph. Locke had not written his *Essay* in order to become a more sociable person. Was the young man up to something very different?

The letter soon makes clear that he was. The tactful opening tone gives way to more direct sentiments. One reason that Ashley had little to communicate was that he was not 'an empiric' who might promote 'new inventions that are to gain credit to the author'. The term 'empiric' was not in this context complimentary, nor was it tactful given that Locke, with his modern view of medicine, could be held to be an 'empiric'.

The young man was just starting. He was not one of 'the men of new systems' who seek to build their work on 'the discredit of those learned men that went before'. He named names and continued his insults: 'Descartes, or Mr Hobbes, or any of their improvers' are as 'jealous about their notions, and DISCOVERIES, as they call them' as any mounteback or apothecary is jealous of their potions (p. 151, emphasis in original). Thus, the young man compared the great Descartes and Hobbes with the sellers of quack remedies.

And who were their 'improvers' with their new enhanced systems to hawk? Ashley did not inform the man who was being hailed as the greatest improver of them all. He added nothing to the effect: 'Of course, dear friend and esteemed teacher, I do not include your great works that are a real improvement upon Descartes and Mr Hobbes'. Nor was he tactful in the way that he dismissed the discoveries that the ambitious empirics sell to the world. The added phrase – 'as they call them' – indicates that, in his view, the 'discoveries' do not merit the term: they are not genuine discoveries. His words were not felicitously chosen. Locke had announced his discoveries to the world four years earlier in the *Essay*. In his Epistle to the Reader, Locke had described how his inquiries had grown, as 'new discoveries led me still on'.

Ashley then proceeded to an issue that lay at the core of his disagreement with Locke. He compared the emptiness of modern philosophy with the 'true philosophers of Socrates's days' (p. 152). In those ancient times, Ashley wrote, philosophers did not espouse systems, but they sought to live genuinely philosophical lives. What is philosophy, Ashley asked, if it does not teach how to live? In a passage that prefigures sections of the *Characteristicks*, Ashley asked Locke 'What signifies it to know (if we could know) what elements the earth was made from; or how many atoms went to make up the round ball we live upon?' Or what signifies it to have an exact system 'of our frames'? Such knowledge is insignificant when compared with 'true learning' – and this is to know 'our selves' and to discover 'what makes us low, and base, stubborn against reason, to be corrupted and drawn away from virtue' (p. 153).

How could Locke possibly agree? The young man was dismissing the very things that he held to be important. The new atomic science – the works of Newton and Boyle – could never be insignificant for Locke. His psychology, by searching for the origins of ideas, sought to reveal the basic atoms of knowledge. Yet Ashley was saying that any exact knowledge of our 'frames' somehow failed to answer the big questions about our characters and our morals. To know how we come by our ideas was trivial when compared to the big question: 'What ideas should we have?' To examine in ever greater detail the cognitive operations of thought would be to condemn philosophy (or psychology) to ever more triviality. This was precisely the stance that Shaftesbury would repeat in *Characteristicks*.

There was also a further theme distancing Ashley from his teacher. Locke had cut himself off from the history of philosophy. He recognized no ancestors as he claimed to have spun his ideas from his own thoughts. By contrast, Ashley was dismissing the new systems and going back into the history of philosophy. As his early letter made clear, Socrates was his intellectual inspiration (and, by implication, his foster-father was not). The young man sketched a picture of philosophical decline from the age of Socrates: the 'Socratic spirit sank much' and 'philosophy and sophistry' began to become entwined (p. 152). Philosophy ceased to be a matter of living of a philosophical life – or, to use more modern terminology, theory became split from practice.

Ashley added that in his quest for understanding he would search 'any age or language that can assist me here' (p. 153). Just because a writer is long dead, or writes in a foreign language, that is no reason to neglect their teaching. He sounds so reasonable, so open-minded. He was rejecting the puritan imperative to value the writings of Christians over those of non-Christians. Yet, he was going further than rejecting religious dogmatism. By stressing philosophy's ancient heritage, Ashley was not putting his faith into the clear and distinct truths of modern, empirical science. Understanding was to be attained through embracing the wisdom of the past, not by breaking with past.

In writing all this to his teacher, the young man was leaving a significant absence. Ashley did not qualify his vision of philosophy, in order to take into account the sensibilities of the man whom he was addressing. He did not say 'how fortunate I am to have a teacher, a foster-father, whose writings can guide me in my quest'. Quite the contrary, he was telling Locke that he was looking elsewhere – to other ages and to other languages – for inspiration. It may have been a sign of independent thinking but it certainly was not good manners.

Ashley ended somewhat abruptly with an apology that he had almost missed the time for posting his letter: 'You see what it is to set me a-talking'. He signed off with his usual mixture of friendship and deference: 'Your entire friend and humble servant' (p. 154). Ashley's next extant letter to Locke, written two months later, contains no philosophical discussion. He talks about his public duties. These, he wrote, hold no pleasures for they prevent him from visiting those 'whom I have a real respect for' (Beer, 1979, p. 193). He was, of course, referring to Locke and the Mashams.

Thereafter Locke and Shaftesbury kept in regular, warm correspondence. But they appear to have avoided discussing philosophy. Neither, it seems, wished to explore the growing differences between their views. The young man had almost overstepped the bounds in that early letter. Locke had possibly excused the insensitivity of his pupil on the grounds of youthful enthusiasm. He might well have been glad that the young man's passions were leading him towards philosophy rather than, like so many young noblemen, towards card tables, drinking clubs and ladies of the night.

As Shaftesbury said in the short memoir of Locke that he wrote for Le Clerc, his foster-father had overseen completely the direction of his education. No system of education, however well thought out in theory, can produce guaranteed results: knowledge of the human frame is too imperfect for that. Locke may have controlled the intellectual material that was to be presented to the young Shaftesbury. The right sensory information may have been delivered. But Locke, for all his theory of human understanding, could not control how the young man would reflect upon his teacher's ideas. There is little in the *Essay* to account for the origins of such rebellion.

Locke had transmitted to his pupil a deep love of learning and philosophical inquiry. Nevertheless, the two could not share their common interest in philosophy. Perhaps, instinctively, Locke and Shaftesbury had realized that their bonds of close affection could only be maintained by skirting around the intellectual interests that simultaneously united and divided them. By tactful practice and intuitive understanding, foster-father and foster-son both demonstrated that there is more to life, and to love, than philosophizing.

Publishing and Not Publishing

Shaftesbury's short memoir of Locke contains an interesting omission. It mentions nothing about Locke's philosophical work, and most notably the *Essay*. Of course, the memoir deliberately concentrated on Locke's connection with the Shaftesbury family. Even so, the third Earl could have told Le Clerc that Locke wrote the bulk of his great work while still working in the first Earl's service. Shaftesbury might even have said that his grandfather encouraged Locke in his philosophical quest for the origins of understanding. The absence of any reference to philosophy is significant.

So is the fact Shaftesbury did not publish his own philosophical works until after Locke's death. There was, it is true, the anonymous preface to Whichcote's sermons; but this was not an extended piece of philosophical writings. His reaction to the unauthorized publication of his 'Inquiry Concerning Virtue' was revealing. He tried to buy up all remaining copies to prevent anyone reading what he had written.

In part Shaftesbury's concern to suppress the unauthorized edition reflected what Michael Prince (2004) has called 'Shaftesbury's obsessive efforts at self-revision' (p. 51). He worked hard at the style of his published writings, drafting and re-drafting so his prose would flow with the elegance to which he aspired. He wanted much more than the plain style that Locke produced. In the third volume of *Characteristicks,* Shaftesbury complained that too many British authors did not engage in the tedious business of *limae labor*, or refining their prose. It was as if they feared the eraser and had become 'intolerably supine, conceited and admirers of themselves' (1711/1999, pp. 448f). The accusation could not be raised against Shaftesbury. In a letter written to a university student in 1709, Shaftesbury described that early unauthorized version of 'Inquiry' as 'an imperfect thing' with a 'disguised, disordered style'. He hoped that one day it would be 'set righter'. He told the student to 'have patience in the meanwhile' (Shaftesbury, 1746, pp. 34–5).

By the time he was writing the letter, Shaftesbury himself could no longer afford to be patient if he wanted to set down his thoughts properly. His health was ebbing away. He worked hard at revising the style of the 'Inquiry' for inclusion in *Characteristicks*. The basic structures of the unauthorized and final versions are identical: they share the same ordering of arguments and arrangements of paragraphs. But virtually every individual sentence shows signs of re-working. The Scottish rhetorician, Hugh Blair, who found Shaftesbury's style too ornate for his own tastes, was to comment on the pains that Shaftesbury took in the construction of his sentences. Blair compared the two versions of the Inquiry: 'We see one of the most curious and useful examples that I know, of what is called *limae labor*; the art of polishing language, breaking long sentences, and working up an imperfect draught into a highly finished performance' (Blair, 1793, p. 364).

There can be little doubting Shaftesbury's concern to avoid hasty, unpolished writing, for in his perspective there was no distinction between form and content, style and message. There is, nevertheless, another reason why Shaftesbury might not have wanted Toland's version of the 'Inquiry' to circulate. Locke was still alive and he would have realized just how far his foster-son's way of philosophizing was departing from his own. Several years after Locke's death, Shaftesbury wrote to General Stanhope, a future Chancellor of the Exchequer. In that letter, Shaftesbury was quite frank about the philosophical differences between himself and his 'old tutor and governor'. Shaftesbury said that he 'ever concealed my differences as much as possible' (Rand, 1900, p. 416). That would explain why he tried to prevent the unauthorized 'Inquiry' from circulating.

It would also explain some curious comments Shaftesbury made in a letter sent to his friend John Somers in October 1705. Shaftesbury sent Somers an early version of 'The moralists, a philosophical rhapsody', which he had arranged to be privately printed in Amsterdam in either 1703 or 1704, and which would later be included in *Characteristicks* (Voitle, 1984, p. 313). Having had the piece printed, Shaftesbury delayed circulating it. When he finally sent the copy to Lord Somers, his accompanying letter suggested that this was the first copy he had shown anyone. The letter contained an odd remark: 'So wholly and solely is the book dedicated to you, that nobody has set their eyes on it, nor shall, besides yourself'. He said that Somers could do what he wanted with the book – 'if you have no fancy for it burn it'. But he must not show it to anyone else (letter in Rand, 1900, pp. 336–7).

Why would Shaftesbury have gone to the trouble of having the work printed and then, first, delayed showing it to anyone and then sending it only to one friend who was instructed not to show it to anyone else? And why, six years later, was there no secrecy when the piece appeared as part of *Characteristicks*? The answer is simple. Shaftesbury did not want to circulate the book while Locke was still alive. His old teacher would have seen how the work contested his own theories. Shaftesbury used the form of the Platonic dialogue to examine questions of morality. One passage confronted Locke's most famous idea. The characters were discussing whether the contents of our mind might be innate. The Socrates-type character, whom Shaftesbury named Philocles and to whom he gave the stronger arguments, claims that 'life and the sensations which accompany life … are from mere nature and nothing else'. Philocles adds: 'If you dislike the word "innate", let us change it, if you will, for "instinct", and call instinct that which nature teaches, exclusive of art, culture or discipline' (1711/1999 ed., p. 325).

When Shaftesbury sent the copy to Somers, Locke had only been dead for a few months. Clearly, Shaftesbury wanted to circulate his book – why else send Somers a copy? At the same time, Shaftesbury would have been aware that to rush into publication, so soon after his teacher's death, would have been in questionable taste. However, with the passing of time, Shaftesbury relaxed his reticence. There are other passages in the *Characteristicks*, which, as will be seen, are almost forthright in their criticism of Locke. But even these are nowhere near as forthright as Shaftesbury could sometimes be in his private correspondence.

Privately Criticizing Locke

When writing to friends, Shaftesbury made some outspoken criticisms of Locke's philosophy. The letter to Stanhope, in which Shaftesbury claimed to have concealed his differences with Locke, was quite blunt. Amongst other things, Shaftesbury criticized Locke for his lack of appreciation for philosophy's history. It was the old complaint: the moderns believe their discoveries are more original than they are. Had Locke, Shaftesbury wrote tartly, 'been tolerably learned in the state of philosophy with the ancients, he would not have heaped such loads of words upon us' (Rand, 1900, p. 416).

Just two months after Locke's death, a friend had sent Shaftesbury a copy of a letter that the dying Locke had written. In the letter Locke had talked of the present life being but 'a scene of vanity, that soon passes away, and affords no solid satisfaction'; Locke said that he was dying 'in hopes of another life' (Rand, 1900, p. 345). Shaftesbury's response to the friend, who had sent him the copy, was caustic. The sentiment, he wrote, 'puts me in mind of one of those dying speeches which come out under the title of a Christian warning piece'. It sounds like the view of a good Christian but 'I should never have guessed it to have been of a dying philosopher' (Rand, 1900, p. 345). Philosophy, he went on, should teach us to live a good life in this world – not to hope to be rewarded in another life: 'For our part, let us, on the contrary, make the most of life and least of death' (p. 346).

These are not the words of someone treading carefully. Shaftesbury is dismissing Locke's last thoughts – he is even implying that Locke on his deathbed was betraying philosophy. Shaftesbury concluded his letter by stating that his own philosophy takes a very different view of life and death: 'I ask no reward from heaven for that which is reward itself' (p. 347). He hopes to find what is heavenly on earth: 'And if this disposition fits me not for heaven, I desire never to be fitted for it, nor come into the place' (p. 347).

The idea that virtue should be pursued in this world for its own sake, and not for the purposes of future gain, was a central theme in Shaftesbury's writings. In his view, this constituted an unbridgeable gap between his philosophy and that of Locke's. He believed that Locke had failed to understand the deep roots of morality in human nature. This came out in a series of letters that Shaftesbury wrote to a young student, whom he was supporting at Oxford. In these letters, Shaftesbury was quite frank about his estrangement from Locke's philosophy. Initially, Shaftesbury had encouraged the young man to read Locke's *Essay*, and had even lent him a copy. He praised Locke's book, claiming that no-one had done more 'towards the recalling of philosophy from barbarity'; and no-one had opened 'a better or clearer way to reasoning' (Shaftesbury, 1746, p. 2). But a few months later, in January 1709, Shaftesbury was warning his protégé of Locke's limitations. More profit would be gained from reading the ancients than studying that philosophy 'which is built upon the comparison and compounding of ideas, complex, implex, reflex and all that din and noise of metaphysics' (p. 17).

There was stronger stuff to come. In the summer of 1709 Shaftesbury wrote again to the young man, advising him what philosophical books to read. He cautioned against Hobbes. He then criticized Locke's *Essay*, for going down the same path. Hobbes had started things with his sceptical philosophy but 'it was Mr Locke that struck the home blow'. Shaftesbury continued: it was 'Mr Locke that struck at all fundamentals, threw all order and virtue out of the world, and made the very ideas of these (which are the same as those of God) *unnatural*, and without foundation in our minds' (Shaftesbury, 1746, p. 32).

This was a harsh judgement. And it was intended to be. Locke, so he told the young man, had followed Hobbes in denying that morality was inbuilt into us, 'imprinted on human minds'. Locke had proposed that morality depends on experience: it is just 'fashion and custom'; there is nothing right and wrong in itself (1746, p. 32). Here Shaftesbury was taking up a theme that he elaborated in *Characteristicks*: namely, we have an inborn sense of morality. He had alluded to it in the preface to Whichcote's sermons. But there he had only identified Hobbes, not Locke, as denying this apparent fact of human nature.

Shaftesbury was not finished. He then proceeded to mock Locke's idea that all our ideas have to be taught and that we have no instincts. Maybe, 'a Lockist' would presume that men have to be taught to love women: 'Perhaps if we had no schools of Venus, nor such horrid lewd books, or lewd companions, we might have no understanding of this, till we happen to be taught by our parents'. And, if such teaching does not occur, 'the race of mankind might perish'. He added: 'This is very poor philosophy' (1746, p. 34). It was a good argument to make to a young man doubtlessly experiencing bodily sensations, whose risings were dependent on neither book learning nor parental instruction.

When Shaftesbury criticized Locke in his private letters, he would stress that he was only criticizing his teacher's philosophical writings. He was in no way impugning Locke's character, which he continued to hold in the highest regard (e.g., 1746, p. 32). Many philosophers have been criticized for not living up to the professed ideals of their philosophy. Down the ages there have been rationalists, who have shown irrational prejudices; moral philosophers who have treated their nearest and dearest with callous indifference and radical revolutionaries who have been seduced by luxury. Shaftesbury's criticisms of his teacher were of the reverse order. It was not that Locke failed to meet his own philosophical ideals. Quite the contrary, his philosophy failed to match the goodness of his character.

Dying as a Philosopher

When Shaftesbury wrote his letters of advice to the young man at university, he knew that he did not have long to live. He had little to gain by reticence. During this period, he was publishing separately the sections of the first two volumes of *Characteristicks*. This was also a time of personal change. Shaftesbury was seeking to marry. He had already approached the family of one prospective bride and had been rejected. The young woman's father, a wealthy man, suspected that Shaftesbury was more interested in his daughter's dowry than her charms. Shaftesbury was distraught to be suspected of such base motives.

In response, he turned his attentions to a young woman of no great family, fortune or, it was said, beauty. She accepted his hand in 1709. Shaftesbury's own family thought he was marrying beneath him. So did his manservant. He forbade the latter from commenting on his bride's social position. In a letter to his manservant, Shaftesbury explained that he was marrying this very young woman 'not for love's sake (since I never saw her till the match was resolved on), nor for riches but for my family's sake only, and for my own ease in a private and country life'. He added that, having now met the young lady, the reports he had received about her appearance were all wrong: she was in his eyes 'a very great beauty' (letter in Rand, 1900, pp. 407f).

In 1711, Shaftesbury's young bride gave birth to a son. This was also the year in which the first edition of *Characteristicks* appeared. Shaftesbury's health by now was in serious decline. Fearing that he would not survive another cold and damp English winter, he moved with his wife to Naples. He enjoyed the climate and the architecture of the city. He was already on friendly terms with a number of Napolitan intellectuals.

Giambattisto Vico, the Italian philosopher, was also living in Naples. Like Shaftesbury, Vico stressed the social and historical nature of humans. In fact, Vico was at that time working out his ideas on the concept of '*sensus communis*', or common sense, although his thoughts would not be published for a good number of years (Pettersson, 2004; Schaeffer, 1990). Shaftesbury had published his own essay 'Sensus Communis' two years earlier. This essay, which will be discussed in the following chapter, had argued that humans have an innate sense of community. There is some debate whether Vico actually visited Shaftesbury in Naples. Nevertheless, there is no doubt that Shaftesbury was befriended by several of Vico's friends, to whom Shaftesbury gave copies of his writings (Vico, 1975, p. 81). There is, therefore, good reason for thinking that Vico may have known about Shaftesbury's ideas on *sensus communis*, either directly or through mutual friends. On the other hand, there is no evidence for supposing that Shaftesbury's earlier essay had been influenced by Vico.

Shaftesbury was not to live long in Naples. He died in February 1713, just short of his forty-second birthday. At the time of his death, he was preparing the second edition of *Characteristicks*. He was planning to include symbolic illustrations to complement his text and had commissioned suitable engravings. Before his death, he entered into a legal contract with his wife (Voitle, 1984, p. 410). She was legally bound on his death to return immediately to England, leaving his body in Naples and putting her own health before any duties of mourning. Shaftesbury insisted on this. If the contract appears odd, then Shaftesbury was ensuring that the interests of his young wife came first. He did not want her left distraught and alone in a foreign country.

More than this, he was facing death philosophically. He did not want to die like Locke. There were to be no Christian death-bed scenes with pious wishes for a better after-life. He would face the prospect of death in a calm, business-like manner, as Socrates had done. He would tidy up his affairs, see that his obligations were fulfilled and attend to the interests of others. And then he would die. That is what his philosophy taught him. And that is what he did.

6

Shaftesbury: Moral and Social Sense

The tone that Shaftesbury used when writing privately to friends about the philosophy of Locke suggests something deeply felt. It is easy to speculate about hidden resentments. Perhaps Shaftesbury felt threatened by the fame that his teacher was enjoying late in life. Locke now belonged to the whole world rather than to the Shaftesbury family. Maybe the young philosopher feared being swamped by Locke's powerful intellect and needed to react sharply to preserve his intellectual independence. Without too much difficulty, the ambiguities of love and aggression – identification and rebellion – can be suspected.

There is, nevertheless, a basic fact that should not be overlooked. As a young man, Shaftesbury was drawn to a very different philosophical tradition than that of Locke. On important issues – such as the nature of morality, truth and the human condition – Shaftesbury's views were diverging from Locke's. As is clear from that early letter, which was discussed in the previous chapter, Shaftesbury was aligning himself with the traditions of ancient stoicism. Once he had done that, a fundamental intellectual rejection of Locke was inevitable.

Central to the difference between Locke and Shaftesbury were their contrasting views on human nature. They differed on so many psychological matters. Locke declared that we are born with empty minds; Shaftesbury postulated that we have innate social and moral feelings. Locke's approach was atomistic, taking apart the workings of the mind to find the basic units. Shaftesbury rejected this: the whole was greater than the sum of its parts. In some respects, Shaftesbury's view of the mind anticipated the views of early twentieth century Gestalt psychologists, who rejected the views of Locke's heirs, the associationists. In other respects, this was a difference between an individual psychology and a social psychology.

Yet, bland descriptions of different psychologies fail to capture the depth of the disagreement. As will be discussed in this chapter, the *Essay's* cognitive processor of sensory information was far removed from Shaftesbury's image of humans as moral and aesthetic agents. The difference also had a potential ideological element. Locke and

Shaftesbury, it is true, shared similar political views, both aligning themselves with the Whiggish politics of the first Earl. Nevertheless, it will be suggested that their psychologies contained very different ideological potentials. Locke's psychology, based on the principle of individual self-interest, would later seem well suited to the world of capitalism. From the awkward aristocrat, by contrast, came a critical vision – the image of the human whose natural sociability was being betrayed by a climate of self-interest.

Epicureans versus Stoics

It would be possible to compile a list of the various psychological topics on which Shaftesbury and Locke disagreed. Such a listing, however, would fail to go to the heart of their disagreement. Another strategy is to ask how the two thinkers themselves might have described their differences. We do not know how Locke would have characterized them. Not only was he habitually discrete, but, of course, he had no opportunity to read Shaftesbury's main writings. Nevertheless, we can imagine his response.

Had Locke lived to read Shaftesbury's *Characteristicks*, he would not have been comfortable with Shaftesbury's wealth of classical sources and his neglect of the new empirical sciences. There are abundant references to Socrates, Marcus Aurelius and Horace, but none to Boyle, Newton and Huygens. On a more personal level, Locke would have noted an absence of praise for himself. Shaftesbury lauded Ralph Cudworth, the old Platonist advocate of innate ideas, calling him 'pious and learned', but there are no similar tributes to his old teacher (1711/1999, p. 264). The self-conscious elegance of Shaftesbury's writing, modelled on classical rhetoric, would have irritated Locke. It differed from the no-nonsense, plain style which Locke advocated for philosophical writing and which he sought to practise. This reflected a basic difference in relation to history. Locke saw himself sweeping away the philosophical garbage of the past. His pupil must have seemed so backward looking. We can imagine Locke perplexed why a young man, growing up in an age of exciting new discoveries, should retreat into the past like an old man fearful of the present.

This imagining of Locke's reaction is, of course, pure conjecture. On the other hand, we do know how Shaftesbury depicted his difference with Locke. He did not see it as a difference between the modern and the old-fashioned. Possessed of a historical perspective, Shaftesbury did not believe that the present was transcending the past. The modernists were not quite as modern they would like to believe: they were showing continuity with the past, rather than rupture. If the 'modernists' were not genuinely modern, then another way of describing them was required.

Such a description should link the so-called modernists to those older traditions of thinking that they sought to disavow.

In October 1706, Shaftesbury wrote to Pierre Coste, a French Protestant who was both his and Locke's friend. Shaftesbury outlined his view that throughout history there had only been 'two real distinct philosophies' – stoicism and Epicureanism (Rand, 1900, p. 355ff). Both traditions owed their origins to academies that were established in Athens around 300 BCE. From then onwards, stoics and Epicureans had argued about practically every philosophical issue. Shaftesbury summed up the difference between the two philosophies: stoicism was 'civil, social, theistic', while Epicureanism was 'the contrary' (p. 359). All subsequent philosophical debate, he wrote, was a reprise of that original, irreconcilable argument.

If Shaftesbury allied himself with the stoics, then he considered his old teacher to be an Epicurean in modern dress. This was not an absurd fantasy. As has been mentioned, there are affinities between Locke's views and those of Gassendi, the great reviver of Epicurean atomism in the seventeenth century. Locke, of course, did not see himself as an Epicurean, or, for that matter, as a supporter of any ancient school of philosophy. In the *Essay*, he described the Epicureans, as a 'philosophical sect', which, like any sect, produced gibberish that was incomprehensible to outsiders (III.x.14). Locke, with his plain English and his belief in modern science, believed he was rejecting all sects, both present and past.

One expert has claimed that in ancient Greece the choice between stoicism and Epicureanism affected one's whole way of living; it was 'decisive not only for one's ethical values and priorities but also for one's understanding of the world's general structure, one's theology, and the importance to be attached to systematic reasoning and the study of language' (Long, 2002, p. 18). In short, everything hung on the decision to be an Epicurean or a stoic. So it must have seemed to Shaftesbury many centuries later. By choosing stoicism as his philosophy, Shaftesbury was accepting an outlook that would inevitably assign Locke to the other side of an unbridgeable divide.

Shaftesbury's personal notebooks, which have become known as his 'Regimen', were filled with quotations from his two favourite stoic philosophers: Marcus Aurelius and Epictetus. Both figures date from the later Roman period of stoicism. They represent the opposite ends of social life. Epictetus was born between 50 and 60 CE and spent his early life as a slave. He managed to obtain his freedom and began to earn his living from teaching philosophy. He was exiled when the emperor Domitian banished all philosophers from Italy. In exile Epictetus established an academy in Nicopolis. Like Socrates, Epictetus wrote little or nothing, but his teachings were collected by devoted followers.

Down the ages, Epictetus's insights, practical advice and earthy wit provided a guide for later stoics.

Marcus Aurelius moved in powerful political circles, becoming emperor of Rome in 161 CE and remaining in that position until his death in 180. Despite his political commitments, Aurelius kept a notebook of philosophical reflections that came to be published as his *Meditations*. Both ex-slave and emperor advocated philosophy as a practical activity. Technical analysis of philosophical issues was considered to be worthwhile only to the extent that it contributed to the living of a moral life. The stoic way of life was open to all; whether high-born or low-born, a slave or emperor, one should aspire to live according to the disciplined virtues of stoicism.

Shaftesbury was attracted to stoic philosophy as a guide for moral self-improvement. He wrote in his Regimen that if philosophical thinking is to mean anything, then it must be 'a matter of practice'. The purpose of his studies was 'my own amendment' and there was little value in 'those speculations' that did not lead 'to my amendment' (1900a, p. 270). Unsurprisingly, he had little but contempt for the abstract metaphysics of the mediaeval schoolmen. This was one of the few philosophical matters on which he and Locke agreed. From Shaftesbury's perspective, however, Locke's analysis of ideas in the *Essay* was too scholastic, too far removed from the practicalities of life to offer scope for self-improvement.

Stoicism advocated a stern morality that taught control over frivolous desire. People should discipline themselves to live 'naturally'. Living 'naturally' certainly did not mean giving way to every impulse or desire. Stoics distinguished desires that are 'natural' (and good) and those that are not natural. Since it is the 'natural' condition of humans to be rational, this meant that humans should attempt, above all, to find happiness by exerting rational discipline over their lives. Desires, which are 'unnatural' or 'neutral', should be controlled. Adherents should keep their minds on higher matters and avoid vain glories and fleeting pleasures. One of Epictetus's great maxims, found in *The Enchiridion*, or 'Manual', encapsulated the stoic code of behaviour: 'Require not things to happen as you wish, but wish them to happen as they do happen, and you will go on well' (Epictetus, 1910, p. 258).

The maxim sounds like a recipe for conservatism. It seems to say that we should learn to accept the world as it is, rather than to change it. However, there was an additional element that saves stoicism from mere fatalism. Stoics should apply their philosophy in the service of others. Unlike Epicureans, stoics did not advocate detaching themselves from social, familial or political life. A stoic emperor was no contradiction, nor was a stoic rebel. By insisting that some desires were natural and others unnatural, stoicism possessed the potential for criticizing prevailing conditions. A society that is seen to be fostering unnatural pleasures is to be resisted and changed.

The great stoic hero was Socrates, who, in the eyes of the stoics, lived the philosophical life to perfection. He cared more for the pursuit of truth than for worldly pleasures. Socrates was no mere conservative, who let the world of affairs go its way while he devoted himself to the world of the mind. Socrates showed no fear in challenging the powerful and questioning their prejudices. He was prosecuted by the authorities of Athens. In refusing to compromise and preferring death to untruthful confession, Socrates was demonstrating supreme stoic virtues.

Later generations of stoics would find inspiration in the life and thoughts of Socrates. In his early letter to Locke, Shaftesbury had referred to Socrates as a great example. Later in *Characteristicks,* Shaftesbury called Socrates 'the divinest man who had ever appeared in the heathen world' (1711/1999, p. 17). According to Shaftesbury, this most divine man showed his greatness by maintaining good humour in adverse circumstances. To Puritan theologians, the description of a heathen as divine was little more than deliberate blasphemy. Shaftesbury was aware of the offence. He was using the example of Socrates and his good humour to show the necessity for opposing the grim, religious dogmatism of his own times.

The stoics, with their veneration of rational control, viewed the Epicurean celebration of sensual experience with distaste. Their image of Epicureanism was not necessarily accurate. Certainly the seventeenth century Epicureans such as Gassendi and Charleton took pains to stress that Epicurus lived a disciplined, morally blameless life. The crucial differences, however, between the Epicureans and the stoics were intellectual rather than personal. Shaftesbury, in his letter to Pierre Coste, stressed the 'social' nature of stoicism. In the opinion of stoics, Epicureanism was a selfish philosophy that encouraged adherents to pursue individual sensory pleasures at the expense of all social duties. Shaftesbury viewed the historic rivalry as a conflict between a philosophy of social morality and one of individual self-interest. This gave force to the comment in his letter to the university student that Locke's philosophy had struck the home blow against morality.

Criticizing Atomism

Atomism was the great attraction of Epicurus's thinking for revivalists such as Gassendi and Charleton. A philosophy stipulating that the universe comprised indivisible, physical atoms seemed stunningly modern. There was an associated methodological principle: if the world is to be understood, it has to be dissected into its component parts. Locke applied this principle to the workings of the mind, breaking down complex ideas into their simple cognitive components.

The stoic reaction was simple. If you search for ever smaller units, you will come up with discoveries of increasing triviality. Epictetus expressed this stoic impatience with atomism as a principle of exploration: 'What does it signify to me … whether the universe is composed of atoms or uncompounded substances, or of fire and earth?' What really matters, he continued, is to know 'the essence of good and evil, and the proper bounds of the desires and aversions' (1910, p. 301). Shaftesbury's youthful letter to Locke contained a virtual paraphrase, dismissing the significance of knowing how many atoms make up the world (see pp. 87–8).

In contrast to the atomism of the Epicureans, stoics adopted a holistic view of the world. The significance of the universe is to be found in the interconnection between the parts, not in the separate elements of those parts. Stoics insisted that each human was a whole person, not a collection of physical atoms. Moreover, humans were not isolated, self-contained units, but were parts of social wholes. If we are to study human nature, then this holistic perspective enjoins us to avoid a two step reduction. We should not decompose social wholes into individual persons and then decompose each individual person into their constituent atomic elements. Locke's work showed this two-step reduction. Society was, Locke argued, merely a contract between individuals, seeking to pursue their own interests. In the *Essay*, he sought to demonstrate that the ideas of the individual could (and should) be decomposed into their simple elements.

There is a passage in the *Characteristicks* where Shaftesbury specifically used the old stoic argument about the triviality of atomism against Locke. Here he identified Locke as an Epicurean. The passage comes in the essay 'Soliloquy', which was the last essay in the first two volumes of *Characteristicks*. Shaftesbury was arguing for the importance of studying the nature of human affections. He referred to 'philosophical speculations' about 'formation of ideas, their compositions, comparisons, agreement and disagreement' (1711/1999, p. 134; see also Regimen, p. 267, for an almost identical passage). The terminology is unmistakably Lockean. Shaftesbury complained that such speculations were worthless. They do not tell us how to judge 'mankind and human affairs'; how to judge the world of 'pleasures, riches, fame, life' (p. 134). He asks: 'What is it to me, for instance, to know what kind of idea I can form of space?' (p. 134).

To hammer home the point, Shaftesbury then quotes 'a renowned modern philosopher'. The quotation is abstrusely worded: 'Divide a solid body of whatever dimension and it will be impossible for the parts to move within the bounds of its superficies, if there be not left in it a void space as big as the least part into which the said body is divided' (pp. 134–5). The quote comes from Locke's *Essay* (II.xiii.23). The wording is not quite exact: if anything, Shaftesbury had tidied up some of the awkwardness of the original phrasing. Shaftesbury ends the quotation with the comment 'Thus the atomist or Epicurean pleading for a vacuum' (p. 135).

Shaftesbury does not stop there. He then imagines the atomist or Epicurean debating with a Plenitudinarian, who was arguing in the manner of Descartes:

> 'Of this', says one, 'I have clear ideas'.
>
> 'Of this', says the other, 'I can be certain'.
>
> 'And what', say I, 'if in the whole matter there can be no certainty at all?' (Shaftesbury, 1711/1999, p. 135)

In a single passage, Shaftesbury had struck at two of the core elements of Locke's philosophy: atomism and foundationalism. Shaftesbury had stated that atomism was trivial as a philosophical procedure. Then he suggested that atomism would not provide a firm foundation for human knowledge, as Locke had hoped it would. He was also questioning the Cartesian method of deducing truths from certain propositions such as *I think therefore I exist*. Shaftesbury was not just doubting whether the methods of Locke and Descartes would be efficacious in finding points of certainty on which knowledge could be built. He was expressing scepticism whether there were any firm, absolute truths of the sort that Locke and Descartes had hoped to find. What if there is no certainty at all? Shaftesbury, here, was questioning the modernist dream of discovering clear, certain truth.

Holistic Perspective

Morally and philosophically, Shaftesbury was reacting against individualism. He believed that it was morally wrong to live one's life having no other purpose than attempting to gain as much benefit for oneself as possible. Any philosophy advocating self-interest as a principle of conduct was wrong both morally and psychologically. In Shaftesbury's view, both Hobbes and Locke had a faulty understanding of human psychology and this was leading them to reduce human conduct to self-interest. Shaftesbury's argument stressed that humans are by their nature social and moral beings. A philosophy of self-interest, although it might be attractive to those who wish to escape from the burdens of higher ethical duties, was nevertheless psychologically 'unnatural'.

As might be expected, Shaftesbury's view of human nature is set within a wider stoic framework. Whereas the Epicureans had depicted the universe as being comprised of millions upon millions of atoms, each pursuing their own individual trajectories, the stoics stressed the interconnectness of all things. Shaftesbury outlined the basic tenets of his holism in 'An Inquiry Concerning Virtue or Merit'. This was the first extended piece that he wrote and he would become increasingly dissatisfied with its style and way of arguing. However, he never rejected its basic principle of holism, although he came to accept that the search for holistic understanding can lead to dilemma and doubt, rather than certainty.

In 'Inquiry' Shaftesbury presented the basic principle that we cannot 'give the least account of a particular part without a competent knowledge of the whole' (1711/1999, p. 167). The limbs serve the body and the leaves the tree: to examine limbs without the body or leaves without the tree would be absurd. Shaftesbury applied the principle to the study of animals: 'To what end the many proportions and various shapes of parts in many creatures actually serve, we are able, by the help of study and observation, to demonstrate with great exactness' (p. 167). Each creature can be considered to be part of larger systems. The males and females of the species will exist to propagate the species and, consequently, male and female will 'have a joint relation to another existence and order of things beyond themselves' (p. 168). Similarly, species do not exist in isolation but are 'parts of another system'. For example, 'to the existence of the spider that of the fly is absolutely necessary' (p. 168). And so on, such that there is 'a system of all animals' (p. 169).

Even the earth is not a complete, self-contained system. It is 'a part only of some other system' for it is connected with 'its sun, the galaxy or its fellow-planets' (p. 169). In the dialogue 'The Moralists', Shaftesbury uses the character of Theocles as a mouthpiece for stoic philosophy. Theocles declares that 'all things in this world are united'. In contemplating things, we should observe 'the system of the bigger world'. Thus, he urges his fellow conversationalists to notice 'the mutual dependency of things, the relation of one to another, of the sun to this inhabited earth and of the earth and other planets to the sun, the order, union and coherence of the whole!' (pp. 274–5).

Shaftesbury's holism contained a metaphysical element. He was suggesting that the various interconnecting systems formed harmonious wholes. Moreover, these harmonies could not have been created by accident. It was impossible to suppose that 'each of these complete and perfect systems were … united in just symmetry and conspiring order, either by the accidental blowing of the winds or the rolling of the sands' (p. 276). There had to be a Creator. Moreover, Shaftesbury was implying that the various systems fit harmoniously such that this created universe is seen to be 'of good order and for the best' (p. 164).

Voltaire was to use a similar argument from design: just as the existence of a watch proved the existence of the watchmaker, so the existence of the universe was proof of a Creator (Dennett, 1995). However, Voltaire was to mock Shaftesbury's complacent optimism that the harmony of the universe indicated, not just an intelligent designer, but a benevolent one. How could, Voltaire asked, a natural disaster, such as the Lisbon earthquake with its massive loss of life, indicate that all is of good order and that everything happens for the best? (Voltaire, 1756/2006).

One might note Shaftesbury's frequent use of the term 'system'. In this, he was showing himself to be an early 'systems theorist'. Organisms should not be studied in isolation but should be understood as functional parts of wider systems. One hundred and fifty years later, similar arguments would be advocated by Herbert Spencer (Young, 1990). In his *First Principles* (1864) Spencer discussed the inter-connections of all matter, from micro-organisms to the planetary systems. In each case, elements had to be understood according to their contribution to the way the system as a whole functioned. Spencer, unlike Shaftesbury, understood the relations between systems as operating according to competitive, rather than benevolent, principles. As a materialist, he suspected no hidden, kindly hand, only a fierce Darwinian struggle for existence.

Shaftesbury may have stressed the systematic nature of the universe, but that does not mean that his own philosophy comprised a system that was intended to reflect the nature of the universe. There is a paradox in his talk about systems – a paradox that will be explored in greater detail in the following chapter. Shaftesbury opposed any sort of systematic philosophy that tried to unite all knowledge around a few basic principles. Locke's *Essay* was far too systematic for Shaftesbury's tastes. Any system necessarily oversimplified the complexities of the universe and, in particular, the complexities of human beings. As will be seen, when he advanced general propositions about human nature, he often tended to contradict his own assertions, as if to stress that humans were too complex to be caught within a simple theoretical net. Only by disrupting systematic thinking can we begin to understand the awkward particularities of human nature. Shaftesbury wrote in *Characteristicks* that 'the most ingenious way of becoming foolish is by a system' (p. 130).

Common Sense

Shaftesbury's general metaphysical point about the interconnectedness of the universe has a direct psychological implication. If all things are interconnected then humans do not live in isolation: not only are we connected to our physical environment, but we are connected also to other humans. It makes no sense to treat humans as if they were separate atoms. Being social is integral to human nature.

When Locke considered the newborn child, he could only see an empty mind, ready to receive sensory inputs. He did not look at the fullness of the infant's situation, being nurtured by other humans within a wider pattern of social relations. Shaftesbury, by contrast, viewed the human infant as bound by social ties. In the 'Moralists' Theocles draws attention to the lengthy, helpless state of the human infant. Why should the human infant be 'the most helpless, weak, infirm' of all species? Why should humans, alone out of all animals, have this defect? He answers his own question: this helplessness engages the infant 'the more strongly to society', for the child cannot exist except 'in that social intercourse and community which is his natural state' (p. 283).

The phrase 'natural state' carried an important political message. Shaftesbury was counteracting the philosophy of individualism associated with Hobbes and also Locke. Both had assumed that in the state of nature individuals pursued their own interests uncooperatively: in other words that it was natural for humans to be selfish. Hobbes had argued that social authority was necessary to provide order. Locke had suggested that the individuals needed to form a social contract in order to protect their own individual interests. Shaftesbury implied that both accounts about the origins of society were absurd. There never was a time when humans lived individually outside of social arrangements. In order to make a social contract, humans must have already been living socially. A social contract was a promise. To make a promise, humans must be able to trust one another. Thus, 'faith, justice, honesty and virtue' must all have been part of the so-called state of nature (p. 51). The social state was the natural state for humans.

In this way, Shaftesbury reacted against Locke's individualist psychology. Far from being born empty-minded, the human infant is born with a predisposition to be social and to form social relations with others. The *Characteristicks* amplified the benevolent view of human nature that Shaftesbury had sketched in his preface to Whichcote's sermons. We do not exist just to receive and combine sensations. We have 'social or natural affections', like those between parents and offspring that 'contribute to the welfare of the whole species' (p. 432). Friendship, benevolence, love of conversation and sociability were all natural human characteristics. The 'cool philosophy' of self-interest ignored these social feelings (p. 43). It could not explain why 'all social love, friendship, gratitude or whatever else of this generous kind ... makes us disregardful of our own convenience and safety' (p. 193).

Shaftesbury rarely contained himself to attacking a single target. As he expanded on the social nature of humans, he could not resist making sarcastic comments against Christianity. He noted that 'private friendship and zeal for the public and our country are virtues purely voluntary in a Christian' (p. 46). Christianity fails to root itself in the details of social life on earth and, in consequence, its 'conversation is in heaven' (p. 47). In this regard, Shaftesbury compared Christianity unfavourably with the Jewish tradition. Elsewhere in *Characteristicks* he might have criticized the Jews for being 'a very cloudy people' (p. 16), but here he praised Judaism for putting social relations, civic duty and commitment to the community at its core: 'Under Jewish dispensation ... each of these virtues ... were in some manner recommended to us as honourable and worthy of our attention' (p. 47). These were not the sorts of remarks to endear Shaftesbury to the stricter sort of protestant theologian. Such comments earned him the notorious reputation of being a 'deist', or someone who believed in God but rejected all official religious doctrines, including those of Christianity.

So, according to Shaftesbury, humans are naturally endowed with some sort of social feeling. In 'Sensus Communis', which is one of the most brilliant pieces in *Characteristicks*, Shaftesbury gives the name 'common sense' to this innate social feeling or social sense. Not just content to link the idea of a 'social sense' with the term 'common sense', he links both terms with the Latin *sensus communis* (which can be literally translated as 'common sense', 'sense of community' and 'the sense of a particular community'). He justified using the term 'common sense' in this way by citing a passage from Juvenal as his authority (p. 48). Shaftesbury's etymological argument might be suspect, but, in a very practical way, he was reacting against Locke's recommendation to link general concepts to a clear and distinct idea. Shaftesbury believed in the poetic uses of language. He was deliberately using a term that resonated with different meanings, rather than seeking to confine it to a single, defined sense.

The upshot is that Shaftesbury's account of common sense takes on an ideological as well as psychological message. Common sense, or sense of community, lies at the heart of human nature. This itself is 'common sense' (or plain, good sense), known to all except religious bigots and individualist philosophers (whose cool, intellectual theories conflict with the good sense of ordinary people). In this way, the argument represents a multi-layered defence of common sense, which is simultaneously depicted as theory, psychological motive and plain, down-to-earth sensibleness.

As regards the last-mentioned meaning, Shaftesbury is to be found praising the 'common honest man', who is 'undisturbed by philosophy' and whose moral reactions can normally be trusted. Indeed, morality is unlikely to gain much by deep philosophical speculation. It is 'best to stick with common sense and go no further', because people's 'natural notions' are generally 'better than those refined by study' (p. 61). But Shaftesbury, as an heir to stoicism, does not really mean that deep study and self-examination were unnecessary. He was suggesting that the speculative philosophy of self-interest is worse than useless: it conflicts with human nature. Common sense was a good baton with which to beat the modern Epicureans and their abstract systems.

National Feeling

But why should we say that it is in our nature to be sociable and cooperative, rather than selfish and competitive? After all, examples of both sorts of behaviour exist. Shaftesbury, like Locke, observes the condition of the human infant, but comes to a different conclusion than Locke. Why was it ordered, Shaftesbury asks, that the human infant should of all species be so infirm? He answers his own question: because it enables the child to live in a social state. Thus, the newborn infant is not the empty vessel that Locke depicted, but possesses natural, social feelings and, most importantly, is the object of natural social feelings displayed by adults. As such, the infant is part of a community, bound by natural ties of dependence and affection from the moment of birth.

Shaftesbury's ideas on an innate social sense are not that different from those of psychologists today who claim that humans possess an 'innate inter-subjectivity' (e.g., Selby and Bradley, 2003; Trevarthen, 1977; Trevarthen et al., 1996). These psychologists have closely observed babies from birth interacting with their parents, participating, as it were, in mutual dialogues of sight and sound. The infant is instinctively drawn to the faces and voices of others. The child, to use Shaftesbury's phrase, lives in a natural state of social intercourse. As Shaftesbury implied, the social sense works in both directions. Adults, too, show a propensity to interact with infants, drawing them into the world of mutual communication. None of this would be possible, as Shaftesbury suggested, if human infants were not born so helpless, and adult humans were not, in their turn, drawn towards the helpless infant.

Shaftesbury saw the naturally helpless state of the human infant as providing the root of all later social feelings. He depicted a continuum of social ties, possessing the same original basis. Originally, the child is drawn to its parents, then to its wider family and from there to wider ties of community. There was, he suggested, a common basis to phenomena such as 'conjugal affection and natural affection to parents, duty to magistrates, love of a common city, community or country, (and) other duties and social parts of life' (p. 283). In this way, common sense as an inborn social sense lays the basis for common sense as the sense of belonging to a community.

These ideas contain an implication of the utmost theoretical and ideological importance. If it is 'natural' to have feelings for other people, and if patriotism is rooted in such feelings, then patriotism, like parental affection, is a 'natural' feeling. Shaftesbury stressed this point. He claimed that the Latin *sensus communis* signifies a 'sense of public weal and of the common interest, love of the community or society' (p. 48). Common sense was as natural for humans as any of the perceptual senses. In fact, he elevated the feelings of common sense above other human emotions: 'Of all human affections, the noblest and most becoming human nature is that of love to one's country' (p. 399).

Such comments make it easy to depict Shaftesbury as an early theorist of nationalism. The modern age might have been the age of individualist capitalism, but its ideology was never wholly individualist. The great political creation of the modern era was the nation-state, in whose name literally millions were to kill and die (Gellner, 1983; Hobsbawm, 1992). The nation-state, as a modern construction, was not yet fully in place when Shaftesbury was writing. It was to be supported by an ideology that claimed to be drawing upon primordial, natural sentiments (Anderson, 1983; Billig, 1995). There were influential intellectuals like Herder who would provide a philosophical justification for nationalism, claiming patriotism to be natural, authentic emotion that should be put at the centre of modern political life. The case for Shaftesbury's influence on later theorists of nationalism, such as Herder, is not hard to make. Ernst Cassirer wrote that the works of Shaftesbury 'were Herder's constant companions from an early age' (1951, p. 199; see also Fowler, 1882, p. 161; see more generally Boyer, 2003, for a discussion of Shaftesbury's influence on the German Enlightenment).

Nevertheless, little is straightforward in Shaftesbury's writings. He was not an author with a single message, to be repeated with endless variations. Nor did he derive his conclusions – and recommendations for self-improvement – from an abstract system. He embraced the stoic ideal that we must use reason to examine our feelings. The feelings of patriotism, important though they might be, were not given special exemption from critical reason. A nation might be, in the words of Benedict Anderson, an 'imagined community', but Shaftesbury was well aware of the partiality and petty-mindedness of the nationalist imagination.

Shaftesbury wrote about the arbitrariness, as well as the naturalness, of patriotism. The relationship between countrymen implies 'something moral and social'. The land must be imagined as a whole, somewhere in scope larger than a hamlet and less than the total globe. The boundaries can be vague. What shall we presume our country to be, he asks? Is it England? Or is Scotland included? If it is Britain, then what of Guernsey, Jersey and 'poor Ireland?' There seems no objective reality: 'Behold, here, a very dubious circumscription!' (p. 402). If the object of our patriotic feelings is hard to define, then those feelings are wont to run beyond the bounds of reason. Shaftesbury noted how the English constantly praise their land and manners unreasonably: 'We tend to have an overweening opinion of ourselves', when in truth 'we are the latest barbarous, the last civilized or polished people of Europe' (p. 403).

By temperament Shaftesbury was more internationalist than little Englander. He traveled widely, especially in his younger days. He spoke

French so well that in France he was often taken for a native speaker. He would die in Italy, whose galleries and collections he had loved from his first grand tour. In *Characteristicks,* Shaftesbury warned against the narrowness of so many English people who refused to travel. In order to find 'the highest politeness in modern conversation', we must go 'further abroad than the little province we call home' (p. 405). As always, he took his inspiration from past times, especially from the ancients of Greece, Rome and the near East. The great figures of those times were, he wrote, 'constant travellers', learning from the peoples whom they visited. But today, the English are sadly inward looking: our inclination is to 'contract our views within the narrowest compass and despise all knowledge, learning or manners which are not a home growth' (p. 404).

Accordingly, Shaftesbury's defence of patriotism did not exclude its rational critique. In this, Shaftesbury resembles Herder, who simultaneously advocated the particularities of patriotism and the universal reason of the Enlightenment (Denby, 2005). How this double-sidedness fits with Shaftesbury's philosophy of thinking remains to be seen. In one respect, it is not surprising that the thesis of nationalism sits side-by-side the anti-thesis of universalism. The stoics never believed that their message was confined to those who had professed loyalty to the stoic academy, nor to the state in which the academy was situated. They had a universal message, addressed to all persons, all nations and all eras. And part of this universal message was to love one's country. So, too, Shaftesbury was universalist: that is why he imagined the past speaking to him directly in foreign languages, telling him to love his native land even as he criticized it. This represented a tension of which Shaftesbury was well aware and which, in his view, reflected a basic tension within human nature.

Moral Sense and the Home Blow

In philosophical circles, Shaftesbury is probably best known for his concept of 'moral sense'. The idea that humans are born with an innate sense of morality was to be taken up by later British moral philosophers. This concept particularly influenced the school of Scottish common sense philosophy, of which Thomas Reid was to be such a notable member. Some of the Scottish philosophers feared to be identified too closely with Shaftesbury because of his heretical reputation. Francis Hutcheson alluded to the problem in his *Inquiry into the Original of our Ideas of Beauty and Virtue.* In using Shaftesbury's concept of a moral sense, he hoped that readers would not associate him with Shaftesbury's 'prejudices ... against Christianity' (1726, p. 12). The sceptical David Hume had no such problems with suggesting that humans have a moral sense that was 'rooted in our constitution and nature' (1740/1964, p. 182).

It is in many ways unfortunate that Shaftesbury became associated with the concept of a moral sense. The concept hardly features in *Characteristicks*. Shaftesbury only used it once in the text and three times as a sub-heading in the margins. All these uses come in the 'Inquiry', which is the earliest essay in *Characteristicks*. As will be suggested, the notion of a moral sense is not satisfactory for understanding the psychology of moral judgement. More importantly, the notion is in conflict with other, more central aspects of Shaftesbury's thinking (see also McNaughton, 1996, for a similar argument). On the other hand, in raising the possibility of a moral sense, Shaftesbury was suggesting a holistic view of sensation. This, in itself, was an important move that contradicted Locke's atomist psychology and prefigured later Gestaltist ideas.

Underlying the notion of an innate sense of morality was an attack on the theory of self-interest. Shaftesbury believed that the atomist theories of mind, such as those developed by Hobbes and Locke, reduced morality to self-interest. These theories dissected moral judgements in just the same way as they dissected other sorts of judgement. Conceiving the mind as a *tabula rasa* at birth, such theorists could find no reason why humans should act, or combine sensations, other than self-interest. Their theories had explicitly excluded the possibility of innate motives that transcended individual pleasure or the avoidance of personal harm. Hobbes had set the trend. In *Human Nature*, Hobbes had written that every person 'calls that which pleases, and is delightful to himself, GOOD; and that EVIL which displeases him' (1650/1999, p. 44, emphasis in original). In this way, Hobbes was implying that moral judgements were nothing more than an expression of a personal preference: when people say 'X is good', they are only indicating that they personally like X.

Locke produced a similar psychological argument in the *Essay*. It followed from his atomist premises. From what simple ideas could beliefs about morality be derived? There can be no moral object that can be perceived in the way that a physical object can be – no 'goodness' or 'badness' whose size, shape, colour, hardness, softness can be sensed in a series of simple ideas. Consequently, when Locke discussed ideas of morality in the *Essay* he introduced a motivational element, just as Hobbes had done. Locke stated that pain and pleasure are simple ideas that we receive from sensation and reflection (II.xx.1). We are motivated to seek pleasure and avoid pain, and Locke suggested that pleasure and pain 'are the hinges on which our passions turn' (II.xx.3, p. 186).

Locke then claimed that what we call 'good' is that which 'is apt to cause or increase pleasure or diminish pain in us'; conversely what we name 'evil' is that which is 'apt to produce or increase any pain, or diminish any pleasure in us' (II.xx.2, p. 186). Locke's argument is similar to that of Hobbes. We think our motives are noble – we give them moral names. But if you look carefully at their underlying psychology, you will see nothing but the desire to increase pleasure and to avoid pain. In this way, judgements of morality are reduced to expressions of personal pleasure and pain. Morality, qua morality, has disappeared.

This explains Shaftesbury's fierce judgement that Hobbes may have begun the destruction of morality but Locke had struck 'the home blow'. Both were proposing an Epicurean philosophy of morality. If there is no natural sense of morality – if all we have is our own desire to increase our own pleasure and avoid pain – then it is moral to pursue individual pleasure. Social duties, or the obligations of individuals to each other and to their society, disappear in this account. All that remains is an individual psychology of pain and pleasure.

In one respect, Shaftesbury was wrong. Locke most certainly had not struck the home blow. There were to be further developments in the philosophy of self-interest. During the nineteenth century, Jeremy Bentham would propose utilitarianism as a moral philosophy for calculating individual interests. Shaftesbury occupies a minor place in the history of utilitarianism. John Brown was one of Shaftesbury's main public critics in the mid-eighteenth century. His *Essays on the Characteristics* achieved instant acclaim, despite Shaftesbury having died almost forty years earlier. Brown, like Locke and Hobbes, suggested that we call actions 'good' if they tend to increase our own happiness. He introduced a notion that would later become central to utilitarianism. Brown claimed that the 'fundamental law' of morality was the production 'of the greatest happiness' (Brown, 1752, p. 134). John Stuart Mill, when writing about the development of utilitarianism, identified Brown as an important precursor: 'We never saw an abler defence of the doctrine of utility than in a book written in refutation of Shaftesbury, and now little read – Brown's *Essays on the Characteristics*' (Mill, 1838/1962, p. 90).

The notion of a moral sense poses a number of problems. One might ask what sort of 'sense' is a moral sense. It would seem implausible to suggest that we can perceive goodness and badness, just as we perceive physical objects in the world. Another problem was noted in Shaftesbury's day. If there is an innate moral sense, then why should there be such differences in moral values between cultures? That should not happen if we were all equipped with the same innate, moral sense. William Wollaston, a somewhat eccentric writer whose *Religion of Nature Delineated* was highly regarded in mid-eighteenth century England, shared Shaftesbury's unease with Locke's psychological account of morality. Nevertheless, Wollaston thought that the concept of a moral sense was problematic. Those who make appeal to *innate* ideas or a common moral sense, he wrote, 'put the matter on a very infirm foot' because 'the sentiments of mankind are not so *uniform* and *constant*' (1738, p. 23, emphasis in original).

Then, there is the developmental problem. The perceptual senses, by and large, seem to be used from birth. If there is a moral sense, then it is a peculiar sense because it cannot be used until mid-childhood. Newborn infants are unable to make moral judgements in the way that they can sense sound, light and cold. In the twentieth century, Piaget was to argue that a series of complex mental developments must occur before the young person becomes capable of thinking ethically. In particular, children must be able to free themselves from their childish, egocentric perspectives of the world (Kohlberg, 1969; Piaget, 1959 and 1968; see Gilligan, 1982, for a classic feminist critique). Today, cognitive psychologists tend to emphasize that the ability to make moral judgements depends upon complex learning processes. It has been suggested that the child must build up prototypes of 'good' and 'bad' behaviours, typically acquiring these prototypical examples from others and then the child must gain practice in matching examples to these prototypes. Paul Churchland writes that this is 'a process that requires repeated exposure to, and practice of, various *examples* of the perceptual or motor categories at issue' (Churchland, 2001, p. 83, emphasis in original). All this is far removed from the idea that we inherit a moral sense that is already primed and ready to use.

Most importantly, the idea of a moral sense contradicted a fundamental aspect of stoic teaching. To be sure, passages from Epictetus's teachings can be found to suggest that humans have an innate moral sense, providing us with moral knowledge (Long, 2002, p. 83). Such an idea, if taken literally, must oversimplify what it means to be moral. In stoic philosophy, it is not easy to live a blameless, ethical life. Epictetus stressed that we should never cease from rigorous self-examination. If a moral sense provided moral knowledge, then there would be little need for self-examination, and certainly not for the tortured self-doubts to be found in Shaftesbury's private Regimen. We would only need to follow the intuitions provided by the moral sense.

There is a more basic problem. The stoics taught that we should not passively receive information from our senses but we should examine our senses. Even if there were a moral sense, then its sensations should not be accepted unquestioningly. In arguing that we need to examine the senses, the stoics were producing a non-atomist view of sensation. Shaftesbury, as part of his reaction against Locke, followed this stoic view.

Aesthetic Gestalts

By raising the possibility of an inborn sense of morality, Shaftesbury was, in effect, doing two things. First, he was stressing that human beings were moral agents. This does not mean, however, that we inherit a moral sense. There might be something about the nature of social living that requires shared ethical codes. Thomas Reid, as will be discussed later, came close to formulating such a notion, when he stressed the links between language and the need to tell the truth.

The second point concerns Shaftesbury's Platonism. Shaftesbury, like Plato, felt there to be an intimate connection between truth and aesthetics. Humans are not just moral agents, but they are also aesthetic ones. Just as we might naturally be drawn to experience the world in moral terms, so Shaftesbury believed that we have an innate sense of beauty (see Kivy, 2003, for a discussion of Shaftesbury's debt to the Platonists in relation to aesthetic theory). In a passage that the poet Keats would famously echo in his 'Ode to a Grecian Vase', Shaftesbury declared that 'the most natural beauty in the world is honesty and moral truth' because 'all beauty is truth' (1711/1999, p. 65).

There was, according to Shaftesbury, a link between aesthetic and moral judgement. When observing the actions of people, the mind 'feels the soft and harsh, the agreeable and disagreeable in the affections, and finds a foul and fair, a harmonious and a dissonant, as really and truly here as in any musical numbers or in the outward forms or representations of sensible things' (pp. 172–3). This happens naturally and spontaneously. The mind cannot withhold 'its admiration and ecstasy, its aversion and scorn, any more in what relates to one than to the other of these subjects' (p. 173).

Shaftesbury's description of the way that the moral sense operates is significant. He was saying that moral judgements depend upon the mind being aware of ethical harmonies and dissonances. This was no mere metaphor. The equation between beauty and moral truth rests upon a psychological assumption: judgements of morality and aesthetics both depend on an innate sense of proportion and harmony. In 'The Moralists' Theocles declares that the human infant is pleased with some shapes but not with others: 'Why is the sphere or globe, the cylinder and obelisk, preferred and the irregular figures, in respect of these, rejected and despised?' (p. 326). Theocles suggests that we have a natural affection for symmetry and harmony: 'No sooner the eye opens upon figures, the ear to sounds, than straight the beautiful results and grace and harmony are known and acknowledged' (p. 326).

Once again, Shaftesbury was opposing the empty tablet theory of mind. We are born ready to experience the world in ways that transcend narrow self-interest. Our minds are so constructed that we automatically apprehend coherence of form. In the words of one perceptive commentator, Shaftesbury's assertions amount to 'what can best be described as a neurological postulate' (Prince, 2004, p. 54). Of course, Shaftesbury was even less interested than Locke in the neurological underpinnings of our judgements. He did not wish to relate, and certainly not reduce, judgements of aesthetics and morality to neurological vibrations in the brain as David Hartley was to do some forty years later (Hartley, 1749/1834). Nevertheless, Shaftesbury was stressing that our aesthetic reactions are not a matter of choice. They happen immediately and spontaneously, because we are constructed to experience the world in this way.

In effect, Shaftesbury was declaring holism to be a basic psychological principle of sensation. He was suggesting that we experience the world holistically by sensing patterns and shapes from the moment that we begin to have sensations. This psychological postulate was opposed to the atomistic psychology that Locke had formulated. Locke had assumed that we build up our view of the world from simple sensations, associating these simple sensations with each other, in order to build up more complex views. Shaftesbury was declaring that the mind operates by very different principles: we sense patterns, not simple ideas.

In the history of psychology, Locke's view tended to predominate, at least during the eighteenth and nineteenth centuries. The later British empiricists saw their task as investigating how different cognitive elements become associated mentally with each other. Behaviourists were to jettison the cognitive aspects, but they retained the principle of association, examining the associations between stimuli and behavioural responses. Both traditions of psychology saw complex behaviour, or thinking, to be comprised of simple units that become associated with each other.

What is extraordinary about Shaftesbury's loosely worded comments on the perception of form is that they anticipate, in broad outline, the theories of Gestalt psychology. In the early twentieth century the Gestaltists opposed associationism (Ash, 1998). According to leading Gestaltists, such as Wolfgang Köhler (1929) and Kurt Koffka (1928), we innately grasp the forms or *Gestalts* of objects, rather than deriving our impression of the whole from combining impressions of the parts. Koffka (1922) specifically claimed that experience is not the sum of its many elements. Structures or wholes were psychologically elementary, but these are not analogous to Locke's 'simple ideas', because they can be broken down into smaller elements. Thus, we can attend to the elements of a structure or Gestalt should we choose to. But our experience of the structure is not derived from combining its associated parts.

When Gestalt psychology was first proposed it seemed quite radical in its implications – at least to those psychologists who had been schooled in the principles of associationist psychology. The situation is much changed now. Ulric Neisser (2002) points out that today's cognitive psychologists have accepted so many ideas from Gestalt psychology that it is hard now to understand why there had been such a fuss (see also Murray, 1995). There is some evidence, as Köhler suggested over fifty years ago, and as Shaftesbury implicitly assumed over two hundred years previously, that the perception of Gestalts is based on innate, physical properties. Some neurophysiological structures have been identified which, if damaged, leave the person able to perceive the constituent parts of objects, but not their overall shape as objects (Goodale, 2003).

As was discussed previously, infants may have a predisposition to prefer facial patterns over other patterns. The preference for facial patterns suggests that there are innate preferences for certain shapes over others – in short, a sort of innate aesthetics. This was something that the Gestaltists suspected. Köhler argued that we have a preference for 'good Gestalts' that are perceived as wholes. Through 'processes of closure', Köhler argued, we automatically turn incomplete Gestalts into 'good', completed ones. This is not something that is learnt. It is as if there is a preference for completeness, for wholeness. The terminology that the Gestaltists used is suggestive: 'good' and 'bad' conveys the idea of an automatic, common aesthetic preference. Again, it is not difficult to see Shaftesbury as anticipating the holistic psychology of the Gestalists. Certainly he was reacting against the atomist associationism of Locke, just as much as the Gestaltists would reject Locke's associationist heirs.

Stoic Sensation and Reflection

Shaftesbury's credentials as an early Gestalt psychologist should not be exaggerated. The parallels between his thinking and Gestaltism refer to perceptual processes, rather than to a general convergence of philosophical outlook. Shaftesbury, in common with the Gestaltists but unlike Locke, saw perception as an essentially active process. We do not passively receive information from outside, but we actively shape what we see. This active element does not necessarily imply conscious direction or intention. With the perception of forms, the perceptual apparatus can work automatically, as the Gestaltists acknowledged. This is one reason why Shaftesbury's parallel between moral judgement and the perception of forms does not hold up. More is involved in morality than an immediate, automatic perceptual response.

The nub of stoic psychology was that we can and should reflect on our perceptions. Even if our perceptions are actively formed as wholes, rather than combined from atomic simples, that does not mean we are excused from the task of judgement. Stoic philosophers sought to teach their pupils how to judge their sensations (Brennan, 2005, chapter six; Long, 1999 and 2002, chapter four). As Epictetus said, 'the first and greatest work of a philosopher is to try and distinguish the appearances, and to admit none untried' (1910, p. 44). In his Regimen, Shaftesbury included a similar quotation from Marcus Aurelius: 'It is the proper work of a man to form a just judgement of plausible appearances – and to scrutinize present impressions so that nothing may enter that is not well examined' (Shaftesbury, 1900a, p. 209).

Accordingly, the stoics considered that it was topsy-turvy to put perceptions over judgement, as the Epicureans had done – and also as Locke did. Animals accept the world as it is perceived, but humans should aspire to more. We should judge our perceptions, rather than assume, as Locke did, that our judgements must be based on simple perceptions. For Shaftesbury, Locke's position meant that, in effect, we cannot judge perceptions except in terms of other perceptions. That is why Shaftesbury denied that certainty could be found in our so-called clear ideas. Once this step is taken, then the balance between Locke's two terms, sensation and reflection, is shifted: reflection, not sensation, is given priority. If we are not to be slaves to perception, accepting uncritically whatever our eyes tell us, then perception should depend on reason – rather than reason upon perception.

Frederic Bartlett, the British psychologist who was greatly influenced by the Gestalt movement, argued that we use 'schemata' to organize our perceptions, shaping, for example, individual components into perceived wholes. Bartlett stressed, however, that our schemata need not bind us to a single apprehension of the world. Instead, we have the capacity to 'transcend' our schemata by using 'the capacity to "turn round one's schemata"' (1932, pp. 200–1). This most important feature of human thinking – this ability for self-reflexivity – distinguishes us from all other creatures. In essence, this is what Epictetus and Marcus Aurelius were teaching when they said that we should train ourselves to judge our senses.

The question, which is as important in today's psychology as it was in ancient stoic thought, is where this capacity for self-reflexivity comes from and how it can be developed. Shaftesbury, in toying with the idea that there might be moral and aesthetic senses, was not coming to grips with the issue. Any postulation of a further sense fails to say how we can distance ourselves from that sense, in order to judge it. As will be seen, when Shaftesbury tackled the issue in later works than 'Inquiry', his position was very different. He pointed to the great gift that humans possess that no animal does – the gift of language. Through dialogue, and particularly through using dialogue in an inner debate with ourselves, we can transcend the perceptual world. That is one reason why the analogy between the perception of forms and moral judgement breaks down. Morality belongs to the world of dialogue, not to sensory perception. Children may be able to perceive shapes from birth, but they cannot become fully moral agents until they have entered into the social world of moral conversations. The perception of shapes and triangles is a simple business when compared with the ability to behave morally. That is why Shaftesbury resisted so strongly

Locke's attempt to reduce judgement to perception, and morality to self-interest.

The Potential for Critique

In the clash between Locke and Shaftesbury, two different psychologies can be discerned, both with the potential for wider social critique. Locke's insistence that the mind is an empty cabinet at birth lays the basis for an egalitarian perspective. All minds are created similar: it is only external circumstances that shape them differently. Shaftesbury, in opposing this view, also postulated a universal psychology. All humans are born with natural predispositions to be social, cooperative and moral. A society that discouraged these natural feelings – a society that sought to promote selfish, individualist behaviour – would be an unnatural society. In fact, it would cease to be a genuine society.

Certainly, many orthodox theologians recognized the dangers of Locke's approach. Generally, Locke and his successors were part of the movement towards the 'naturalization of the soul', to use the apt phrase of Martin and Barresi (2000). What had previously been called the 'soul' was now referred to as the 'mind'. Hartley had stressed that the mind depended upon the body, but, as the second part of *Observations on Man* makes clear, he was keen to stress that his model of thinking was consonant with a Christian perspective. In France, thinkers such as Helvétius, Holbach and Condorcet were to develop the materialist implications of this shift from soul to mind. These French followers of Locke brought out the anti-religious implications of reducing knowledge to sensations, and then sensations to biological processes.

The sensationalist approach in France was to reach its political apotheosis after the revolution with Destutt de Tracy's *Élémens d'Idéologie* (1803–1815). This huge work aimed to synthesize all knowledge around the new biological study of ideas. De Tracy coined the word 'ideology' to describe this science of mind. The ambition was Lockean: the analysis of the mind would provide the foundation for knowledge and would expose the prejudices of past ages. De Tracy had written *Élémens* to be the core textbook for the whole educational curriculum in the schools of post-revolutionary France. For a brief period, while de Tracy was in charge of education, this aim was realized. Then, Locke's theory of ideas lay at the heart of France's educational system, supposedly determining what was to be taught and what could be ignored.

It would not last. Napoleon distrusted de Tracy and his fellow ideologists. Moreover, the word 'ideology' did not retain the meaning that de Tracy had designed for it. Napoleon used the term derisively, much to de Tracy's distress. The decisive semantic shift, however, occurred when Marx and Engels published their *German Ideology* (1846/1970).

From describing a materially based science of ideas, 'ideology' came to be a term for disparaging the sort of airy speculation that changes nothing and that gives succour to existing arrangements of power. In this new critique, the sensationalists found themselves being bracketed with other philosophical conservatives.

At first glance, Shaftesbury's blend of classicism, stoic self-discipline and patriotism seems to prefigure the sort of muscular Christianity and classicism that Thomas Arnold was to promote among the privately educated classes of Victorian Britain. Yet, Shaftesbury's popularity began to dip at precisely the same time as the classicism of Arnold became popular as an education fit for imperialists. There was something about Shaftesbury's message that did not appeal to the earnest Victorians. Perhaps it was his playful cynicism, his self-questioning and, above all, his critical detachment from orthodox Christian theology. He was never going to pretend that Juvenal and Horace, or Epictetus and Socrates, were English, pipe-smoking Christians. In personal terms, Shaftesbury was not the sort of team-player who would muddy his knees on the playing-fields of England.

In a more surprising way, Shaftesbury's ideas presaged the new world. For all his posturing as backward-glancing aristocrat, there was one aspect of his thinking that lent itself to a radical critique of capitalism. Unlike Locke and his French followers, Shaftesbury resisted relativism: good and bad were not to be based on the psychological criteria of pain or pleasure. Instead there were objectively natural and unnatural desires. A degenerate social climate that led its members to pursue false pleasures – to seek goals that conflicted with human nature – was, then, to be condemned regardless of whether or not its members professed to be happy.

Shaftesbury suspected that the society of his day, with its stress on profit and success, was encouraging the false 'economical self' at the expense of the natural self (Shaftesbury, 1900a, pp. 124ff). Marx would propose similar ideas especially in early works such as the *Economic and Philosophic Manuscripts* (1844/1973). Like Shaftesbury, Marx argued that contemporary society, with its worship of the individual, was destroying the natural sense of community. The concept of 'alienation' was crucial to Marx's early critique of capitalism: workers were becoming alienated from the products of their labour and from their human nature. The idea of alienation would become even more important among Marxists in the twentieth century, especially as capitalism produced wealth rather than increasing poverty. The Frankfurt School argued that late capitalism was creating alienating desires and pleasures. Alienation referred to the objective characteristics of society and its failure to accord with human nature; it did not refer to the subjective happiness of individuals (e.g., Fromm, 1971; Marcuse, 1968; more generally, see Jay, 1984).

Shaftesbury may have written of the way that the selfishness of modern society was destroying the natural social nature of its members. He did not use the concept of 'alienation' to describe this estrangement from human nature. However, one does not have to wait until Marx to see the word so used. A family connection with Shaftesbury can be traced. Shaftesbury's nephew James Harris wrote several books on philosophy, aesthetics and grammar. He greatly respected his uncle whose influence is clear in Harris's writings. Harris dedicated his first book, *Three Treatises,* to Shaftesbury's son, the fourth Earl. In that work, Harris followed some of his uncle's themes. He wrote that most people have a natural social feeling and that few are 'alienated from it'. So obvious was this, Harris declared, that few would choose to be isolated: 'What would be more absurd, than to be *indifferent* to their own *welfare*; or to be *alienated* from it, as though it was *foreign* and *unnatural*?' (Harris, 1744, pp. 144–5, emphasis in original). So, here is an English author, born into an aristocratic family, using the concept of 'alienation' exactly a century before Marx and doing so in a recognizably similar sense.

The world of the eighteenth century was not divided, ideologically speaking, into separate classes of stoics and Epicureans. The same persons might purchase, study and enjoy books by both Locke and Shaftesbury. The Epicurean foster-father and stoic foster-son could enjoy each other's company, mix in similar circles and share mutual friends. In mid-eighteenth century France, the brothers Bonnot – Gabriel and Étienne – were to provide another remarkable example of stoic and Epicurean philosophies within the same family.

Neither brother published under their shared family name. Étienne, who used the name Condillac, was the Epicurean. In the introduction to his *Essai sur l'origine des connaissances humaines* (1746), he claimed to be developing the work of Locke. He sought to show how all experience, not just knowledge, was based on sensation. The subtitle of the English translation of his *Essai*, which appeared in 1756, described Condillac's book as 'a supplement to Mr Locke's *Essay on the Human Understanding*'. Condillac did not accept all that Locke had said. Locke had written that if a man blind from birth is suddenly able to see, he would not immediately recognize the depth of objects. Condillac disagreed (1756, pp. 153ff). Later, in *Traité des Sensations*, Condillac changed his position and graciously acknowledged the superior strength of Locke's argument (1754/1798, pp. 8ff).

In both his *Essai* and *Traité*, Condillac addressed various technical questions about the nature of sensation and association. He discussed the relations between the different senses; whether all perception is necessarily conscious, whether the perception of objects is learnt or innate and so on. One can see in his works the move towards making these empirical issues, rather than doctrinal or metaphysical ones.

Of course, Shaftesbury would have viewed such technical discussions as typifying the triviality of atomism.

On the other hand, Condillac's brother, the Abbé de Mably, took the stoic line. He was deeply interested in history, believing that the study of the past contained lessons for the conduct of contemporary politics. Today, Mably may be less well known than his brother, but in his own time his works were read widely. In his various writings Mably combined classical stoicism with utopian socialism. Mably's most popular work was his *Conversations of Phocion* (1767). Shaftesbury would have appreciated the way that the work was presented to the public – as if it were an ancient manuscript that had lain unnoticed for centuries in an Italian monastery. Many readers were taken in by the literary conceit.

The work describes Phocion discussing matters of morality and politics with his fellow Athenians. Phocion, like Socrates, champions the simple virtues; he distinguishes between false, unnatural pleasures and natural ones. The literary device that Phocion was talking about ancient Athens enabled Mably to criticize his own society in ways that would otherwise have been dangerous. Phocion bemoans that 'the thirst for money, which devours us, has suffocated the love for one's country' (p. 31). Laws were needed to prevent individuals from acquiring great fortunes. Nature, he wrote, had not made humans in order that they might possess great treasures, but the poor man was born with the same needs as the rich man (p. 150). In other works, particularly in his *De la Législation*, Mably specifically advocated the abolition of private property, identifying private ownership as the source of modern social ills (Mably, 1765 and 1766). As such, Mably was advocating a form of egalitarian socialism.

Shaftesbury would have found little to dissent from Phocion's critique of selfishness and his championing of plain, civic virtues. However, Shaftesbury cannot be seen as a utopian socialist, either in his writings or in his way of life. He was not advocating the redistribution of wealth, certainly not his own. He does not seem to have had difficulties with his family's economic interests in slavery. Shaftesbury felt that his civic duty was to administer, not redistribute, the family estates. His message was, above all, directed inwards, towards self-amendment and self-improvement, in order to set examples to others. This was not a message for amending the economic arrangement of the social whole (Eagleton, 1990).

The example of Mably illustrates that in the eighteenth century the stoic position was not necessarily tied to a single political position. The latter-day stoics and Epicureans were not neatly divided by class or religion. Even within the same family, stoics and Epicureans could happily converse together, each believing that the old order was giving way to the lights of reason. Those who seemed to be looking backwards, were not simple reactionaries. Shaftesbury and Mably were using history to transform conceptions of the present, rather than vainly trying to turn time backwards. In so doing, they were helping to construct a way of criticizing the society which was coming into being and whose outlines they could only imperfectly discern.

7

Shaftesbury: Almost a Pre-Post-Modern Figure

• • • • • • • • • • • • • • • • • • •

S haftesbury would not deserve to occupy more than a minor place in the history of psychology, if his contribution to understanding the human mind were limited to his ideas about humans having innate social, moral and aesthetic senses. There would, then, be little need to imagine him as an ancestor of today's critical psychology, which, it must be said, is inhospitable to theories of instincts or innate senses. But there is much more to Shaftesbury's writings, especially in the parts of *Characteristicks* that he wrote not long before his death. In these later writings, we can find ideas – and, most importantly, ways of presenting such ideas – that make Shaftesbury appear a much more congenial figure today.

When the third Earl discussed the nature of truth, language and humour, he produced some ideas that might seem surprisingly familiar to today's social scientists. As will be seen, his ideas about the relations between dialogue and thinking, and about the possibilities for splitting the self, sit comfortably with a number of themes now being proposed by critical psychologists. This is not just a matter of mixing and matching particular psychological hypotheses. There is much more in Shaftesbury's way of thinking that seems to leap across time. He expressed a distrust of grand systems, a sense of irony and playfulness, and a sceptical ability to reflect on his own claims to knowledge. All these characterize what today is often identified as a post-modern sensibility.

The previous chapter discussed a passage from *Characteristicks* in which Shaftesbury imagined Locke and Descartes debating where to find certainty. Shaftesbury asked ironically: and what if there is no certainty in the whole matter at all? This today can seem a very post-modern reaction, as post-modernists are sceptical of claims to certainty and truth. They stand back from what Lyotard (1984) called the grand narratives of modernity. Marxism, scientific progress, Enlightenment are all distrusted, just as Shaftesbury distrusted Locke's claims for the truth of clear and distinct ideas, and Descartes's belief that certainty could be rooted in rational cogitation. And what if there is no certainty at all? Three hundred years ago such doubt might have been shocking, amidst all the doctrinal certainties and scientific hopes of the early modern period. But today it seems familiar. We no longer feel as confident as Locke did that we are about to enter a future filled with clean, scientific truths.

Today's distrust of modernism seems to echo Shaftesbury's scepticism at the very birth of the modern age. The present chapter will offer parallels between Shaftesbury's ideas and those of Mikhail Bakhtin (1895–1975). As will be seen, there are a range of similarities that help to identify Shaftesbury, not as the toga-wearing reactionary that he might have once seemed, but as a thinker with messages for later times – or, at least, for our times.

Scholars have disputed whether or not Bakhtin can be considered as a prototypically post-modern thinker. Some doubt whether the description is apt (see, for instance, Gardiner and Bell, 1998). But, in a strict sense, this hardly matters. There is no doubt that Bakhtin has become an intellectual hero in post-modern times. Twenty-five years ago, his name was little known outside of Russia. Today, he is considered one of the twentieth century's great intellectual figures. In academia there has been an outpouring of Bakhtin studies. One commentator has said that the Bakhtin industry has been like a successful retail chain, opening franchises in the most far-flung disciplines (Steinglass, 1988). Whether or not Bakhtin himself should be described as post-modern, he has been saluted by intellectuals as a thinker with important messages for today's post-modern world. This could not have happened if Bakhtin's general message had not matched the general, intellectual and political climate of today.

In a range of matters, Shaftesbury and Bakhtin appear as soul mates battling against doctrinaire authorities. Both, as will be seen, championed the importance of dialogue, the philosophical role of humour and the need to resist fanatical certainty. This is more than mere coincidence. It is not that the world had to wait until Bakhtin's message before it could possibly begin to understand Shaftesbury – as if Bakhtin's genius throws light backwards in time. The situation may be more prosaic. Bakhtin owed an unacknowledged debt to Shaftesbury. Because the debt was unacknowledged, Shaftesbury's influence has tended to remain hidden. But, now, as the roots of Bakhtin's work become clearer – and secrets have been revealed – Shaftesbury can emerge in his own right and stand as more than a representative of his distant times. He can be made to appear as a pre-post-modern figure.

Confronting Religious Enthusiasm

One reason for the freshness of Shaftesbury's message (or, at least, parts of his message) is that he addressed a problem that is very much present in today's world. In Shaftesbury's time, the problem was called 'religious enthusiasm'. Now it goes by the name of 'fundamentalism'. In today's world, the Western press frequently presents the problem of fundamentalism as if it were a property of Islam – almost as something that emerged from outside the Western tradition. Three hundred years ago the problem was very much a Christian one. In fact, Shaftesbury suspected that non-Christian religions may have been less prone to the dangers of zealotry than was Christianity.

As Shaftesbury discussed the problem of enthusiasm, so he displayed the distinctive features of his philosophy. The importance he assigned to the issue was evident. Shaftesbury chose his 'Letter Concerning Enthusiasm' as the opening part of *Characteristicks*. This piece, which ostensibly is a letter dated September 1707 and is addressed to an anonymous Lord, takes us to the heart of Shaftesbury's political and psychological thinking. Shaftesbury writes as if commentating upon a group of French Protestants who have recently arrived in England. He does not name the group, but they can be identified as the Camisards who had sprung up in the Cévannes region of France. They were a millenarian group who claimed direct links with God. Their members were liable to fall into trances, speak with tongues, howl ecstatically and generally show disdain for the sort of urbane manners that Shaftesbury so valued. More problematically, they were given to bouts of violence, having been responsible for massacring Catholic priests in France. Were the Camisards still active today, the British headline writers would have little difficulty in condemning them as 'alien fundamentalist terrorists'.

Shaftesbury's response to the Camisards was not theological. He was not concerned to show how their form of Christianity might have been based on misinterpretations of biblical texts. His reaction was, at root, based on moral and psychological factors, which were, according to his stoic perspective, deeply intertwined. In addition, he felt that the group presented a serious threat to liberty. Shaftesbury, along with many Englishmen of his generation, had a deep distrust of Protestant extremism. He had heard from his own family just how dangerous times had been during the Civil War and the rule of Cromwell. Whatever liberties had been obtained since then had to be jealously protected. As the opening section of the opening part of *Characteristicks* made clear, he believed that the enthusiasms of religion challenged the politics of freedom.

Shaftesbury asked what the basis of enthusiasm was and offered a psychological explanation. He wrote that 'there is a melancholy that accompanies all enthusiasm' (1711/1999, p. 9). As Lawrence Klein (1999) points out in his editorial notes to *Characteristicks*, this was a reference to one of the four humours which classical medical psychology believed to determine human temperament. Melancholy, based upon black bile, led to unreason and mental disease, unless tempered by other humours. In this way, Shaftesbury associated religious enthusiasm with mental disorder. He did not assume that melancholy was an inborn condition, affecting individuals who were prone to enthusiasm. The melancholic state was brought about by external factors. There are 'melancholy occasions' when the panics of enthusiasm grow: 'For vapours naturally rise and, in bad times especially, when the spirits of men are low, as either in public calamities or during the unwholesomeness of air or diet ... at this season the panic must needs run high' (p. 10).

Shaftesbury's descriptions of the melancholy occasions, when the panics of enthusiasm spread, resemble the descriptions that later crowd psychologists would give of mass behaviour. Shaftesbury talked about the fury of panics, which transforms individuals, putting them 'beyond themselves' (p. 10). In this state, the mood is 'infectious', as 'the fury flies from face to face, and the disease is no longer seen than caught' (p. 10). Gustav Le Bon in his book, *The Crowd* (1896), was to write in similar ways about the emotional contagions of crowds and the suggestible mental states of crowd members. Le Bon's account not only influenced Freud's *Group Psychology* (1921/1985), but also modern psychological theories of deindividuation (Diener, 1979; Zimbardo, 1969; see also Farr, 1996; Moscovici, 1985; van Ginneken, 1992). Modern psychologists might not talk of crowd members being put 'beyond themselves', as Shaftesbury did. Nevertheless, they have retained the idea that the psychology of individuals can be dangerously transformed by the contagious, emotional atmosphere of crowds.

Shaftesbury's main concern in his 'Letter' was not to describe the psychological state of enthusiasm, or to uncover its bodily correlates. His primary problem was how to deal with such enthusiasm. He was addressing a problem that remains important today. Should the state, when confronted by the threat of violent fundamentalism, respond by restricting liberty, prosecuting those who preach beliefs that are deemed to be dangerous? On the other hand, should the state seek to protect strong religious feelings by prohibiting certain forms of mockery, thereby using the law to restrict free expression in the name of mutual respect?

Shaftesbury stood firmly in favour of free expression both for the zealots and for those who wish to ridicule them. He wrote against those who advocated repressive measures against the religious enthusiasts. Shaftesbury's words have resonance today, when state authorities and the popular press seek to ban and imprison fundamentalists. Such measures, Shaftesbury argued, are largely counter-productive. Far from stopping the zealots, they actually increase their resolve. Just as physicians can make matters worse by trying to allay all bodily eruptions, so the 'body politic' can be set into uproar by 'the specious pretence of healing this itch of superstition', thereby turning 'a few innocent carbuncles into an inflammation and mortal gangrene' (p. 9). The authorities would be doing the enthusiasts a favour were they to hang or imprison them. That would grant them the martyrdom that they seek and 'blow up their zeal and stir afresh the coals of persecution' (p. 15).

The way to oppose the melancholy of enthusiasm was to maintain good humour and to protect the freedoms on which good humour depends. The religious enthusiasts were deadly serious, with their grim, religious visions. They were the enemies of humour and laughter. Shaftesbury wrote that 'gravity is the very essence of imposture' (p. 8). Instead of restricting liberty, we must recognize that 'it is only in a nation such as ours, that imposture has no privilege' (p. 7). Thus, the melancholy spirit with its violent and unreasoning tendencies must be countered, not by the seriousness of repression, but by its opposite: the humour of ridicule. Shaftesbury took delight in describing how the religious enthusiasts had been mocked at Bartholomew's Fair by puppet shows. The crowd laughed with delight as the puppets imitated their 'strange voices and involuntary agitations' (p. 15). If freedom is threatened by fanaticism, then ridicule and humour are its defenders.

Shaftesbury urged that we must not be cowards in the defence of freedom. We must not say some topics 'are too grave', too important, to be ridiculed, thereby establishing laws to restrict what can be said (p. 8). There can be no freedom if 'any peculiar custom or national opinion' is declared to be 'exempted from criticism' (p. 7). All opinions should be open to debate and mockery. Above all, we must not be afraid to let our own beliefs 'stand the test of ridicule' (p. 8). In writing thus, Shaftesbury was assigning a weighty role to ridicule, giving it the very highest moral, political and psychological significance.

The Dialogic Way of Understanding

In his 'Letter Concerning Enthusiasm', Shaftesbury was sketching the outlines of a very important view on truth and understanding. Shaftesbury would elaborate this position in later sections of *Characteristics*. His approach turned Locke's assumptions upside-down. Locke had suggested that the way to truth was through matching ideas with perceptions. The individual should check that complex concepts could be justified in terms of simple ideas. The locus for such checking was the individual mind. Only if we are sure that our ideas are clearly and distinctly derived from perceptions should we then communicate them to others.

Shaftesbury's approach to truth was very different. Truth was not a matter of sorting out the ideas in our mind – something that we have to do on our own. Instead, Shaftesbury suggested that we arrive at truth through conversation. Dialogue was not the means of communicating individually checked truths from one mind to another. It was the means by which ideas could be produced and assessed. As such, Shaftesbury was providing a dialogic and, thereby, inherently social approach to knowledge. He was advocating an approach that bears more than chance resemblance to that which Bakhtin would propose more than two centuries later.

Shaftesbury may have introduced the notion of ridicule as a test of opinion in the opening piece of *Characteristiks*, but it was in the next essay 'Sensus Communis' that he really developed the theme. Significantly, this was the piece where he argued that humans have an inborn social sense that draws us to our fellows. If truth is related to the practice of dialogue, and dialogue is a mode of social association, then truth and error are not matters of individual perception, as Locke had supposed: they are intrinsically social and dialogic matters.

On one matter Locke and Shaftesbury were in agreement: we should not uncritically accept the views of authorities. Instead, we must subject all views to critical inquiry. Shaftesbury asserted in 'Sensus Communis' that we may be charged with 'wilful ignorance and blind idolatry' if we take opinions 'upon trust' and not test them 'in open light' (p. 29). But how do we test our notions? Truth, he writes, might be supposed to 'bear *all* lights' (p. 30, emphasis in original). One of the principal lights that truth should bear is the exposure to mockery. If an opinion cannot stand mockery, then it will be revealed to be ridiculous. Accordingly, Shaftesbury writes 'in commendation of raillery' (p. 29). Mockery was not just to be reserved for the opinions of religious enthusiasts, on whom we might look with ironic detachment. Mockery should be applied to all serious claims to knowledge.

This was a stunning proposal. In the late seventeenth and early eighteenth centuries, there was great interest in the issue of politeness. New forms of meeting places were being developed – such as salons in France and coffee-houses in Britain. These were neither strictly public nor private meeting places. Nothing like the coffee houses had existed in the dire, suspicious times of the Civil War. Many people were uncertain how they should behave. Books of etiquette, instructing readers how to converse politely, became popular (Burke, 1993). Shaftesbury's own work was part of the movement to examine the nature of politeness (Klein, 1994).

The guides to etiquette generally viewed ridicule as something to be avoided. Polite people did not engage in mockery: it was not genteel. Two years before Shaftesbury's 'Sensus Communis' appeared, an English edition of the Abbé de Bellegarde's guide to politeness was published under the title of *Reflexions on Ridicule and the Means to Avoid It*. The book advised against ridicule: 'Men are made for society, and therefore the most useful of all sciences is the art of living, which guards us perpetually against ridicule, and teaches us to avoid whatever may disgust the persons we converse with, and diminish the pleasure they taste in our conversation' (Bellegarde, 1707, pp. 1–2). In other words, we do not enjoy being ridiculed and we spoil conversations for others if we engage in ridicule.

Shaftesbury, in praising ridicule, was, thus, countering the etiquette of his times. He emphasized that he was not recommending all forms of ridicule – after all, he was as concerned, as were the writers of the etiquette books, with the problem of politeness. Polite conversation, however, cannot exclude ridicule if it is to fulfil its highest tasks of testing views. Nor should it encourage all types of ridicule. There was a world of difference, Shaftesbury wrote, between genteel wit and 'scurrilous buffoonery', or between false and true raillery (p. 31).

Shaftesbury did not offer firm criteria to distinguish true from false raillery: 'that would be as hard a matter, and perhaps as little to the purpose, as to define good breeding' (p. 31). His refusal to offer clear distinctions did not stem from evasion. It derived from the stoic belief that the truths of philosophy should be discovered in practice, not in formal definitions. The same applied to the conduct of behaviour. Thus, Shaftesbury suggested in the 'Letter' that good judgement and politeness can only 'come from the trial and experience of what is best' (p. 7). We can only discover through dialogue what the acceptable ways of conversing are. The principles cannot be set down in advance.

Although 'true raillery' could not be defined in the abstract, Shaftesbury offered some clues about how it should be practised. Without ridicule, we will run the risk of holding fast to ignorant prejudices, pandering each other by politely agreeing with all ill-considered opinions. Shaftesbury quoted (and somewhat adapted for his own argumentative purposes) Aristotle's quotation from the orator Gorgias. Shaftesbury rendered the quotation as 'humour was the only test of gravity, and gravity of humour' (p. 36; Aristotle's quote comes in *Rhetoric*, III. xviii.7). Shaftesbury states that any subject that would not 'bear raillery was suspicious'. He had in mind the sort of religious fundamentalists who refused to allow their beliefs to be mocked. On the other hand, a jest, which would not bear serious examination, 'was certainly false wit' (p. 36). Shaftesbury was not recommending buffoonery for its own sake: ridicule needed to serve the serious purposes of exploring matters of significance. Humour, thus, is not the enemy of seriousness, but the two supposed opposites need each other, otherwise we will lapse into unthinking dogmatism or foolish buffoonery.

Shaftesbury also gave hints about the conditions in which ridicule can flourish. He wrote that true raillery occurs in conversations where there is freedom, enjoyment and mutual respect between the participants: 'A freedom of raillery, a liberty in decent language to question everything, and an allowance of unravelling or refuting any argument may disgust the persons we converse with, and diminish the pleasure they taste in our conversation' (Bellegarde, 1707, pp. 1–2). In other words, we do not enjoy being ridiculed and we spoil conversations for others if we engage in ridicule.

Shaftesbury, in praising ridicule, was, thus, countering the etiquette of his times. He emphasized that he was not recommending all forms of ridicule – after all, he was as concerned, as were the writers of the etiquette books, with the problem of politeness. Polite conversation, however, cannot exclude ridicule if it is to fulfil its highest tasks of testing views. Nor should it encourage all types of ridicule. There was a world of difference, Shaftesbury wrote, between genteel wit and 'scurrilous buffoonery', or between false and true raillery (p. 31).

Shaftesbury did not offer firm criteria to distinguish true from false raillery: 'that would be as hard a matter, and perhaps as little to the purpose, as to define good breeding' (p. 31). His refusal to offer clear distinctions did not stem from evasion. It derived from the stoic belief that the truths of philosophy should be discovered in practice, not in formal definitions. The same applied to the conduct of behaviour. Thus, Shaftesbury suggested in the 'Letter' that good judgement and politeness can only 'come from the trial and experience of what is best' (p. 7). We can only discover through dialogue what the acceptable ways of conversing are. The principles cannot be set down in advance.

Although 'true raillery' could not be defined in the abstract, Shaftesbury offered some clues about how it should be practised. Without ridicule, we will run the risk of holding fast to ignorant prejudices, pandering each other by politely agreeing with all ill-considered opinions. Shaftesbury quoted (and somewhat adapted for his own argumentative purposes) Aristotle's quotation from the orator Gorgias. Shaftesbury rendered the quotation as 'humour was the only test of gravity, and gravity of humour' (p. 36; Aristotle's quote comes in *Rhetoric*, III. xviii.7). Shaftesbury states that any subject that would not 'bear raillery was suspicious'. He had in mind the sort of religious fundamentalists who refused to allow their beliefs to be mocked. On the other hand, a jest, which would not bear serious examination, 'was certainly false wit' (p. 36). Shaftesbury was not recommending buffoonery for its own sake: ridicule needed to serve the serious purposes of exploring matters of significance. Humour, thus, is not the enemy of seriousness, but the two supposed opposites need each other, otherwise we will lapse into unthinking dogmatism or foolish buffoonery.

Shaftesbury also gave hints about the conditions in which ridicule can flourish. He wrote that true raillery occurs in conversations where there is freedom, enjoyment and mutual respect between the participants: 'A freedom of raillery, a liberty in decent language to question everything, and an allowance of unravelling or refuting any argument

other humours. In this way, Shaftesbury associated religious enthusiasm with mental disorder. He did not assume that melancholy was an inborn condition, affecting individuals who were prone to enthusiasm. The melancholic state was brought about by external factors. There are 'melancholy occasions' when the panics of enthusiasm grow: 'For vapours naturally rise and, in bad times especially, when the spirits of men are low, as either in public calamities or during the unwholesomeness of air or diet ... at this season the panic must needs run high' (p. 10).

Shaftesbury's descriptions of the melancholy occasions, when the panics of enthusiasm spread, resemble the descriptions that later crowd psychologists would give of mass behaviour. Shaftesbury talked about the fury of panics, which transforms individuals, putting them 'beyond themselves' (p. 10). In this state, the mood is 'infectious', as 'the fury flies from face to face, and the disease is no longer seen than caught' (p. 10). Gustav Le Bon in his book, *The Crowd* (1896), was to write in similar ways about the emotional contagions of crowds and the suggestible mental states of crowd members. Le Bon's account not only influenced Freud's *Group Psychology* (1921/1985), but also modern psychological theories of deindividuation (Diener, 1979; Zimbardo, 1969; see also Farr, 1996; Moscovici, 1985; van Ginneken, 1992). Modern psychologists might not talk of crowd members being put 'beyond themselves', as Shaftesbury did. Nevertheless, they have retained the idea that the psychology of individuals can be dangerously transformed by the contagious, emotional atmosphere of crowds.

Shaftesbury's main concern in his 'Letter' was not to describe the psychological state of enthusiasm, or to uncover its bodily correlates. His primary problem was how to deal with such enthusiasm. He was addressing a problem that remains important today. Should the state, when confronted by the threat of violent fundamentalism, respond by restricting liberty, prosecuting those who preach beliefs that are deemed to be dangerous? On the other hand, should the state seek to protect strong religious feelings by prohibiting certain forms of mockery, thereby using the law to restrict free expression in the name of mutual respect?

Shaftesbury stood firmly in favour of free expression both for the zealots and for those who wish to ridicule them. He wrote against those who advocated repressive measures against the religious enthusiasts. Shaftesbury's words have resonance today, when state authorities and the popular press seek to ban and imprison fundamentalists. Such measures, Shaftesbury argued, are largely counter-productive. Far from stopping the zealots, they actually increase their resolve. Just as physicians can make matters worse by trying to allay all bodily eruptions, so the 'body politic' can be set into uproar by 'the specious pretence of healing this itch of superstition', thereby turning 'a few innocent carbuncles into an inflammation and mortal gangrene' (p. 9). The authorities would be doing the enthusiasts a favour were they to hang or imprison them. That would grant them the martyrdom that they seek and 'blow up their zeal and stir afresh the coals of persecution' (p. 15).

The way to oppose the melancholy of enthusiasm was to maintain good humour and to protect the freedoms on which good humour depends. The religious enthusiasts were deadly serious, with their grim, religious visions. They were the enemies of humour and laughter. Shaftesbury wrote that 'gravity is the very essence of imposture' (p. 8). Instead of restricting liberty, we must recognize that 'it is only in a nation such as ours, that imposture has no privilege' (p. 7). Thus, the melancholy spirit with its violent and unreasoning tendencies must be countered, not by the seriousness of repression, but by its opposite: the humour of ridicule. Shaftesbury took delight in describing how the religious enthusiasts had been mocked at Bartholomew's Fair by puppet shows. The crowd laughed with delight as the puppets imitated their 'strange voices and involuntary agitations' (p. 15). If freedom is threatened by fanaticism, then ridicule and humour are its defenders.

Shaftesbury urged that we must not be cowards in the defence of freedom. We must not say some topics 'are too grave', too important, to be ridiculed, thereby establishing laws to restrict what can be said (p. 8). There can be no freedom if 'any peculiar custom or national opinion' is declared to be 'exempted from criticism' (p. 7). All opinions should be open to debate and mockery. Above all, we must not be afraid to let our own beliefs 'stand the test of ridicule' (p. 8). In writing thus, Shaftesbury was assigning a weighty role to ridicule, giving it the very highest moral, political and psychological significance.

The Dialogic Way of Understanding

In his 'Letter Concerning Enthusiasm', Shaftesbury was sketching the outlines of a very important view on truth and understanding. Shaftesbury would elaborate this position in later sections of *Characteristicks*. His approach turned Locke's assumptions upside-down. Locke had suggested that the way to truth was through matching ideas with perceptions. The individual should check that complex concepts could be justified in terms of simple ideas. The locus for such checking was the individual mind. Only if we are sure that our ideas are clearly and distinctly derived from perceptions should we then communicate them to others.

Shaftesbury's approach to truth was very different. Truth was not a matter of sorting out the ideas in our mind – something that we have to do on our own. Instead, Shaftesbury suggested that we arrive at truth through conversation. Dialogue was not the means of communicating

individually checked truths from one mind to another. It was the means by which ideas could be produced and assessed. As such, Shaftesbury was providing a dialogic and, thereby, inherently social approach to knowledge. He was advocating an approach that bears more than chance resemblance to that which Bakhtin would propose more than two centuries later.

Shaftesbury may have introduced the notion of ridicule as a test of opinion in the opening piece of *Characteristiks*, but it was in the next essay 'Sensus Communis' that he really developed the theme. Significantly, this was the piece where he argued that humans have an inborn social sense that draws us to our fellows. If truth is related to the practice of dialogue, and dialogue is a mode of social association, then truth and error are not matters of individual perception, as Locke had supposed: they are intrinsically social and dialogic matters.

On one matter Locke and Shaftesbury were in agreement: we should not uncritically accept the views of authorities. Instead, we must subject all views to critical inquiry. Shaftesbury asserted in 'Sensus Communis' that we may be charged with 'wilful ignorance and blind idolatry' if we take opinions 'upon trust' and not test them 'in open light' (p. 29). But how do we test our notions? Truth, he writes, might be supposed to 'bear *all* lights' (p. 30, emphasis in original). One of the principal lights that truth should bear is the exposure to mockery. If an opinion cannot stand mockery, then it will be revealed to be ridiculous. Accordingly, Shaftesbury writes 'in commendation of raillery' (p. 29). Mockery was not just to be reserved for the opinions of religious enthusiasts, on whom we might look with ironic detachment. Mockery should be applied to all serious claims to knowledge.

This was a stunning proposal. In the late seventeenth and early eighteenth centuries, there was great interest in the issue of politeness. New forms of meeting places were being developed – such as salons in France and coffee-houses in Britain. These were neither strictly public nor private meeting places. Nothing like the coffee houses had existed in the dire, suspicious times of the Civil War. Many people were uncertain how they should behave. Books of etiquette, instructing readers how to converse politely, became popular (Burke, 1993). Shaftesbury's own work was part of the movement to examine the nature of politeness (Klein, 1994).

The guides to etiquette generally viewed ridicule as something to be avoided. Polite people did not engage in mockery: it was not genteel. Two years before Shaftesbury's 'Sensus Communis' appeared, an English edition of the Abbé de Bellegarde's guide to politeness was published under the title of *Reflexions on Ridicule and the Means to Avoid It*. The book advised against ridicule: 'Men are made for society, and therefore the most useful of all sciences is the art of living, which guards us perpetually against ridicule, and teaches us to avoid whatever without offence to the arguer, are the only terms which can render such speculative conversations any way agreeable' (p. 33). Of course, Shaftesbury, with his evocation of the codes of gentlemanly behaviour, allowed the assumptions of class and gender superiority to affect his guidelines – hence his comments, quoted much earlier, about the liberty of the gentleman's club (see above, p. 76).

There was no necessity, even by Shaftesbury's own logic, to restrict 'gentlemanly' behaviour to males. His friend Lady Masham could more than hold her own in the sorts of discussions that Shaftesbury was recommending. In her *Occasional Thoughts in Reference to a Virtuous or Christian Life*, Lady Masham wrote that 'there is no so constant and satisfactory a pleasure, to those who are capable of it, as rational conversation gives' (1705, p. 4). She added a comment that Shaftesbury would have done well to have noted. In her experience, the persons who afforded such agreeable and rational conversations were 'the greater part of them ladies' (p. 6). Her husband Francis Masham, good solid fellow that he was, was not one for intellectual discussion.

Shaftesbury was not attempting to re-write the etiquette books, as if he were seeking to replace codes that discouraged mockery with those that encouraged it. His aim was much more philosophical. In fact, he was discussing something that would become an important issue in mid-twentieth-century thinking: namely, the ideal conditions for speech. Jurgen Habermas (1987 and 1989) was to argue that it was politically and socially important to maintain the theoretical possibility of an ideal speech-situation in which people could talk openly, equally and without constraint. Habermas's ideal speech situation was a much more sober-minded business than Shaftesbury's gentlemanly conversations: Habermas did not envisage that these situations would be filled with the laughter of mockery. Hannah Arendt (1959) was to deal with the same basic issue of the ideal conditions for dialogue, albeit from a somewhat different perspective than Habermas. Neither Habermas nor Arendt would, of course, have dreamt of excluding Lady Masham and her friends on the grounds of gender.

Shaftesbury may not have offered a strict definition of the ideal dialogue, but he did have exemplars to which he could point. His ideals were the Platonic dialogues, in which Socrates and his friends discussed the weightiest of issues with humour, sharpness and vivacity. Lady Masham, as a Platonist, could also point to the Socratic dialogues as a model of rational conversation. These were not conversations in which the participants came together to report the results of their solitary deliberations. In these discussions, the participants were actually engaged in the activity of thinking, as Socrates goaded his fellows into discussing things that they had previously taken for granted. And, nearly always, the discussions end in disagreement, as the participants agree to meet again to talk about things further.

What drew Shaftesbury to Plato was not so much the Platonic theory of essences; even less was he attracted by the image of the ideal, regulated, authoritarian society depicted in Plato's *Republic*. In fact, the *Republic* is one of Plato's least dialogic works. Socrates does not really debate with his fellow conversationalists in the *Republic*. It is more of a question-and-answer session, in which Socrates offers definitive answers about the ideal state. Here, the literary form matches the message. In the ideal state, thought and debate would be tightly controlled by elite philosopher-rulers, who were convinced of their knowledge of truth. In terms of the *Republic*, Shaftesbury was not a Platonist.

But in terms of the earlier dialogues, Shaftesbury was most certainly a Platonist in dialogical spirit. This was in keeping with the stoic tradition. The surviving thoughts of Epictetus are also fundamentally dialogical. They are, in the main, records of conversations between Epictetus and his pupils. Sometimes, Epictetus is to be heard giving a monologue, but, even then, he is often conducting an imaginary conversation. He imagines, for example, what an Epicurean might say and how he would reply as a stoic, and how the Epicurean might reply to his reply and so on. As Long (2002) writes, the discourses of Epictetus, regardless of their form, are 'consistently dialectical or dialogical' (p. 61).

Shaftesbury loved Plato's philosophical writings. They were, according to Shaftesbury, 'a kind of poetry' (p. 87). Plato dramatized dialogues whose participants 'had their characters preserved throughout, their manners, humours and distinct turns of temper and understanding maintained'. It was not enough, Shaftesbury continued, that Plato's dialogues treated issues of morality fundamentally, but they 'exhibited them alive and set the countenances and complexions of men plainly in view' (p. 87). Above all, Socrates, was 'the philosophical hero of these poems'; he was presented as 'a perfect character' (p. 87). The perfection did not reside in his possessing a truthful system but in his way of conducting himself. Socrates had his moods and his different tones. Shaftesbury particularly loved Socrates's use of humour, his 'exquisite and refined raillery'. Socrates could treat the highest subjects and the most ordinary: 'in this genius of writing, there appeared both the heroic and the simple, the tragic and the comic vein' (p. 87). Socrates showed how to answer seriousness with jest and jest with seriousness.

Shaftesbury took Plato as a literary model. The *Characteristicks* includes a philosophical dialogue, the 'Moralists'. The Socratic character is Theocles, who expounds views that are close to Shaftesbury's own. However, Shaftesbury writes from the point of view of another character, Philocles, whose views are far more sceptical than those of Theocles. The aim of Theocles is not to triumph over the others, overpowering their arguments and forcing them into silent acceptance of his own views. Theocles wants to keep the dialogue alive with its clash of opinions. At one point Theocles delivers a lengthy speech that happens to mirror some Shaftesburian themes about the naturalness of beauty. Theocles finishes and then tells Philocles that he would be scandalized if Philocles merely commended him and did 'not choose to criticize some part or other of his long discourse' (p. 278). Philocles duly obliges and the conversation continues. In this way, Shaftesbury, who writes the dialogue from the perspective of Philocles, presents himself as a critic of the views that he elsewhere espouses in the *Characteristicks*. As will be seen, this aspect of self-criticism and self-reflection was deeply embedded into the very structure of *Characteristicks*.

Heteroglossia and a Wonderful Contrariety

It is not difficult to draw parallels between the views of Shaftesbury, which have been outlined above, and those to be found in the writings of Mikhail Bakhtin. The commendation of mockery, the distrust of serious enthusiasm, the defence of liberty and the championing of dialogue are all important themes in Bakhtin's work. At root, both thinkers shared a fear of political authorities that try to impose uniformity of opinion in the name of doctrinal correctness.

Bakhtin, like Shaftesbury, had good reason to fear the totalitarian spirit that persecuted dissent. Shaftesbury feared the enthusiasms of religion, but Bakhtin lived in a time when enthusiasm was marching under the banner of secular, scientific politics. There was another difference between their respective fears. Shaftesbury may have feared a future return to the intolerances of a recent past. But he did not live in times of active persecution. Bakhtin, by contrast, did. He lived his adult life under the Soviet regime. He was a young student during the Bolshevik revolution and later he managed to survive the Stalinist tyranny, when so many intellectuals were condemned to death for failing to support the correct political line. Bakhtin suffered greatly, especially during the periods of food shortage. The details are hard to come by and myths about his life have multiplied. Even the facts of his education are unclear. It is said that his circumstances were at one time so desperate that he used his manuscripts as cigarette papers. What is not doubted is that he spent long periods in exile, working in remote regions of the Soviet Union, avoiding the attentions of the authorities (on Bakhtin, see Clark and Holquist, 1984; Coates, 1999; Emerson, 2000; Hirschkop, 2001; Holquist, 2002).

Bakhtin had to be circumspect in his criticisms of tyranny: dissent that was too openly expressed would have meant imprisonment and possible death. Bakhtin's chosen field was literary criticism and the analysis of language, but it is not difficult to detect wider allusions in his writings. Exactly what his views were on political issues is a matter of controversy – there is even debate about which writings should properly be ascribed to him. Even so, there is a parallel with Shaftesbury. Just as Bakhtin could not openly express his political and religious views, so Shaftesbury had to be careful in his criticisms of Christianity. When Shaftesbury professed to being a Christian – despite his numerous critical and sarcastic asides – it is not clear whether he was politely paying lip-service to orthodoxy, expressing a cultural attachment to the atmosphere of English churches, or expounding a genuine theological belief. Given the immediate dangers to Bakhtin's life and the uncertain conditions under which he was forced to work, his rhetorical evasions needed to be all the greater.

Like Shaftesbury, Bakhtin viewed mockery as essential to the condition of freedom. One major theme in his work, especially in his book on Rabelais, was the celebration of the carnival (Bakhtin, 1984). The voice of mockery subverts the seriousness of authority. As Bakhtin wrote in *Speech Genres*, 'only dogmatic and authoritarian cultures are one-sidedly serious' (1986, p. 134). The politics of violence tries to curb humour, for 'violence does not know laughter' (p. 134). Thus, Bakhtin contrasted humour, especially the riotous merriment of the carnival, with the grimness of doctrinaire politics. Shaftesbury's delight in the London carnival crowd mocking the Camisards can today appear positively Bakhtinian.

Bakhtin clearly loved the early Platonic dialogues, seeing them as a creative source for the modern novel with its heroes and other characters. The Platonic dialogue constituted, in his view, a new form of writing (but he excluded later dialogues, such as *The Republic*; see Zappen, 2000). Plato's portrayal of Socrates, according to Bakhtin, represented 'a new type of prose heroization' (1981, p. 24). Plato's writings, unlike the systems and theories of so many philosophers, do not display a single, monological voice of seriousness insisting on its own correctness. Instead there are 'living people' and 'diversity of speech and voice' (Bakhtin, 1981, p. 25). Like Shaftesbury, Bakhtin said that it was of the 'utmost importance' that the Platonic dialogues contained humour, for humour is more than mere jest: it has a serious philosophical role. Thus, Bakhtin wrote of the Platonic dialogues that 'we have laughter, Socratic irony, the entire system of Socratic degradations combined with a serious, lofty and for the first time truly free investigation of the world, of man and of human thought' (1981, p. 25).

Bakhtin's writings, let alone the way he conducted his life, also contain stoic elements. Caryl Emerson (2000), a notable Bakhtinian scholar and English translator of several of Bakhtin's works, has suggested that the stoic philosophers were Bakhtin's intellectual role models. She specifically connects Bakhtin's love of the carnivalesque with stoicism: 'with full justification ... we might interpret the laughing carnival moment in Bakhtin as the stoic moment' (Emerson, 2000, p. 260). In *Dialogical Imagination* Bakhtin claimed that the writings of Epictetus and Marcus Aurelius prefigured later literary forms, most notably the *Bildungsroman* (literally: educational novel) (1981, p. 350). Bakhtin's claim, however, does little to quieten doubts that he may have derived his knowledge of classical writing from secondary sources (Hirschkop, 2001). Had Bakhtin read any of Epictetus's discourses, he would surely have been aware that Epictetus, just like Socrates, was a teacher and conversationalist, not an author.

The central theme of Bakhtin's work is the importance of dialogue. One commentator has described 'dialogism' as the 'master key' to Bakhtin's work (Holquist, 2002, p. 15). Bakhtin argues that language does not exist as a formal system, as grammarians sometimes suppose, but it exists to be used in dialogue. Every utterance is a response to previous utterances and a prelude to further ones. Bakhtin writes that an utterance cannot have a single, self-contained meaning but its meaning comprises two meanings that 'meet and accompany one another' (Bakhtin, 1986, p. 146). Even what seems to be a monologue will have a dialogical context, from which it takes its meaning. A single-author book, such as a piece of systematic philosophy, might seem to be a monologue, in that the author writes without interruption. However, the book will be a response to other books, other utterances, other responses. It takes its place within a wider chain of responses and answers. Moreover, the book is addressed to an audience – it is in dialogue with that audience. In this regard, it participates in the condition of all understanding, which is 'actively responsive' (1986, p. 69). Accordingly, understanding is not a cognitive process of processing information, but, according to Bakhtin, 'understanding is always dialogic to some degree' (1986, p. 111). As will be seen, Shaftesbury, too, believed that dialogue provides the path towards understanding.

Bakhtin's work on the dialogical nature of language is part analysis and part celebration. Because language is dialogical, it is marked by 'heteroglossia' or a diversity of voices. Novels illustrate this heteroglossia. In a novel, there is not just a single authorial voice: there are different characters with their own individual voices. Also, a single novel will contain different literary forms, such as letters, quotations, dialogues, descriptions, etc. In this way, modern novels reproduce the heteroglossic character of language, just as the Platonic dialogues did with their different moods and different characters.

For Bakhtin, heteroglossia was not merely a necessary fact of human understanding: it was something to be cherished. Indeed, Bakhtin considered that dialogue, and the freedom of speech on which it depends, was being seriously threatened in the twentieth century. He lived under a regime that was attempting to impose a single, ideological conformity – an official, monological voice. Bakhtin viewed the trend towards monologue and the curtailment of diversity as a threat to language itself and, thereby, to the very conditions of human existence. This is why heteroglossia – or a multiplicity of positions – was so important.

A celebration of diversity is also clear in Shaftesbury's depiction of Socrates as a man of different moods, different tones and different voices. Shaftesbury describes him as 'the philosophical patriarch' who 'containing within himself the several geniuses of philosophy, gave rise to all those several manners in which the science was delivered' (p. 114). Socrates, far from espousing a single, methodically constructed system, gave birth to the varying and contradictory systems of later philosophers. It was his genius, not his weakness, to contain the seeds of all these contradictions, all these diverse voices.

In the 'Letter on Enthusiasm', Shaftesbury depicts the golden age of philosophy as a time of intellectual diversity and freedom of debate. In ancient Athens, 'visionaries and enthusiasts of all kinds were tolerated' and philosophy was permitted 'a free course' to argue against superstition. While the Pythagoreans and later Platonists may have allied themselves with religious enthusiasms, they were not able to impose a grim seriousness on the order of the day: 'the Epicurean, the Academic and others were allowed to use all the force of wit and raillery' against them (p. 11). As a result, comments Shaftesbury, in Athens 'matters were balanced'. Reason and science flourished and 'wonderful was the harmony and temper which arose from all these contrarieties' (p. 11).

It does not matter whether or not this is an accurate description of ancient Athens – a society in which slavery was permitted and women were denied the right to participate in public life. What counts is Shaftesbury's depiction of the ideal state of affairs. This is not Plato's republic where the zealous guardians seek to cultivate a single perspective. In Shaftesbury's ideal state, there is debate, difference and, above all, mockery. The Epicurean and stoic will argue with each other, and both will argue against the Pythagorean and the mystic. None is permitted to impose silence on their rivals. In this image of utopia, the lion does not lie down in silence with the lamb, but the Epicurean and stoic meet again and again to argue, to seek truth and to laugh.

This image seems to be at variance with the stoic vision of harmony, which Shaftesbury outlined in his 'Inquiry' and which Voltaire mocked. In 'Inquiry', Shaftesbury had imagined the universe to be a single inte- grated whole with all its parts harmoniously fitting together. Shaftesbury in the 'Letter' is still using the language of stoic holism: there is a harmony and a balance. But this harmony is constituted by continual contrariety, argument and ridicule. In other words, the harmony, to be a genuinely human harmony, cannot be harmonious: it must be based on contrariety.

The history may be cloudy, but the politics are clear. Shaftesbury is celebrating difference. It is the sort of difference that Socrates – rationalist and mystic, believer and sceptic, tragic and comic hero – contained within himself. As a stoic, Shaftesbury argues with the Epicureans, but realizes that if the wonderful balance of contrarieties is to continue, there need to be Epicureans to argue with. The aspiration is not to sweep them away with the rubble of history. In the same way, Locke is not just personally loved, but his philosophical views are necessary *because of* (not *despite*) their lack of congeniality. Hence, as was seen in chapter five, Shaftesbury recommended that his protégé read Locke's *Essay*. By the same token, Shaftesbury criticized the zealots and divines of his own day who wished to pursue 'a new sort of policy', using the law to enforce 'uniformity of opinion (a hopeful project!)' (p. 11).

The comment is extraordinarily prescient. Shaftesbury, early in the era of modernity, sees the politics of uniformity as a new sort of policy. Of course, he was well aware that this new sort of policy was not quite so new. After the decline of Athens, he wrote, there arose a narrow-minded outlook in which 'doctrinal tests were framed' and 'religious massacres' were practised (p. 365). The 'spirit of bigotry' was spread, as zealots demanded 'a strict and absolute assent' (p. 373). Shaftesbury saw a resurgence of this spirit in the politics of his grandfather's times.

With hindsight, and especially with the examples of twentieth century totalitarianism in mind, it is easy to read Shaftesbury's words as a warning against a new age of politics that would demand strict assent and uniformity of opinion. Shaftesbury would have deplored Bakhtin's term 'heteroglossia' as both redundant and ugly. But he would have recognized the justness of its meaning as a word that described the operations of language and warned against those who sought to restrict human possibilities in the name of absolute truth. Bakhtin, like himself, had good reason to celebrate the wonderful contrariety of opposites against a grimly serious politics that was intolerantly convinced of its own truthfulness. But Bakhtin, living in supposedly more advanced and enlightened times, had greater reason to express himself allusively, to hide behind technical jargon, lest his meaning became too apparent.

A Dialogical View of Thinking

Shaftesbury's warnings against enthusiasm contain an important psychological element. He was describing a state of being – a grim melancholia – that he considered dangerous. Using stoic terminology, this state could be described as 'unnatural'. Of course, the stoic conception of 'natural' was both prescriptive and descriptive. To call a mental state or desire 'unnatural' was to say that it did not conform to the essential conditions of human nature – or at least to the stoic conception of human nature. Thus, selfishness was deemed 'unnatural' because it was 'natural' for humans to be socially minded (not that all humans followed their so-called 'natural' desires). Similarly the melancholia of enthusiasm was, in Shaftesbury's view, the very antithesis of rationality: it could be seen as 'unnatural' because, as the stoics stressed, being rational was an integral part of human nature. That is one reason why Shaftesbury believed that the irrational intolerance of enthusiasm should be countered with rational good humour, not with further enthusiasm.

This antithesis between tolerance and intolerance – grim zealotry and good humour – contains an implicit assumption about the nature of thinking. To be in the grips of enthusiasm is to have relinquished the power of rational thinking. Shaftesbury depicted the enthusiast rather similarly to the way that later psychologists have described the so-called 'authoritarian personality'. Authoritarians are presumed to have psychological fears that prevent them from accepting the complexities of the world in a rational manner; in consequence, they seek the security of a single doctrinaire and intolerant truth (Adorno et al., 1950; Altemeyer, 1981 and 1988; Duckitt, 2003).

Any psychological description of the failures of thinking implies that there is a better way to think. In the 'Letter concerning enthusiasm', Shaftesbury contrasted the grimness of religious enthusiasm with the humour of Socrates in debate. This contrast not only links good humour with reason, but, most crucially, locates dialogue as the site of reasoning. The image of the thinker as a conversationalist rests on a psychology of thinking that is very different from the cognitive account which Locke presented in his *Essay*. Shaftesbury was expressing ideas that resemble those being proposed today by critical psychologists, who have been influenced by Bakhtin. To show this, it will be necessary to say a few words about the contrast between individual cognitive accounts of thinking, such as Locke's, and the more social and dialogical accounts that can be found in Shaftesbury and Bakhtin.

Locke's account, as has been said, tied thinking to perception. Thinking occurs when we reflect on perception. Locke did not really explain what the skills of reflection are, or where they come from. Some later followers, most notably Condillac in his *L'essai sur les origines des connaissances humaines*, argued that the skills of reflection were themselves derived from perceptual processes, with the result that thinking, at root, was entirely a perceptual process. Even so, that still leaves the question where the skills of perception are derived from: how do we organize the perceptual field into objects that can be recognized from one time to another?

There is a further question: what agent of the mind carries out the tasks of reflection? Locke's psychology implies that there is such an agent. The self, the ego, the thinker, or whatever it is called, reflects on simple ideas, combining them into complex ones. It is the same agent that can direct the attention, to receive some sensations but not others. This implies that there must be what Daniel Dennett has termed 'a Central Executive' in the mind, directing operations (Dennett, 1991). Certainly, Locke wrote about the origins of our feelings of enduring selfhood: we believe our minds to exist across time. According to Locke, consciousness always accompanies thinking and this consciousness 'makes everyone to be what he calls self'; this is the basis of 'personal identity, i.e., the sameness of a rational being' (II.xxvii.9, p. 286).

Locke's phrase 'the sameness of a rational being' is indicative. A rational being is one that shows some sameness or consistency in their thinking. It is not rational to think one thing on one day and then to have the entirely opposite thought on the next day. Locke's prescriptions for thinking are designed to bring order into the mind. Complex ideas must be arranged so that their links with simple ideas are made explicit. The Central Executive should be an efficient administrator, allowing the clear and distinct processing of information. In this, Locke's psychology presumed that there was an underlying strong ego, just as much as Descartes did. If the Cartesian ego has the job of weeding out beliefs that are not derived from rational certainty, then the Lockean ego must tidy up the unruly mess that the senses are continually bringing into the mind.

Just like the ability to reflect, this ego must have its origins within the mind itself. It constitutes the precondition for having organized perceptions and, thus, despite some of Condillac's ingenious arguments, it cannot be derived from the external world. The ego cannot bring itself in from the outside. This is an implication of Locke's individualism. The mind is considered to operate in splendid isolation. It works out how to receive, understand and organize sensations all by itself. The ego, in this regard, is an autochthonous entity.

Today, critical psychologists and theorists of post-modernity have taken issue with the concept of the strong, independent ego. It is often said that the image of the ego is a fiction that has dominated western thinking about the mind since the era of Descartes and Locke. Post-modern thinkers talk about the need to 'de-centre' the ego – to knock it from its presumed place at the centre of the mind. It has been said that 'reflexive historical sociologists' oppose the idea of 'a fixed self, a transcendental subject or ego that is the foundation of all knowledge' (Szakolczai, 2000a, p. 89). Feminist theorists have argued that the image of the ego reflects masculine fantasies of the untrammeled, rational being, who can dominate the world with pure thought and no emotions. Certainly, the ideal of thinking that Locke proposed is one in which order dominates over disorder, rationality over emotion. His Central Executive is a somewhat bloodless bureaucrat.

The critics suggest that this ego-dominated image of thinking fails to match the realities of the way people actually think. Our minds are not so tidily organized: we cannot dispel uncertain and unclear thoughts, let alone eradicate the cross forces of competing emotions. And even if we could achieve such mental tidiness, it would be undesirable. We would be diminished, not enhanced. The image of the rational, controlling ego is not one to which we should aspire. The totally rational individual is, in the stoic sense, 'unnatural'. Accordingly, the critics argue that the fantasy of the controlling ego must be de-centred from psychological thinking.

A number of critical psychologists have been proposing a dialogical conception of thinking. They have claimed that this entails a very different conception of the mind than that which has long dominated standard cognitive psychology (see, *inter alia*, Billig, 1996; Edwards and Potter, 1993; Gergen, 1994 and 2001a; Harré and Gillett, 1994; Hermans and Dimaggio, 2007; Kvale, 1992b; Markova, 2003; Potter and Wetherell, 1987; Shotter, 1991 and 1993a; Shotter and Billig, 1998; Wertsch, 1991). The assumption is that much human thinking is dependent on language and, thereby, on dialogue. To think about ethics, the dilemmas of social life, the characters of other people and so on, we need to use language. There is, in consequence, a qualitative difference between the perception of objects and language-based thinking. Animals can perceive objects; they can remember stimuli; they can learn to react to different categories of object. But they cannot think ethically, hold opinions or, in the stoic sense, examine their perceptions critically. For all that, language is necessary.

Being in possession of a language does not mean primarily that one is equipped with syntax and vocabulary whose prime purpose is to name objects or to transmit inner thoughts to others, as Locke had supposed and as any theory of 'telementation' assumes. It means belonging to the world of dialogue, as Bakhtin emphasized. The skills of language are acquired through dialogue and interaction. Language is a means by which we relate to others. Through learning to speak, we become part of the dialogic world. Then, and only then, do we develop the capability of thinking by ourselves. We do this by internalizing dialogue – that is, speaking to ourselves. When we can do this, we can properly be said to be able to think.

There are two points about this perspective that are particularly worth noting. The first is the developmental aspect. It is assumed that we learn to think by learning to talk. The ability to think is not something that is present at birth. Nor is it presumed that the infant child is born with a strong, autonomous ego. Thinkers are dialogical selves – selves who can conduct conversations with others and with themselves.

The dialogical self must develop out of the practices of conversation. In this way, the self-reflecting self develops out of the ability to use language dialogically. The dialogic self must be a social self. It develops in dialogical relations with others. Unless we lived in a social world – a world saturated by the practices of dialogue – we could not become this dialogical self. As such, human thinking has a social origin.

The second implication is that thinking cannot be a purely hidden, internal process. It is out there, existing in the practices of language. The child learns to think by copying the ways others talk. It can hear others engaging in criticism and justification, questioning and answering. It can learn what are considered to be adequate criticisms and justifications; what count as answers and what count as further questioning of answers and so on. It hears the thinking of dialogue, just as the readers of Plato can enter into the world of Socrates's thinking. Moreover, children can try out their own questioning and answering, receiving responses that tell them whether they have done so adequately.

If thinking is just a matter of internal cognition – the arranging of sensations, impressions and general ideas – then there would be nothing for the young child to copy; there would be no way of learning to think. All the processes of thinking, which Locke described and which cognitive psychologists write about, are out of sight. No one can observe cognitions, memory stores or information-processing. If, on the other hand, thinking is directly observable in the practices of dialogue, then, in a real sense, children have models to copy, and, most importantly, the rhetorical processes of thought can be taught. Moreover, thinking is a practical task that children must engage in when they too participate in dialogues.

This dialogical approach to thinking is very much in keeping with Bakhtin's ideas. Bakhtin (1986), for example, referred to the 'inner dialogism' of thinking. Even more clearly are such ideas to be found in Volosinov's *Marxism and the Philosophy of Language* (1973). Volosinov was a member of Bahktin's circle and some scholars believe that Bakhtin may have been the real author of *Marxism and the Philosophy of Language* (Clark and Holquist, 1984; Holquist, 2002; but see Emerson, 2000; Morson and Emerson, 1989). Volosinov clearly argued that consciousness is formed by outward action, rather than vice versa. Psychological phenomena are not located within the mind, but are located '*without* in the word, the gesture, the act' (Volosinov, 1973, p. 19, emphasis in original). Of course, these outward manifestations of language can be internalized. Thus, the patterns of dialogue can give rise to the patterns in individual thinking: that is why thinking has the character of 'the alternating lines of a dialogue' (Volosinov, 1973, p. 38).

The psychologist who expressed this notion most clearly was Bakhtin's Russian contemporary, Lev Vygotsky (1896–1934). Like Volosinov, Vygotsky suggested that children absorb language through dialogue.

Thinking is a form of 'inner speech' and that is why the construction of the child's internal world is dependent on the acquisition of the skills of dialogue (Vygotsky, 1987). This idea has been enormously influential in recent developmental psychology (see, for instance, Rogoff, 1990; Rogoff and Lave, 1999; Werstch, 1991). Vygotsky's perspective links the learning of concepts to dialogue and, thereby, in the words of Jerome Bruner, it presumes thought to be 'both an individual achievement and a social one' (1987, p. 4). The cognitive capacities of the child do not grow according to some internal logic of development, as Piaget assumed: they grow in relation to the child becoming part of the dialogical world of social life. Vygotsky's theory, therefore, is much closer to Bakhtin's ideas on dialogue than it is to Piaget's cognitive theory (Dore, 1986; Emerson, 1996).

The dialogical perspective makes a very important assumption about the nature of thinking. If thinking is a form of inner debate, and debate requires different voices, then thinking requires different voices. This implies that the thinking person should not possess one single voice, style of reaction, state of being. Instead, thinkers must internalize the heteroglossia of language so that they are able to think reflectively. In order to think – to debate with oneself – one must have internalized a contrariety of opinions. This is why the grimly serious enthusiast was, in Shaftesbury's opinion, a danger to rationality. Such a person seeks the sort of internal mental uniformity that excludes self-doubt, self-debate and, thus, thought. It is the same in psychology's image of the authoritarian personality. Self-questioning is held at bay by a ferocious conviction of rightness. The ferocity of that conviction, according to the theory of authoritarianism, is derived from an underlying fear of the world. It also prevents the authoritarian from thinking openly.

The individual/cognitive and the dialogical perspectives present two opposing images of thinking. According to the Lockean cognitive perspective, thinking is an individual, inner process that is the product of a self-directing ego. The ideal is internal consistency and the matching of ideas to evidence. The dialogical perspective sees the thinker altogether differently. Thinking is socially produced in the outer world of dialogue. It can be internalized, but to do this the thinker needs to have internalized different opinions and a diversity of voices. Such deliberative thinking requires what Shaftesbury described as the wonderful harmony of contrarieties. Consistency and uniformity, then, are threats to thinking. So is the belief that a strong, unified ego is a requirement for rationality.

The Divided Self
....

Shaftesbury's views on thinking appear in the essay 'Soliloquy, or advice to an author', which is the final essay in the first volume of *Characteristicks*. Here Shaftesbury links thinking to conversation. Significantly, it is 'Soliloquy' which contains the imagined dialogue between the Epicurean (Locke) and the Plenitudinarian (Descartes). In this passage, Shaftesbury dismissed Locke's search for the origins of ideas as trivial. Does it matter where my ideas come from, Shaftesbury had asked pointedly. What counts is their value.

'Soliloquy' starts by complaining about current literary standards. Too many writers were rushing into print before they had worked out exactly what they wanted to say. Shaftesbury had particularly harsh words for authors of 'the sanctified kind', who were publishing 'uncontrollable harangues' and who were claiming that their views 'must neither be questioned nor contradicted' (pp. 75–6). Never one to resist an opportunity to ridicule clerics, Shaftesbury feared that such holy writers might 'suffer much by crudities, indigestions, choler, bile and particularly by a certain tumour or flatulency' (p. 76). They were being so public spirited that they were rushing into print without affording 'themselves the least time to think in private' (p. 75).

But how should one think in private? 'Soliloquy' offers helpful hints. Thinking is no easy matter: 'Our thoughts have generally such an obscure implicit language that it is the hardest thing in the world to make them speak out distinctly' (p. 78). In Shaftesbury's view, the remedy was not to trace verbal ideas to underlying sensations, removing the misleading evocations of words, as Locke had suggested. The remedy was the reverse: 'The right method is to give them (our thoughts) voice and accent' (p. 78). In all such cases, it was necessary to 'self-converse' (p. 75).

This is more than simply saying 'think before you speak or write'. In Shaftesbury's view, the speaker or writer needs to practise in private the same sort of task that will be done in public: thinkers must engage in a conversation with themselves. In taking this line, Shaftesbury was following stoic teaching. The model, as always, was Socrates. As Epictetus said, Socrates argued with others, leading them to examine their thoughts and his own. If there was no-one else to hand, then Socrates 'argued with, and examined himself' (Epictetus, 1910, p. 69). Shaftesbury's notebooks – his 'Regimen' – are, in essence, a record of his own self-questioning. His literary model was Marcus Aurelius, whose great work has become known as his *Meditations*. But the word 'meditation' does not do justice to what Marcus Aurelius was doing. In 1701, Jeremy Collier published an English translation, whose title well caught the spirit of the emperor's stoic philosophy: *The Emperor Marcus Antoninus, His Conversation with Himself*. Shaftesbury, of course, had no need of an English translation: he read and quoted the original Greek.

But how should we set up an internal argument with ourselves? Shaftesbury gave a crucial clue. As was typical, he looked back to classical times. He claimed that the ancient Greeks imagined that everyone carried within themselves a guardian-spirit. They would have considered it to be an impious sacrilege 'to slight the company of so divine a guest' by refusing them access to their innermost thoughts and not following their advice when offered (p. 77). In consequence, the ancients imagined themselves to possess 'a certain duplicity of soul', in the sense of being double beings.

Shaftesbury recommended cultivating this sense of double self-hood as a means for thinking. The basic way to conduct an internal soliloquy was to achieve the internal division that the ancient Greeks took for granted. He suggested that the famous inscription at the Delphic oracle 'Recognize yourself!' meant, in point of fact, '"Divide yourself!" or "Be two!"' (p. 77). Accordingly, Shaftesbury wrote that the 'chief principle' of his philosophy was 'the doctrine of two persons in one individual self' (p. 83).

The principle is implied by the very notion of self-conversation. The sort of social dialogue that Shaftesbury considered necessary for the examination of opinions needs a multiplicity of voices and opinions. A conversation consisting of people all saying the same things would not be a real dialogue. That is why Shaftesbury was scathing about polite conversations where the participants flattered one another, uttering polite pleasantries. Similarly, an inner dialogue, in which one voice – one tone – predominated, could not be thoughtful. To have a proper dialogue, or a genuine conversation of the self with the self, there must be division and contrariety. The self must be able to oppose its own seriousness with jest and vice versa. Heteroglossia must be internalized: or, to use Shaftesbury's language, the self must be divided.

Such divisions can be found in Shaftesbury's work. As was discussed in the previous chapter, Shaftesbury simultaneously wrote in support of the naturalness of patriotism while also criticizing the narrowness of national feeling. Two voices, or two opinions, were in opposition, the one arguing for the virtues of particular loyalties, the other arguing for the virtues of universality. In Shaftesbury's view, it was not as if one voice were wrong and the other correct. Both were needed to criticize the other. Only by debate can one examine whether it is appropriate to be nationally partisan or universally minded in a given situation. No theoretical system can determine this in advance. Each case and each instance has to be examined in its own right. Debate and self-criticism are vital if one is to think about the dilemmas of life, rather than reacting to them in an unthinking manner.

The message was particularly appealing to those living within two cultural conditions. Shaftesbury was not saying, as Locke had implied, that the rational person must sweep old, non-empirical traditions into the dustbin of history. Tradition could be used to criticize the claims of enlightenment and vice versa. The doubleness of Shaftesbury's message was attractive to the young, German philosopher, Moses Mendelssohn. Altmann (1973), in his biography of Mendelssohn, recounts the excitement that the young man felt on first reading Shaftesbury. The Englishman's defence of dialogue and multiplicity struck a deep chord, as Mendelssohn conducted his own dialogues between the traditions of Judaism, in which he was raised, and the rationality of the Enlightenment, to which he was philosophically drawn. Mendelssohn went on to publish books of Enlightenment philosophy and also of Jewish theology. There was no reason to make a choice between the two, as if one had to be either Jewish or enlightened but not both. Mendelssohn rejected neither voice, nor did he subordinate one to the other. Shaftesbury had provided an inspiration for believing that there could be – indeed, there needed to be – a harmony of contrarieties.

Continual Self-Reflection

It might be questioned whether division should be a permanent feature of the self. Why should not the division be a temporary stage, during which one searches for the truth? And then having found the truth, should not the self be united again? Shaftesbury's message, however, was that the search for truth was unending. There was no point at which one could say 'Now that I have found certainty, there is no need for further thinking'. According to stoic teaching, the searching, the self-questioning and the internal doubting were never to be finished. That is why Theocles, in Shaftesbury's dialogue 'The Moralists', asks Philocles to criticize him. If thinking is never finished, then the self should be continually divided. A unified self would signify self-satisfaction and the avoidance of thinking, not a natural wholeness.

Many years later, Freud would write about the division of the self. Like Shaftesbury, he would claim that desire conflicted with both duty and reason and that it operated in roundabout, self-deceiving ways. Indeed, Shaftesbury could sound almost Freudian when writing about desires. Appetites are, he wrote, 'strangely subtle and insinuating', for they possess 'the faculty to speak by nods and winks' and to 'conceal half their meaning' (pp. 84–5). However, it would be a mistake to imagine Shaftesbury as a pre-Freudian. There was one huge difference. Freud believed that the self is inevitably divided. Id and ego collide from early life, and then the ego is split into a sense of reality and a sense of conscience. By contrast Shaftesbury viewed the sense of division as something that has to be painfully achieved. There are all manner of temptations to keep us from the task of dividing ourselves.

Shaftesbury recommended in 'Soliloquy' that we use the model of Plato's dialogues to accomplish the division of the self. The dialogues should be like a 'looking-glass' in which we 'discover ourselves and see our minutest features nicely delineated' (p. 87). Readers who studied the dialogues would 'acquire a peculiar speculative habit, so as virtually to carry about with them a sort of pocket-mirror, always ready and in use' (p. 87). In this pocket-mirror, 'two faces' present themselves to our view: the face of 'the commanding genius' and the other face 'like that rude and undisciplined and headstrong creature whom we ourselves in our natural capacity most exactly resembled' (p. 88). When we have acquired the habit of using this looking-glass, then 'we should, by virtue of the double reflection, distinguish ourselves into two different parties'. In this way our work of 'self-inspection' would continue 'with admirable success' (p. 88).

In this extraordinary passage, Shaftesbury appears to be describing the processes of identification; but, of course, he possessed neither the word 'identification' nor the psychological concept as such. Shaftesbury seems to imply that the Socratic dialogues present an idealized self – the figure of Socrates – and secondary, more ordinary characters. There is a double identification, as we recognize the ideal self that we should aspire to become and the imperfect self that we are. In outline, this resembles Freud's theory of identification, which he expounded in *Group Psychology and the Analysis of the Ego* (Freud, 1921/1985). Freud wrote about identification being a dual process. In the primary process, we identify with a leader, a hero or father-figure. In secondary identification, group members note that they have all identified with the same great leader and, in consequence, they establish bonds of similarity between themselves. This dual identification reflected, according to Freud, the split between superego and ego.

For Freud, this splitting of the self, based on two processes of identification, was something unavoidable. By contrast, Shaftesbury saw it as all too avoidable. It is so easy not to look into the pocket-mirror and thereby to avoid noticing our own imperfections. The opening pages of *Characteristicks* declare that people are 'wonderfully happy in a faculty of deceiving themselves' (p. 5). Shaftesbury returned to the theme in 'Soliloquy'. We resist being as harsh with ourselves as with others. We may criticize others freely, but it is 'insupportable' to appear as 'fools, madmen or varlets to ourselves' (p. 79).

Part of the problem lay in the nature of ridicule, which is the prime way of exposing folly in others. It is hard to laugh at ourselves in our solitary, self-dividing dialogues. Whatever raillery we 'may use with others', we can by no means endure 'to hold with ourselves' (p. 79). This failure to mock ourselves reflects the intrinsically social nature of laughter. As Henri Bergson was to suggest, laughter demands an audience: it stands 'in need of an echo' (Bergson, 1911, p. 5; see Billig, 2005, for an argument that links the social functions of laughter to embarrassment). We need to laugh with others as we laugh at another person. It is not easy to laugh simultaneously *with* and *at* ourselves, acting at the same moment as scoffer, victim and audience. That is one psychological division too far.

Characteristicks and Self-Reflection

Self-mockery may be easier to accomplish in writing than in self-dialogue, as the ridiculing of the self is played out before an imagined audience of readers. *Characteristicks* offers an example. It is not presented as a standard piece of systematic philosophy, but it has a form that exemplifies self-reflection and self-critique. In its literary structure, the book practises what the author preaches. In this, *Characteristicks* can be seen as possessing features that we have come to associate with post-modern sensibility – being more Derrida than Locke, even more Bakhtinian than Bakhtin himself.

Bakhtin may have championed the need for dialogue but he wrote in fairly conventional formats. He did not experiment with self-reflexive forms of writing. The conventional, monological essay or book was his medium. Of course, he could have defended himself by pointing out that philosophical monologue always takes place within a wider dialogue: the apparently monological book is an answer to previous writings and, in its turn, it will provoke further responses. Shaftesbury, by contrast, sought to incorporate the practice of self-criticism and self-division within his own writing.

Characteristicks contains a mixture of literary genres. The 'Inquiry' was the nearest Shaftesbury gets to straightforward philosophical exposition. The 'Moralists' was an imagined dialogue, employing a form much used by other eighteenth century philosophers (Prince, 1996). Shaftesbury's additional element was to write from the perspective of a character who was apparently criticizing Shaftesbury's own views. Thus, within the dialogue, Shaftesbury was displaying a literary division of the self. 'The Letter Concerning Enthusiasm' appears as if it were a letter to 'Lord *****', while 'Sensus Communis' is ostensibly a letter addressed to a friend, recalling a conversation that they had 'the other day', when the letter-writer aired his views on raillery (p. 29). 'Soliloquy' appears as 'advice to an author'. Shaftesbury, in these pieces, adopts the literary conceit that he is not doing philosophy, so much as partaking in friendly or literary dialogues.

More remarkable than the literary conceits of the first two volumes is the third and final volume of *Characteristicks*. Here Shaftesbury provides a practical, rhetorical demonstration that dialogue must be continual. This third volume was written when Shaftesbury knew that his health was deteriorating. It comprises five 'Miscellanies', as the author presents himself as engaging in the 'happy method' of the 'miscellaneous manner of writing' (p. 339). It is as if Shaftesbury has become an Addison or a Steele, discoursing in the educated, light and entertaining style of the early eighteenth century, by writing essays to entertain the coffee-house habitués.

There is one crucial difference between Shaftesbury's miscellaneous writings and those of Addison or Steele. Shaftesbury was not reviewing the latest works of theatre or literature. His five miscellaneous pieces comment on each of the five essays of the previous two volumes. The author of the 'Miscellanies' writes as if he were commenting on the works of another writer. No reader is expected to be fooled by the conceit. Here then is a form perfectly matched to the demands of Shaftesbury's dialogic philosophy and its principle of dividing the self.

The five Miscellanies deal with the preceding essays in turn, commenting on their limitations. As Shaftesbury claimed at the start of the fifth 'Miscellany', it is absurd 'to assert a work or treatise, written in human language, to be above human criticism or censure' (p. 434). The First Miscellany points out that the author, having criticized the spirit of enthusiasm, turns out himself to be an enthusiast for his own views. The Miscellany is demonstrating that the issues of free speech and dogmatism are not easily disposed of; instead, accusers can have their own arguments turned back against themselves as debates continue. The Third Miscellany discusses the 'Soliloquy', also turning its argument against itself. The Miscellany complains that the author did not present his full project but 'muttered to himself in a kind of dubious whisper or feigned soliloquy' (p. 396). Following Gorgias's (and Shaftesbury's) maxim that humour should be countered with seriousness, the Miscellany complains that 'what he discovers of form and method is indeed so accompanied with the random miscellaneous air that it may pass for raillery rather than good earnest' (p. 396).

The Fourth Miscellany, dealing with the 'Inquiry', is the fiercest of them all. The 'Inquiry' was the earliest piece in *Characteristicks*, written before Shaftesbury fully developed his dialogic perspective. Of all the essays, it most resembles conventional philosophical writing. In the Miscellany Shaftesbury attacks his own 'methodic' way of writing. The author of the 'Inquiry', he says, reveals himself 'openly as a plain dogmatist, a formalist and man of method, with his hypothesis tacked to him and his opinions so close sticking as would force one to call to mind the figure of some precise and strait-laced professor in a university' (p. 396). He continued to mock the author of the 'Inquiry' as 'our grave inquirer' (p. 425) and 'a system-writer, a dogmatist and expounder' (p. 418).

Today, some philosophical writers, most notably Jacques Derrida, have experimented with different ways of writing philosophy, especially as they criticize the hidden assumptions contained in traditional ways of writing philosophy. Derrida teaches that so-called rational philosophy employs language that bears extra-rational, literary meanings. This is not a message that can be conveyed in a neutrally rational language, at least without risk of self-refutation. Thus, Derrida continually displayed the surplus rhetoric of rational philosophy as he confronted its classic texts with his own seriously playful, self-reflexively aware and exuberantly surplus language (e.g., Derrida, 1982 and 2002). In the social sciences, a number of post-modern writers have explored the unacknowledged rhetoric of standard social scientific language by self-reflexively and playfully commenting on their own use of language (e.g., Ashmore, 1989; Ashmore et al., 1995; Clifford and Marcus, 1986; Mulkay, 1991; Pinch and Pinch, 1988).

It is easy to suppose that such playful self-reflexivity encapsulates the post-modern spirit in its rebellion against the seriously unaware voice of modernity. However, the example of Shaftesbury cautions against assuming the novelty of the new. Dialogism, reflexivity, playful self-reference and a de-centring of the ego – it has all been done before. Furthermore, it was done by a man so steeped in the classics that he never claimed to be doing anything new.

Something Borrowed, Something Lost

The issue of Shaftesbury and Bakhtin has to be confronted. As has been suggested, there are numerous parallels between the ideas of the two thinkers. It is not difficult to suggest that Shaftesbury was pre-Bakhtinian. But, is this just a matter of coincidence? Did Shaftesbury once shine as a leading intellectual light, only for his reputation to dim and his works to become forgotten? And, then, were his ideas re-invented independently, in another time, country and language, by a great thinker who knew nothing of his predecessor? If so, then Bakhtin can be given the credit of reviving Shaftesbury's spirit through his own self-generated genius. To use Locke's phrase, he would have spun out the ideas from his own mind. Bakhtin would, then, have given unwitting confirmation of his own maxim that 'nothing is absolutely dead; every meaning will have its homecoming festival' (Bakhtin, 1986, p. 170).

The history of ideas contains precedents for chance re-inventions. A few years ago, this is where the matter of Bakhtin and Shaftesbury might have rested. Then Bakhtin would be credited with invention; and the parallels with Shaftesbury would be noted as intriguing curiosities rather than as evidence of an actual link of continuity. But today it is not possible to be so sure. Locke's critics felt that he had not entirely spun his ideas from his own mind, but that he had failed to acknowledge his intellectual debts. Now, thanks to the fine scholarship of Brian Poole (2001 and 2002), Bakhtin no longer appears as the sole originator of his own ideas. Shaftesbury belongs to Bakhtin's story, although his part was concealed.

There may be scant evidence that contemporary thinkers in the social sciences, especially critical psychologists, have been directly affected by Shaftesbury's work. But an indirect link of continuity can be traced through Bakhtin. Shaftesbury was greatly appreciated by one philosopher, who was held in high repute in the mid-twentieth century. Ernst Cassirer's seriousness of purpose and his scholarly command of European philosophy's history make him today seem like a figure from a different age. In his books *The Platonic Renaissance in England* (1953) and *The Philosophy of the Enlightenment* (1951), Cassirer praised Shaftesbury as the last and greatest of the English Platonists. According to Cassirer, Shaftesbury's thinking was situated in the Renaissance tradition of the sixteenth century. Philosophers such as Nicolas of Cusa had formulated a tolerant view of the world. This tolerance was particularly attractive to the English Platonists, in whose works, according to Cassirer, 'differences of doctrinal opinion are not only tolerated, but welcomed' (1953, p. 38).

Shaftesbury, in Cassirer's view, took forward the spirit of the Renaissance into the modern age. He was the 'one great writer' who would make Cambridge Platonism 'a philosophic force in the centuries to come' (1953, pp. 159–60). Shaftesbury recognized the philosophical power of humour, ascribing to the comic 'the power of love' and seeing it as a bastion of freedom (p. 171). In the modern era, Shaftesbury's Platonism entered into the history of German thought, 'giving it a fresh impetus which none of the truly creative minds escaped' (p. 198). Cassirer mentions, for instance, the way that Moses Mendelssohn took up the notion of 'disinterested pleasure' from Shaftesbury; and Cassirer describes how this idea came to be developed by Kant (p. 186).

The time and place of Cassirer's praise for Shaftesbury as an influence on German thought are significant. Cassirer was acknowledging the humane, humorous celebration of difference just when such values were being destroyed in his own land by an even more violent outbreak of enthusiasm than Shaftesbury could ever have imagined. Cassirer's *Platonic Renaissance* was published in Germany the year before Hitler came to power. To identify Mendelssohn as a German thinker was politically pointed. Cassirer, the first Jewish rector of a German University, was removed from his position and forced to flee to England. From there, he went to live in Sweden and then the United States.

Whereas there is no evidence that Bakhtin actually read *Characteristicks*, Cassirer provides a missing link. Sorting out the figures that influenced Bakhtin has proved a difficult business. As the earlier comments on Bakhtin and Epictetus suggest, Bakhtin sometimes borrowed from secondary sources without due acknowledgement – and sometimes giving a false impression of familiarity with the primary sources. Brian Poole (2001 and 2002), however, has demonstrated Bakhtin's debts to Cassirer from 1936 onwards (see also Brandist, 1997). Previously, Bakhtin had not written on the philosophical importance of humour. But after reading Cassirer, Bakhtin's thought developed in significant new directions.

Like Cassirer and Shaftesbury, Bakhtin came to recognize the creative, philosophical power of humour. Poole shows that Bakhtin's book on Rabelais actually contains five pages copied word for word from Cassirer without acknowledgement. Bakhtin's uncompleted work on the *Bildungsroman* assimilates themes not only from Cassirer's *Platonic Renaissance* but also from *Philosophy of the Enlightenment*, in which Cassirer also discusses Shaftesbury. Amongst the themes that Bakhtin developed, having read Cassirer, are the unity of opposites, the depiction of temporal forms in terms of visual images, the celebration of religious tolerance because of the unattainability of a single truth and the idea of laughter as philosophically purifying. Poole comments that Cassirer's work on the Renaissance was perhaps 'the most important source for Bakhtin's philosophical thought on comedy' (2002, p. 133).

Poole, an admirer of Bakhtin, seemed shocked by his discoveries. It was not what he had been looking for when studying Bakhtin; nor, having noticed the faults, could he look away. Bakhtin's borrowings are made worse by examples where he seems to have cited Cassirer but does so in ways that conceal the extent of the borrowing. Poole does not hesitate to use the term 'plagiarism', saying that we cannot condone faults which we would censure in undergraduate work. Poole also shows generosity, acknowledging that Bakhtin did not work in conditions conducive to careful scholarship. Showing the same spirit of generosity, Poole suggests that it may be appropriate to talk of Bakhtin assimilating, rather than simply copying, Cassirer's thoughts, for Bakhtin recreated his borrowings in new contexts.

This, of course, gives a new twist to Bakhtin's remark that no meaning is completely dead, for every meaning can have its own homecoming festival. Cassirer's ideas – and with them Shaftesbury's – are given something of a festive homecoming in Bakhtin's work. The problem is that Cassirer appears only as a background figure at the festival, attending on other celebrants, unobtrusively filling their glasses. Shaftesbury was not even invited to attend his own festive homecoming. He would have known how to bear the disappointment stoically.

8

Thomas Reid: A Common Sense Psychology

A part from the connection with Bakhtin, there is another line of intellectual continuity that can be traced from Shaftesbury. This is a line that leads initially to the Scottish philosopher, Thomas Reid (1710–1796) and then from him to a number of twentieth century ideas about language. Most psychologists today will not have heard of Reid. Even many philosophers, especially those not educated in Scottish universities, will be unfamiliar with his work. It may come as a surprise that Reid's reputation once vied with that of Kant. Victor Cousin, who for a while during the first half of the nineteenth century dominated the teaching of philosophy in France, claimed that Reid and Kant were the 'two greatest thinkers about the human mind of the eighteenth century' (1864, p. 273). According to Cousin, Reid – that 'modest and hard-working pastor from a poor Scottish parish' – was the 'true Socrates' of the modern era (p. v). Reid's reputation, however, did not endure. The editors of the *Cambridge Companion to Thomas Reid* write that Reid, after 'enjoying enormous popularity in the United States, Great Britain, and France for almost one hundred years after his death', then 'disappeared from the philosophical canon' (Cuneo and van Woudenberg, 2004, p. 1). There may have been a renaissance in the past twenty years – being the subject of a *Cambridge Companion* is evidence of this. However, this is only a slight upturn in otherwise declining fortunes.

The point is not to boost the importance of Shaftesbury by showing that his thinking directly and indirectly influenced someone who was once considered the equal of Kant. The issue is simultaneously more interesting and more perplexing. In drawing a connection between Shaftesbury and Reid, a connection will be made to ideas in today's critical psychology. It will be suggested that Reid, in his analysis of the human mind, followed Shaftesbury by proposing a social perspective that was sharply distinguished from Locke's individualist perspective. Reid developed Shaftesbury's notion of 'common sense', becoming the major figure in what was known as the Scottish school of 'common sense philosophy'.

Importantly, Reid formulated two ideas that have great resonance in the so-called ordinary language philosophy of the twentieth century and also in today's critical psychology. First, Reid argued for an anti-cognitivist perspective. He rejected Locke's theory of ideas, denying that our knowledge of the world must be mediated through ideas, sensations or what today might be called 'cognitive representations'. Reid, for reasons similar to those that Wittgenstein would later give, questioned the reality of these inner entities. Second, Reid had a very different view of language to that of Locke. Reid stressed that we do things with words, using them pragmatically rather than to express inner thoughts. Again, Wittgenstein was to advance similar views.

Just as the similarities between Shaftesbury and Bakhtin raised questions of direct and hidden influences, so do the similarities between Reid and what in the twentieth century became known as Speech Act Theory. Is it just chance that Reid in the eighteenth century formulated ideas that were to emerge again in the twentieth century? Or, is there point of continuity that has become hidden, just as Cassirer's role in carrying forwards the ideas of Shaftesbury to Bakhtin became concealed? To provide some sort of answer, there need to be two lines of excavation. One starts from the eighteenth century and moves forward, tracing Shaftesbury's ideas through Reid and the Scottish school. The other begins in the present and digs backwards. The issue is whether these two lines of excavation can be joined at a single point, or whether each meets hard bedrock that continues to separate the two excavations.

The line leading from the present will trace today's versions of Reid's ideas back to Wittgenstein, Austin and Speech Act Theory – and then a little bit further back to the Cambridge philosopher G.E. Moore. It is there that this line of excavation will meet the drilling that started from the past and moved towards the present. As with the story of Bakhtin – not to mention the story of Gassendi and Locke – this tale includes accusations of plagiarism, as well as suspicions of debts being unacknowledged. It will provide a further example that the spinning of psychological ideas has not always been entirely straightforward in the modern period.

Reid's Life

Thomas Reid's life spanned the greater part of the eighteenth century. He was born in 1710 in Aberdeenshire, in the highlands of Scotland, a year before Shaftesbury's *Characteristicks* was published. He died in 1796, having lived a quiet, provincial life. Unlike Shaftesbury and Locke, Reid did not move in high political or aristocratic circles. He earned his living first as a clergyman and then as an academic. In the nineteenth century, his admirer, the Scottish philosopher Campbell

Fraser, commented that Reid's life 'cannot be expected to offer incident for the gratification of the lovers of brilliant external adventure' (1856, p. 77). Fraser, nevertheless, managed to gather sufficient material for a short biography of his hero (Fraser, 1898; for more recent, brief accounts of Reid's life, see, *inter alia*, Broadie, 2004; Wood, 2004).

Reid was brought up in a religious home in the remote parish of Strachan, west of Aberdeen. His father was a clergyman, who, according to Campbell Fraser, was well respected for his 'piety, prudence and benevolence' (1898, p. 10). Having been educated locally, Thomas went to study at Marischal College in Aberdeen. He then followed in the footsteps of this father by becoming a church minister, serving the quiet rural parish of New Machar for fourteen years. Reid was inclined to the more liberal, intellectually minded wing of Scottish Presbyterianism. His sermons were probably too dry for his parishioners, who would have preferred a somewhat livelier, hell-fire version of evangelism.

It seems that some parishioners were not taken with Reid's habit of reading his sermons. On one occasion he was accused of reading a sermon by John Tillotson, the latitudinarian English theologian, whom Shaftesbury had warmly praised in the final pages of *Characteristicks*. Reid denied that his Sunday sermon had been one of Tillotson's and was embarrassed when proof was produced (McCosh, 1875, p. 184). It is a mystery why Reid, who earned a reputation for the utmost probity, should have denied his borrowing. Unlike the world of academia, the world of Presbyterian preaching did not value originality for its own sake. There was nothing to prevent a humble country parson from reading out a whole sermon written by a great theologian. The offence lay in the denial. On that, the worlds of academia and preaching were, and still are, in agreement: repetition does not necessarily constitute plagiarism, so long as it is openly admitted. Woe to anyone attempting to pass off another's words as their own.

It seems that Reid's congregation warmed to him over time. He was a kindly careful man who took his pastoral duties seriously. In between attending to the needs of his congregation, Reid devoted his time to philosophical and scientific studies. During this period, Reid took two brief trips to England, the only times he was to leave Scotland. The second trip was undertaken with the purpose of marrying his first cousin, Elizabeth. His wife belonged to one of Scotland's foremost intellectual families. In 1751, Reid managed to obtain an academic post in King's College Aberdeen, principally on the basis of a single article that he had published. Apparently, he hesitated before accepting the post but Elizabeth insisted that the opportunity, with its intellectual, social and pecuniary advantages, was not to be missed.

Her insistence was felicitous. At Aberdeen, Reid joined a remarkable group of scholars with likeminded philosophical, scientific and theological interests. Together with George Campbell, James Beattie,

Alexander Gerard and James Dunbar, Reid was an active member of the Aberdeen Philosophical Society, which came to be known affectionately as the 'Wise Club'. The society met at an inn on the second and fourth Wednesdays of each month to present papers and to discuss intellectual topics of mutual interest. They were liberal minded, religious men – as keen to oppose the intolerance of strict Calvinism as to find ways of combining rational science with Christian faith. Reid presented early drafts of his great work *An Inquiry into the Human Mind* to the Wise Club. This was, as Reid later recalled, the happiest period of his life.

In 1764 Reid moved to Glasgow University as Professor of Moral Philosophy, succeeding Adam Smith. The new position offered better prospects in terms of status and financial remuneration. Reid spent the rest of his days in Glasgow, often overburdened by the teaching and administrative duties that he fulfilled assiduously. In those days, many Scottish professors were responsible for delivering the whole curriculum to their students, rather than just lecturing on their specialist areas. Reid was to complain that his duties at Glasgow prevented sufficient time for his own scholarly pursuits. *An Inquiry* had been first published in 1764, the year he moved to Glasgow. There was to be a further, long gap before Reid's next book was published: *Essays on the Intellectual Powers* appeared in 1785, by which time Reid was well into his seventies. This was followed by *Essays on the Active Powers of Man* in 1788. Both these later two books were based on courses of lectures that Reid had delivered at Glasgow.

Reid's later years would be overshadowed by loss. Elizabeth was to die in 1792. Only one of their nine children was to outlive their father. Compared with the life of the modern academic, with endless rounds of international travel, conferences and opportunities for self-promotion, Reid lived humbly. He was by circumstance and temperament a provincial. He was not even drawn to live in Scotland's capital Edinburgh, which in the mid-eighteenth century still retained the air of a provincial city (Buchan, 2004). Certainly, Reid had no ambitions to make a stir in the intellectual worlds of London or Paris. Nevertheless, this plain-living, quiet family man was to be a central figure in the Scottish Enlightenment, that flowering of intellectual life which, according to at least one writer, gave birth to the modern world (Herman, 2002).

Combatting Scepticism

While the young Reid was ministering to his congregation at New Machar, he could look forward to a life of pastoral work with opportunities for occasional scientific, theological or philosophical publications. But one event, more than any other, transformed him from country parson to a man with a philosophical mission. This was the publication of David Hume's *Treatise of Human Nature* in three separate volumes between 1739 and 1740. Hume completed this book before he was twenty-six. Bishop Stillingfleet might have complained that Locke's way of ideas contained the seeds of scepticism. Had he lived to read Hume, he would have felt vindicated. Hume had taken the plain historic method of Locke's *Essay* and pushed it towards sceptical conclusions. Locke, to use Shaftesbury's phrase, no longer could be seen to have struck the home blow. The honour, or shame, belonged to Hume, whose analysis of mind delighted radicals and shocked the pious. Reid and his Wise Club colleagues belonged to the latter group.

Before Hume, Bishop Berkeley had taken a decisive step in his *Treatise Concerning the Principles of Human Knowledge* (1710). Berkeley had followed the logic of Locke's method. Since all our knowledge of the world rests upon our sensations, then if there is no sensation of a thing, its existence cannot be known. Thus, the existence of all things depends on their being perceived. The argument, which seems to deny the independent existence of the material world, was saved from outright scepticism by Berkeley's premise that there was an all-seeing God, who was watching over the world. In this way, divine perception guaranteed the continual existence of the material world. Berkeley was a churchman, who had no intention of calling into question the principles of his faith. His ideas tended to be more mocked than feared. Samuel Johnson was once in conversation with a friend who defended Berkeley's view. When the gentleman bid leave to depart, Johnson said, 'Pray, sir, don't leave us; for we may perhaps forget to think of you, and then you will cease to exist' (Boswell, 1906, vol. II, p. 334).

The church establishment, especially in Scotland, could not easily laugh Hume off. He was seen as a genuine sceptic and atheist. His *Treatise* dissected – one might say psychologically de-constructed – the origins of human knowledge. If all knowledge, as Locke had stipulated, was the product of sensation and reflection, then many cherished beliefs were exposed as reflecting the nature of our minds rather than the constitution of the external world. Beliefs in causes and effects were the products of sensations being brought into regular contiguity: we cannot actually perceive anything that connects the cause to the effect. Similarly, we have no genuine identity: our sense of being an independent agent is merely the result of successive impressions in our minds. And so on. One after another cherished belief was demonstrated to be just a psychological illusion.

Most offensive to religious believers was Hume's questioning of miracles. Hume applied the principles of psychological dissection to the testimonies provided by the scriptures. Unlike Berkeley, Hume postulated no all-seeing God to rescue the slide into scepticism. The human construction of knowledge was left without a divine prop.

There was no reality beyond our fleeing perceptions. No wonder, then, that the church authorities ensured that Hume never obtained a university position in Scotland. He was not a man fit to be entrusted with the education of the young and impressionable.

Reid would recall that Hume's book had made him question his own philosophical principles. As Reid wrote in *Essays on the Intellectual Powers of Man*, as a young man he had accepted Berkeley's ideas so firmly 'as to embrace the whole of Berkeley's system' (Reid, 1785/1854, p. 82). Hume's book, however, shook Reid: this way of doing philosophy was leading to unpalatable conclusions. Dugald Stewart, Reid's pupil and follower, recounted, in a short biography of his teacher, that from then onwards Reid began to question the 'established opinions on which Mr Hume's system of scepticism was raised' (Stewart, 1822, p. 16). Reid began to search for an entirely different way to reconstruct the basis of knowledge.

The members of the Wise Club were united in their belief that Hume's views were not just intrinsically dangerous but represented the prevailing mood of the times. James Beattie wrote in 1766 to his friend Sir William Forbes that 'sceptics and their writings (which are the bane, not only of science, but also of virtue)' were, in his view, 'so much in vogue in the present day' (Forbes, 1824, p. 42). Beattie was later to write in his book *An Essay into the Nature and Immutability of Truth* that 'scepticism is now the profession of every fashionable inquirer into human nature' (Beattie, 1804, pp. 9–10). Similarly, James Oswald, another member of the Wise Club, claimed that in present times scepticism is 'in such vogue that scarce any are ashamed of it' (Oswald, 1766, p. 2). Thus, an answer to Hume was imperative to halt the general slide into scepticism.

Reid's response to Hume's work, as he wrote in his *Inquiry*, was to undertake 'a serious examination of the principles upon which this sceptical system is built' (1769, p. vii: all quotations are taken from the third, revised edition). The principles on which Hume's approach rested needed to be exposed and then critically assessed. Reid claimed to have been surprised to find that Hume's philosophy rested 'upon a hypothesis, which is very ancient indeed, and hath been generally received by philosophers, but of which I can find no solid proof' (p. vii). The hypothesis in question was that we do not actually perceive the external world, but the mind only sees images or impressions of things. Therein, he suggested, lay the root of scepticism.

When Hume first heard that a clergyman from a parish outside of Aberdeen was preparing a criticism of his *Treatise*, he feared the worst – another clod-hopping, anti-philosophical tract, defending doctrinal orthodoxy with far more moral rectitude than philosophical insight. No doubt, Hume felt he knew exactly what to expect when he further heard that the clergyman in question was going to mount his attack in the name of common sense. Hume wrote to his friend Hugh Blair, who was also a friend of Reid: 'I wish that the parsons would confine themselves to their old occupation of worrying one another, and leave philosophers to argue with temper, moderation and good manners' (quoted in Stewart, 1822, p. 17).

Through Blair, Reid sent Hume some early drafts of his *Inquiry*. Hume was clearly taken aback by the depth of Reid's thinking and the humour of his writing. Put Reid in a lecture-hall or on a pulpit and he seems to have delivered his message in a dry, uninspiring manner. Even the devoted Dugald Stewart conceded that 'in his elocution and mode of instruction, there was nothing particularly attractive' (1822, p. 23). But on paper Reid's prose sparkles with caustic wit. Hume could appreciate that something special in both content and style was coming from the far north. He wrote to Reid: 'It is certainly very rare, that a piece so deeply philosophical is written with so much spirit, and affords so much entertainment to the reader' (quoted in Stewart, 1822, p. 18). And it is certainly rare in the history of ideas that two intellectual opponents – the one seeking to undermine the very basis of the other's thought – could display such warm, mutual appreciation. The spirit of Socrates, which Shaftesbury had lauded for its playful seriousness and argumentative fellowship, was by no means defunct.

Scottish School of Common Sense Philosophy

Reid has become known as the leading figure of the Scottish school of common sense philosophy. The Scottish school sought an alternative to Locke's empiricism and Descartes's rationalism. Instead of claiming that perception or rational deduction provided the basis for knowledge, the Scottish philosophers looked to common sense. What the Scottish philosophers meant by 'common sense' was not always clear, nor did they necessarily agree among themselves. But in Reid they had an original and profound defender of the concept (Wolterstorff, 2004).

The use of the term 'common sense' suggests the influence of Shaftesbury whose impact on eighteenth century Scottish philosophy has been long recognized. James McCosh wrote in his classic history of Scottish philosophy that it was Shaftesbury 'who exercised the most influence on the earlier philosophic school of Scotland' (1875, p. 29; see Richards, 2004, for a discussion of McCosh's own influence on early American psychology). According to McCosh, Reid took the term 'common sense' from Shaftesbury (p. 203). Shaftesbury's notion of 'common sense' indicated that humans are intrinsically social creatures. If common sense is to be taken as the basis of knowledge, then this implies that our knowledge of the world is related to our nature as social beings, and not just to our individual ability to perceive the external world.

Certainly, it is not difficult to find the influence of Shaftesbury in the writings of Reid's Scottish predecessors. John Turnbull (1698–1748), who was Reid's teacher at Marischal, is a case in point. In his *Observations on Liberal Education* (1742) Turnbull quoted Shaftesbury – that 'excellent author' – on the dangers of speculative philosophy, reproducing several pages of *Characteristicks* to illustrate his theme (1742/2003, pp. 200–5). In *Principles of Moral Philosophy* (1740/2005), Turnbull discussed Hobbes's views and commented that 'my lord Shaftesbury refutes this gloomy pernicious doctrine' (p. 323). Turnbull then quoted copiously from Shaftesbury's 'Sensus communis' in support of his argument that humans have benevolent, social feelings and are not driven solely by self-interest.

Francis Hutcheson (1694–1746), who taught philosophy at the University of Glasgow before Reid and was also a Presbyterian pastor, drew upon Shaftesbury, although, as was noted in an earlier chapter, he took pains to distance himself from the Englishman's disparagement of Christianity. Hutcheson in *Essay on the Nature and Conduct of the Passions* (1728) claimed that there were four natural powers, or senses, of the mind. The first power is the perception of external objects. Hutcheson's descriptions of this power follow Locke in a fairly orthodox fashion. Hutcheson's other three natural senses are precisely those that Shaftesbury had discussed. According to Hutcheson, the human mind possesses: an aesthetic power, based on the perception of 'regular harmonious uniform objects'; a sense of public feeling or 'sensus communis'; and lastly a 'moral sense' by which 'we perceive virtue or vice in ourselves or others' (Hutcheson, 1728, p. 5; see also Carey, 2000 and 2006, for Shaftesbury's influence on Hutcheson). Hutcheson made it plain that the strength of feeling excited by the social sense exceeded that of the ordinary perception of external objects: Who would not prefer the sensations of pleasure deriving from friendship, mutual love and sociability to 'the enjoyments of the external senses?' (p. 139). He added that the matter had been fully treated by Shaftesbury in his 'Inquiry concerning virtue'.

It is not surprising that these philosophers were drawn to Shaftesbury's view of the moral and social nature of humans. A cold philosophy of self-interest was inimical to the traditions of Scottish Presbyterianism. These university philosophers wanted to imbue their pupils with a sense of social duty, and not encourage the mere pursuit of pleasure and self-interest (Sher, 1991). Respect for stoicism provided a further link with Shaftesbury. According to one historian, the stoics offered 'a morality sufficiently congenial to the Calvinist mind' (Stewart, 1991a, p. 291; see also Stewart, 1991b, for further discussion of the use of stoic philosophy in Scottish university teaching during the eighteenth century). Hutcheson, in fact, published a translation of Marcus Aurelius, although his name was not publicly associated with the book. Hutcheson's anonymous preface to his translation risked the wrath of the strict Calvinists by suggesting that non-Christians could be pious and holy (Marcus Aurelius, 1742). Temperamentally, stoicism suited Reid. He may not have praised the stoics in his philosophy, but nothing could have been more stoical than the way he bore the hardships of his later years. He never complained of his lot, beyond the occasional ironic aside. Nor did he deviate from his religious faith and his commitment to pursuing truth.

The Scottish philosophers adapted Shaftesbury, rather than slavishly following him. They avoided his suspect attitude towards Christianity and they drew back from copying his grand, rolling style of writing. They preferred a more modest, less showy mode of expression. It might be said that Locke's plain historic method was combined with Shaftesbury's social view of human nature. In many respects, Hutcheson represented a mid-point between the psychology of Locke and that of Shaftesbury (Carey, 2006). As Victor Cousin put it, Hutcheson's work represents Shaftesbury 'transported into Scotland and into a university chair' (1864, p. 25).

The university context is important. Neither Shaftesbury nor Locke held university posts. Reid's writing is far more disciplined, even disciplinary, than Shaftesbury's. His *Inquiry* looks at first sight as if it were a textbook on the various perceptual senses. There are separate chapters on the sense of smell, taste, hearing, touch and sight. It seems innocently conventional. To call it a psychology textbook would not be entirely anachronistic. Like most of the books of the Scottish school, Reid's *Inquiry*, was intended to be used as a university text. By the end of the eighteenth century, Reid's fellow Wise Club colleagues were describing their analyses of mind as 'psychology'. Alexander Gerard, the first professor of moral philosophy at Marischal College, called his lectures on the nature of the mind 'psychology' (Wood, 1991, p. 140). James Beattie's *Elements of Moral Science* (1790) was sub-titled 'a class book at Marischal's College'. The first part of this two-part work dealt with 'the philosophy of the human mind', and Beattie entitled this part of his book 'Psychology' (p. xiv). Reid, however, preferred the term 'pneumatology' to 'psychology', suggesting that pneumatology described the branch of study that 'treats of the nature and operations of minds' (Reid, 1793, p. x; see also Reid, 1788/1820, p. 432).

The psychology (or pneumatology) that Reid was presenting may have looked superficially as if it were an extension of Locke's analysis of understanding. Certainly, Reid discussed the individual senses with great insight and originality. According to Norman Daniels, Reid's analysis of the way that the light from objects strikes the curvature of the retina anticipated developments in non-Euclidean geometry (Daniels, 1989). It is not Reid the psychologist of the senses that is of interest here. As will be seen, Reid drew a sharp distinction between the individual and the social senses. In doing so, he was showing just as much brilliance as when analyzing the processes of individual perception. In that distinction, which can be traced backwards to Shaftesbury, can be found a line of argument that leads forwards to the linguistic philosophy of the twentieth century and from there towards critical psychology.

Philosophy and Common Sense

At its heart, Reid's *Inquiry into the Human Mind* sought to expose the unreasonableness of philosophical reason. The philosophers of his times, he wrote, 'have waged open war with common sense and hope to make a complete conquest of it by the subtleties of philosophy' (1769, p. 16). Philosophy had been brought into ill repute because ordinary people were finding the views of philosophers quite ludicrous. It was absurd to argue that the world only exists when we see it; that there are no real causes and effects; that we can doubt everything except our own existence; and so on. Samuel Johnson was not the only person laughing at the philosophers.

Reid does not ask: What is the logical weakness in the sceptic's reasoning? Instead he asks: Why should we choose the philosopher's way of reasoning over that of common sense? The question changes everything. It forces philosophy onto the defensive. In Reid's words, philosophy had called common sense 'to the bar' and had tried to submit ordinary knowledge to its own jurisdiction. The aim had been to find certainty, but the result was that philosophy had attracted 'the contempt and disdain of sensible men' (1769, p. 15). In this contest between common sense and philosophy, it is the latter that 'will always come off both with dishonour and loss' (p. 15). So the relations between philosophy and common sense needed to be reversed. Philosophy had to justify itself in terms of common sense, rather than vice versa.

It has been pointed out that Reid was following Shaftesbury's maxim of using ridicule as a test of truth (Kuehn, 1987, pp. 30f). Certainly Reid mocked the pretensions of philosophy. Philosophers were showing what he called 'metaphysical lunacy' (1769, p. 379). An ordinary person who doubted their own existence would be considered mad. Yet, Descartes, who doubted everything, clearly was not mad. This is because it was evident that he was in control of his senses and 'never seriously doubted of his existence' (p. 11). The problem was not that philosophers had approached their tasks with insufficient intelligence. Quite the reverse: it is 'genius, and not the want of it, that adulterates philosophy, and fills it with error and false theory' (p. 9). In short, the philosophers were too clever by half. It was time to bring them down to earth and show them a bit of common sense.

By contrasting the ridiculous lunacies of philosophy with common sense, Reid was using 'common sense' as a synonym for plain, good sense. He specifically asserted that the common sense of mankind was marked by 'good sense' (p. 378). Had he left the matter there, his writings would not be worthy of close attention: they would constitute yet another bashing of intellectuals in the name of sound sense. But Reid was doing more. He was analyzing the nature of common sense and relating it to a vision of human nature. Reid's notion of 'common sense' implied that good sense is a shared, social sense. Reid was arguing, like Shaftesbury before him, for the priority of social sense over individual sense.

Reid considered the case of Hume. When on his own, Hume seemed to be attacked by bouts of metaphysical lunacy and scepticism. The mood would pass as soon as he spent time in the company of others: 'Society, like daylight, dispelled the darkness and fogs of scepticism and made him yield to the dominion of common sense' (1769, p. 18). Even so, Hume could not really have been a thorough-going sceptic even in the isolation of his study. Had he been, he would not have bothered to have written for the benefit of others. Instead he would have doubted the existence of his potential readers – and certainly doubted that it was worthwhile addressing these phantoms. Thus, Reid states that Hume's *Treatise* contains 'manifest indications that the author every now and then relapsed into the faith of the vulgar, and could hardly, for half a dozen pages, keep up the sceptical character' (pp. 18–9).

There was, according to Reid, a general rule. Metaphysical lunacy is 'apt to seize the patient in solitary and speculative moments'; but as soon as the patient enters into society, 'common sense recovers her authority' (1769, p. 379). Social life depends on shared common sense. Philosophers may have their moods of doubt and scepticism, but even during these times they are sharing some of the assumptions of common sense. It is quite absurd to suppose that our sense of knowledge must be based on these moods – as if any belief must be rejected if it cannot pass the unreasonably high standards of proof that we demand when we sit gloomily on our own.

The similarity between Reid's arguments and those of Wittgenstein in his later work has been noted by some modern day scholars of Reid's work (e.g., Gallie, 1989; Michaud, 1989; Wolterstorff, 2001). Wittgenstein, like Reid, imagined that he was curing philosophy of a malady. In *On Certainty*, Wittgenstein argued that it was impossible to doubt everything. In order to doubt, one has to be sure of the meaning of the word 'doubt'. In this respect, doubting presupposes certainty: and if one tried to doubt everything, one 'would not get as far as doubting anything' (Wittgenstein, 1975, p. 125). Or, as Wittgenstein said in *Zettel,* 'a person can doubt only if he has learnt certain things' (1981, remark number 410).

Reid's point was that philosophizing cannot be spun out of a single mind, as Locke had supposed. The philosopher lives a life in the social world and philosophical activity is part of that life. One cannot meaningfully wish away that life, in order to pretend to start with the activity of doubt – or, indeed, to start with a blank mind and only accept empirically grounded truths. Wittgenstein was to say much the same: 'I want to say: it is characteristic of our language that the foundation on which it grows consists in steady ways of living, regular ways of acting' (Wittgenstein, 1993, p. 397). Philosophy cannot exempt itself from this: 'Isn't the real point this: we can't start with *philosophical speculation*?' (p. 399, emphasis in original).

So where do we start? Reid had no doubt. We must start with ordinary life. And this means we start with common sense, not with philosophy. Reid declared with uncharacteristic drama: 'I despise philosophy, and renounce its guidance: let my soul dwell with common sense' (1769, p. 14).

Rejecting the Way of Ideas

The big metaphysical lunacy that Reid addressed was not Descartes's method of doubting. It was Locke's way of ideas. This lay at the root of Hume's scepticism. If the way of ideas could be excised, then a moment of madness would pass, and philosophy might be reunited with common sense. As will be seen, Reid's attempt to reject the doctrine of ideas would be repeated by Wittgenstein and J.L. Austin in the twentieth century. And it resembles critical psychology's rejection of cognitivism. Shaftesbury may have criticized Locke's study of ideas for its triviality, but Reid was not driven by impatience with empirical investigations of the mind. Quite the contrary, as he stated at the start of *Inquiry*, the mind must be studied by means of 'observation and experiment' (p. 3). Like later anti-cognitivists, he was to claim that careful observation and experiment failed to reveal the existence of ideas or other ghostly mental substances.

According to Reid, the way of ideas inevitably leads to scepticism. Locke had assumed that we receive ideas or impressions of the world. Our knowledge of external reality is built out of these ideas or impressions. Since ideas constitute the contents of our mind, then we can only know our ideas of things, not the things themselves. Our ideas, thus, come between us and the world. The implication, which Hume emphasized, is that our supposed knowledge of things is just a series of associated ideas. Even my conception of my self is just another idea. As Reid wrote, if I take this line, 'I see myself, and the whole frame of nature, shrink into fleeting ideas, which like Epicurus's atoms, dance in emptiness' (1769, p. 22).

It sounds reasonable to assume that our minds contain impressions of things, rather than the things themselves. The assumption is to be found in today's cognitive science. It is assumed that the brain stores representations of objects, which have impinged upon our senses; and we build our knowledge of the world from these representations. Reid asked what the evidence was for the existence of such ideas or impressions; or for what today might be called cognitions or representations. He raised the question in his *Inquiry* and took up the theme in his *Essays on the Intellectual Powers*.

According to Reid, philosophers had assumed that images of the world are formed in the brain and that the mind, being seated in the brain, then perceives these images. But there is no proof of this. The brain has been dissected many times and its parts held up to microscopes, but 'no vestige of an image of any external object' was ever found. In fact, the brain seems to be 'the most improper substance that can be imagined for receiving or retaining images, being a soft moist medullary substance' (1785/1854, p. 50). Nor did Reid hesitate to ridicule David Hartley's attempt to supply Locke's theory of ideas with a physiological model, based on supposed neurological vibrations. Reid pointed out that the existence of such vibrations was never proved and Hartley was reduced to 'heaping supposition upon supposition, conjecture upon conjecture, to give some credibility to his hypothesis' (Reid, 1785/1854, p. 45).

Reid criticized the language of those who supported the way of ideas. In the *Inquiry*, Reid wrote that he could understand what is meant by an impression of a figure on wax, or upon a physical body, 'but an impression of it upon the mind is to me quite unintelligible' (p. 164). He doubted whether it was meaningful to talk of 'ideas' as the objects of perception, for we do not see ideas – we see things. In the *Intellectual Powers*, Reid wrote that the mind having impressions of objects is 'either a phrase without any distinct meaning, and contrary to the propriety of the English language, or it is grounded on a hypothesis which is destitute of proof' (1785/1854, p. 48). Reid did not just direct this argument against the concepts of 'ideas' and 'impressions' as used by Locke, Berkeley and Hume. He said that the same objection could be raised against the 'shadows' of Plato, the 'species' of Aristotle and the 'films' of Epicurus (1785/1854, p. 137). Moving forward, Reid's argument can be applied equally to the 'cognitions' and 'representations' of cognitive science. And many of today's cognitive models are just as hypothetical as were Hartley's descriptions of the vibrations and vibratiuncles that supposedly carried ideas around the nervous system.

Reid was aware that he was criticizing a well-entrenched philosophical tradition. But, all the concepts of ideas, impressions, shadows, and so on are deficient in two essential ways: 'We neither have any evidence for their existence, nor, if they did exist, can it be shown how they would produce perception' (1785/1854, p. 137). If no-one has ever successfully demonstrated the existence of ideas, then it is better to stop talking about ideas in this way. We risk stretching ordinary language beyond the point of meaningfulness if we insist on claiming that we can only know our ideas or impressions. We should talk about seeing objects themselves, not having ideas or impressions of objects.

Again and again, Reid charges philosophers, such as Locke, Berkeley and Hume, with misusing ordinary language – and thereby undermining common sense. The philosophers and their admirers claim that the discovery of ideas is the great discovery of modern philosophy. Yet, there is a paradox, suggests Reid. What has been 'universally esteemed as a great discovery' rests 'on nothing else but an abuse of words' (1769, p. 139). Philosophers may claim that ordinary language needs to be reformed because it fails to use words as philosophers believe they should be used. However, Reid is on the side of ordinary language: 'The vulgar have undoubted right to give names to things which they are justly conversant about'. On the other hand, the philosophers abuse language 'when they change the meaning of a common word, without giving warning' (1769, p. 141).

Many of Reid's arguments about 'ideas' presage both the tone and the content of J.L. Austin's *Sense and Sensibilia* (see de Barry, 2002, for a discussion of these similarities). Like Reid, Austin was arguing against the philosophical doctrine that people only have access to their 'ideas' or 'sense-data' about the world – rather than sensing the world directly. Austin traced this doctrine back to Locke and Berkeley. Austin argued, just as Reid had done, that the doctrine flew in the face of the experiences of ordinary people, who claim that they really do see objects. Austin criticized philosophers for taking a superior stance, implying that 'the plain man is really a bit naïve' (1964, p. 9). Like Reid before him, Austin was presenting himself as the defender of ordinary people: their so-called naivety is, in fact, more sensible than the speculations of philosophy. Austin also blamed philosophers for abusing ordinary language. Philosophers, Austin wrote disparagingly, 'often seem to think that they can just "assign" any meaning whatever to any word' (p. 62).

When Austin's *Sense and Sensibilia* was first published in 1962, the ordinary language movement in philosophy was at its height. The ordinary language philosophers were accusing philosophers and psychologists of abusing ordinary language when they talked about psychological matters. Gilbert Ryle's *Concept of Mind* claimed philosophers and psychologists with making category mistakes by talking about minds, ideas, impressions as if they were physical objects. Above all, Wittgenstein in *Philosophical Investigations* suggested that philosophers should pay attention to the ordinary usage of words, especially 'psychological' words such as 'see', 'think', 'believe' and so on. These words do not denote inner ideas, as philosophers and psychologists often suppose. Philosophers, Wittgenstein argued, only muddle matters when they try to use such words in special senses.

Again, the side of ordinary language – or common sense – was being taken.

What may be surprising is that Thomas Reid had advanced similar arguments almost two hundred years earlier. There is no mention of Reid in Austin's *Sense and Sensibilia*, in Wittgenstein's *Philosophical Investigations* or in Ryle's *Concept of Mind*. It was as if these twentieth century writers, when defending ordinary language accounts, were spinning out ideas afresh from their own minds. A philosophical tradition seemed to have been forgotten.

Common Sense

Central to Reid's defence of ordinary language and his attack on the theory of ideas was the notion of 'common sense'. It was also central to his social approach towards understanding the nature of human thinking. The term 'common sense' became emblematic of Scottish philosophy. Fellow Wise Club colleagues, James Beattie and James Oswald, wrote popular works challenging scepticism and defending religious faith in the name of common sense. Their uses of the concept were derived from Reid's but tended to lack his philosophical subtlety.

Having criticized philosophers for using ordinary language in extraordinary ways, Reid did not want to use 'common sense' in a new, technical sense. Like Shaftesbury he used the term in two ordinary ways. First, his contrast between philosophy and common sense indicated that 'common sense' was the plain, unsophisticated understanding of ordinary people. Second, the defence of the ordinary person's understanding indicated that 'common sense' was good sense. Indeed, these two ordinary meanings were in harmony: it could be said that to follow common sense (ordinary sense) was common sense (good sense). And this could be taken as a credo of common sense philosophy.

However, the elaboration of common sense philosophy required a bit more than the disparagement of philosophy for its failure to show good sense. As will be seen, in defending common sense, Reid introduced a third and crucial meaning of the term. He did not extend the term 'common sense', as Shaftesbury had done, to indicate a sense of community. Nevertheless, Reid used the notion of common sense to indicate why we have social natures. His psychology, like that of Shaftesbury, went beyond the individual, cognitive psychology of Locke.

In the *Inquiry*, Reid approached the notion of common sense indirectly. He analyzed the senses individually and argued that existing accounts were unsatisfactory because they failed to appreciate the interconnections between perception and judgement. Reid did not elaborate in *Inquiry* why this implied that humans by nature possess a 'common sense'. However, in *Essays on the Intellectual Powers* Reid devoted the second chapter of the sixth essay to 'common sense'. Here he makes clear why he believed that his critique of Locke's theory of perception entailed recognizing that the possession of common sense was integral to the human condition.

Reid starts the chapter by comparing ordinary and philosophical notions of 'sense'. He suggests that modern philosophers from Descartes onwards have been using 'sense' in a very particular way. They have used 'sense' to describe how we supposedly receive ideas or impressions of the world. Reid points out these philosophers are suggesting that the processes of sensing are separate from those of judgement. Locke argued that we sense simple ideas; and having received these impressions, we then reflect upon them. Thus, modern philosophers 'consider sense as a power that has nothing to do with judgement' (Reid, 1785/1854, p. 266). Interestingly, Reid, in this passage, attributes to Hutcheson (but not to Shaftesbury) the notion that we have a sense of harmony, a sense of beauty and a moral sense. Reid argues that the concept of a moral or aesthetic sense also rests on the assumption that sensing is independent of judgement. Hutcheson had assumed that we apprehend directly and without reflection harmony, beauty and morality.

Reid points out that the philosophers' use of 'sense' conflicts with ordinary use of the word. In ordinary talk, 'sense' almost always implies judgement. To call someone a person of sense is to say that they possess good judgement, not that they possess perceptual faculties. Good sense means good judgement: it does not mean above average perceptual acuity. Thus, in 'common language', Reid noted, sense 'always implies judgement' (1785/1854, p. 267). He goes on to say that we call seeing and hearing 'senses', not because we have ideas by them, as philosophers imply, but 'because we judge by them' (p. 267).

In the *Inquiry*, Reid had argued this point in detail, criticizing Locke's account of the senses. Reid's arguments are sophisticated. Locke had said that we make judgements on the basis of perceptions. For instance, we judge that there exists a world beyond our perceptions. To do this, we must reflect on the perceptions that we have received from our senses. According to Reid, this was nonsense. There never is a moment when we just passively receive sensory information, which we then later reflect upon.

Reid began with an analysis of the powers of smell. He argued that the smell of a rose is different from the memory of the smell of a rose. We do not first sense the smell and then reflect on the smell in order to judge whether it is a memory or a present sensation. We know automatically how to distinguish present sensation from the memory of a sensation. We can do this because the present sensation of a rose involves more than a 'pure' sensation of smell: it is experienced as the sensation of an object, which is presumed to exist beyond the body. Reid writes: 'By the original constitution of our nature, we are both led to believe that there is a permanent cause of the sensation, and prompted to seek after it' (1769, p. 59). We sense a smell and, because of our innate constitution, we suppose that an object is causing this smell. There is, thus, a 'principle of human nature' predisposing us to think in terms of causes and effects (p. 54). This is why perception, contrary to the views of Locke and others, is intrinsically an active, not passive, process (pp. 60ff).

Something similar occurs with the visual sense. We have difficulty in attending to the mere visible figure of a body. We see more than the visual surface of an object. We see the object as an object: 'Nature intended the visible figure as a sign of the tangible figure and situation of bodies'. This occurs naturally 'by a kind of instinct', for, 'it is as unnatural to the mind to stop at the visible figure, and attend to it, as it is to a spherical body to stop upon an inclined plane' (pp. 165–6). Having considered the senses in turn, Reid concludes that sensory experience involves judgement – and, in particular, the judgement of the existence of physical objects including one's own body.

In the final chapter of *Inquiry*, Reid writes: 'Every operation of the senses, in its very nature, implies judgement or belief, as well as simple apprehension' (p. 377). If I feel gout in my toe, I not only have the sensation of pain, but a belief that this pain is occasioned by my toe. This belief does not arise by comparing ideas, as Locke had assumed, but is integral to the very nature of sensation. Similarly, I see a tree and 'my faculty of seeing gives me not only a simple notion or simple apprehension of the tree, but a belief of its existence' (p. 378). This is a basic property of sensation and such judgements are, concludes Reid, 'a part of that furniture which nature has given to the human understanding' (p. 378).

In this, Reid was opposing the atomism of Locke's approach. Like Shaftesbury, Reid was proposing a view that was more akin to what would be the theories of the Gestaltists. Reid, however, was arguing for this position in a much more systematic and detailed way than Shaftesbury ever did. The position also agrees with work of contemporary cognitive scientists, such as Zenon Pylyshyn (2001 and 2004), who claim that our ability to perceive objects *qua* objects is automatic. Kant would also argue something similar. This is one reason why Victor Cousin bracketed Reid with Kant.

On its own, Reid's argument about perception does not necessarily imply anything about common sense. Reid, however, took the extra step in his *Essays on the Intellectual Powers*. If sensation involves judgement, then one can ask whether there are some judgements that all humans make. Does the furniture of our minds predispose us to judge the world in a particular manner? If so, all humans would share a common judgement – they would possess a common sense. This common sense would be the source of judgements which all reasonable people would find self-evident. This is not the common sense of a particular community – a common sense, which another community might find absurd. This is a common sense that unites humans (with the exception of lunatics and modern philosophers in their gloomiest, most isolated moments).

Reid suggests there are a number of judgements, which we universally make and consider to be self-evident: that objects exist in the world; that other people exist; that I exist and have powers of action; that there are causes and effects. Such judgements are made automatically: they do not have to be inferred from simple sensations. When philosophers question such things, they are not displaying superior wisdom, but metaphysical lunacy – or, they are engaging in a game, rather than really believing in what they are doing. To question these self-evident beliefs would be to fly in the face of our natural constitution and to contradict our common sense. It is unnatural to ask us for logical proof or empirical evidence that the world exists. When philosophers seek to prove such things, they are engaging in a very silly task.

In arguing thus, Reid's three meanings of 'common sense' come together. Ordinary people do not doubt the existence of the world. Our common, self-evident sense of the world provides us with the basis of ordinary sense. Moreover, when it comes to matters of philosophy, this ordinary sense is 'good sense'. It is certainly bad sense to deny this 'good sense'. Thus, Reid's argument for common sense is rooted in a theory of sensation. But, at this point in the argument, the transition from individual psychology to social psychology has not yet been made. The arguments about perception, pain, smell, etc. do not, by themselves, say why humans need to share their common sense and why this common sense is, as Shaftesbury insisted, a social sense.

Some Murky Business

Before discussing Reid's theory of the social aspects of the mind, there is some murky business to attend to. Reid may have taken the general notion of common sense from Shaftesbury, via the Scottish philosophers James Turnbull and Francis Hutcheson. However, he gave the concept a special interpretation by using it to denote self-evident principles that were common to all humans. One can ask whether Reid derived this notion of common sense from any previous thinker, or whether it was his own invention. And here, we enter very unpleasant territory. A charge of plagiarism was made against Reid in the eighteenth century. It was said that Reid had pilfered his notion of common sense from Claude Buffier, an obscure French Jesuit, whose philosophical works appeared almost fifty years before Reid's *Inquiry*.

Father Buffier (1661–1737) wrote on a wide variety of topics, publishing works on geography, grammar and exercises for improving the memory. His interests also included the philosophy of mind. He sought to reconcile the rationalism of Descartes with the empiricism of Locke; and to reconcile both those thinkers with the demands of faith. Buffier's *Traité des premières vérités* was first published in 1717. In it Buffier argued that Descartes and Locke had been mistaken in searching for the basis of knowledge either in logically indubitable propositions or in the certainties of sense perception. Instead, Buffier sought to outline the 'first truths' or 'principles of common sense' on which knowledge rests and which are common to all humans (1717/1846, pp. 33ff).

These common principles included a general trust in the senses and in the existence of the world. Buffier argued that the senses generally report faithfully what appears to them. Almost always the senses conform to 'the truth in things which it is important for men to know'; and that it is easy to discern when the witness of our senses can be doubted (pp. 55ff). Buffier concluded his *Éléments de Metaphysique* (1724/1846) with the claim that only people who have lost their reason would doubt first truths, such as the existence of the world or the existence of other minds. Since nature makes us in this way, 'let us not believe that to be a philosopher it is necessary to renounce common sense; rather let us make common sense the foundation of all our philosophy' (1724/1846, p. 308). The similarity with Reid is hard to overlook.

In 1780, fifteen years after the first edition of Reid's *Inquiry*, an English translation of Buffier's *Traité* was published. It contained an anonymous preface that claimed, on the title page, to be a 'detection of the plagiarism, concealment and ingratitude of the Doctors Reid, Beattie and Oswald'. The charge was ugly and the language was even uglier, as the anonymous writer mixed personal slur with anti-Scottish bigotry. The preface alleged that it was a national characteristic of the Scottish to steal their ideas from others: 'Whatever is to be found of genuine merit, real learning and superior intellect, in their literary manufactures, is generally purloined and unacknowledged' (1780, p. xv).

How to deal with the charge of plagiarism and intellectual dishonesty? Reid's supporters have tended to downplay the charges. McCosh (1875) suggested that Reid may have taken from Buffier without due acknowledgement, but Buffier almost certainly took from Shaftesbury, whose essay 'Sensus Communis' was translated into French a year before the first English edition of *Characteristicks*. But that is merely to answer one charge with an unverifiable counter-charge. Marcil-Lacoste (1982), in an extensive discussion of the issue, has defended Reid. She suggests that Reid's use of the term 'common sense' differs in detail from Buffier's and that when Reid wrote *Inquiry*, he probably had not heard of Buffier.

Nevertheless, there are sufficient broad similarities between Reid and Buffier that render a detailed analysis of their respective uses of 'common sense' somewhat beside the point. Had Buffier been born a generation later, lived in Aberdeen and been a Presbyterian rather than a Jesuit, he would certainly have been classed as a Scottish common sense philosopher. After all, neither Beattie nor Oswald used the term 'common sense' in quite the same ways as Reid. Francisque Bouillier, Buffier's nineteenth century editor, wrote that Buffier was Reid's precursor, because at start of the eighteenth century Buffier played 'precisely the same role in philosophy that Reid played at the end of the century' (1846, p. xlvi). Even Bouillier, who was keen to rescue Buffier's philosophical reputation from obscurity, acknowledged that Reid possessed the wider philosophical range and the greater depth of analysis (pp. xxxv and xlv).

It is not difficult to offer a defence of Reid. There is no evidence that he had read Buffier's *Traité des premières vérités* when he was writing his *Inquiry*. Had there been such evidence, then any failure to cite Buffier's earlier use of 'common sense' would indeed constitute academic malpractice. Nine years after the first edition of *Inquiry*, Reid clearly had read Buffier's *Traité*. He cited it in a piece about Aristotle that he wrote for Lord Kames's *Sketches of the History of Man*, which was published in 1774. Reid commented that 'I have *lately* met with a very sensible and judicious treatise, written by father Buffier about fifty years ago' (emphasis added). Reid praised Buffier generously, commenting that Buffier's ideas about first principles heralded, after the eras of rationalism and empiricism, 'a third grand era in the progress of human reason' (Kames, 1774, p. 240; Reid, 1774/1822, p. 127). Reid wrote these comments before he was accused of perjury.

Reid also praised Buffier in *Essays on the Intellectual Powers*, which appeared after the accusation. There, Reid summarized Buffier's ideas on common sense and first principles (1785/1854, pp. 331ff). Reid commented that there was more originality in Buffier's book than in 'most books of the metaphysical kind' (p. 332). In a roundabout way, Reid alluded to the charge of plagiarism. He mentioned that Oswald, Beattie and Campbell 'have been led into a way of thinking somewhat similar to that of Buffier', but that Oswald and Beattie developed their ideas without knowledge of Buffier (p. 332). Campbell's *Philosophy of Rhetoric*, which was published after Reid's essay on Aristotle, contained references to Buffier (Campbell, 1776/1856, pp. 60f). Reid declared that all three writers 'have my high esteem and affection' (p. 333). Oswald and Beattie (and also, by implication, Reid himself) were able to come to their conclusions independently of Buffier because anyone acquainted with Hume's work would realize that human knowledge must rest on 'other principles' than those of Locke and Descartes. Nevertheless, priority has to be given to Buffier who 'must be acknowledged to have the merit of having discovered this, before the consequences of the Cartesian system were so fully displayed as they have been by Mr Hume' (p. 332).

So, it looks quite straightforward. Reid and his colleagues in the Wise Club worked out their ideas on common sense in innocent ignorance of Buffier. When Reid came upon Buffier's work – probably some time in the early 1770s – he made amends by publicly acknowledging Buffier's priority and praising his originality. There seems no reason to suspect any scholarly misconduct. And yet, something does not fit. Reid said that Oswald had written his book on common sense without knowledge of Buffier. However, in his *An Appeal to Common Sense*, Oswald included a lengthy quotation from Buffier's discussion of Locke (Oswald, 1766, pp. 67ff; the quotation is not a verbatim translation but is taken, with omissions and additions, from Buffier, 1724/1846, pp. 225f). The quotation includes reference to 'the faculty of apprehending simple truths that are the objects of common sense' (Buffier, 1724/1846, p. 227), as well as Buffier's criticism of Locke's failure to account for the first principles of knowledge.

So, it appears that Reid's colleague Oswald had read Buffier before 1766. Why should Reid have been convinced that Oswald had not known of Buffier's work, especially when the evidence of Oswald's book makes it so plain that he had? If Oswald had known of Buffier's ideas on common sense, would he not have mentioned it to Reid? The two men were colleagues and friends who shared their ideas and manuscripts regularly, at least before Reid left Aberdeen in 1764. In any case, Reid would have had an opportunity after the publication of Oswald's *Appeal* to make corrections to his own *Inquiry*, when the third, and corrected, edition appeared in 1769. Reid added no correction to remedy the lack of reference to Buffier. By his own admission he seems to have delayed reading Buffier for several years.

Perhaps there is a parallel between Reid's treatment of Buffier and Locke's treatment of that earlier French, Catholic thinker, Pierre Gassendi. As was discussed previously, there is *prima facie* evidence that Locke avoided reading Gassendi's metaphysical works. This is not plagiarism but a form of academic avoidance or scholarly amnesia: a scholar avoids reading the work of another scholar who seems to have produced similar ideas. Reid had taken years to write the *Inquiry*. He must have been in the final stages when Oswald read Buffier's *Traité*. We can only speculate. Perhaps Oswald had mentioned Buffier at a Wise Club meeting. If so, Reid, normally so sharp and intellectually inquisitive, may have temporarily suffered from a scholarly deafness. Certainly Reid did not seem in a hurry to chase up Buffier's work.

One can imagine Reid's dread of discovering that his labours had been in vain. During the long years of writing, he might have privately imagined that he was inaugurating the new age of reasoning – although he was far too modest ever to make such a claim publicly. Having finally read Buffier, Reid knew that the honour must be given to the obscure Jesuit priest. It is to Reid's great credit that he said so publicly.

The later charge of plagiarism must have upset this pious, upright man, as he had been disturbed by a similar accusation about his sermons many years earlier at New Machar. What, if anything, is the significance of this? If Reid, who was a genuine scholar of great personal virtue, could be accused of plagiarism, then this is not so much a reflection on his character. It hints at something much more important – the social condition of the scholar in the modern world of discoveries.

Social Operations of the Mind

If Claude Buffier deserves credit for formulating the concept of 'common sense' in the way that it was to be used by the Scottish philosophers, then why is this chapter not devoted to him? Surely Buffier, rather than Reid, should be acknowledged as one of the hidden originators of critical psychology. To a limited extent, that is true. As Reid himself recognized, Buffier does deserve more recognition. But it would be hard to draw a simple line from Buffier to present-day ideas in critical psychology. Any line would still have to come through Reid and from Shaftesbury. It was Reid, not Buffier, who took the concept of 'common sense' out of individual psychology and explicitly into a social understanding of the mind. In so doing, Reid produced ideas that anticipated twentieth century Speech Act Theory. Buffier's understanding of 'common sense' did not possess these crucial extra dimensions.

Reid, especially in his later essays, stressed that humans were social beings by their nature. In this, he was following Shaftesbury and the English latitudinarians such as Whichcote and Butler, as well as the Scottish philosophers such as Turnbull and Hutcheson. He was even following Adam Smith, whose first book *The Theory of Moral Sentiments* (1759/1976) was based on the idea that humans have basic social feelings of sympathy for each other (see Force, 2003, for an argument that Adam Smith, far from being an individualist, was in the tradition of stoic philosophers). Reid's philosophical position fitted his moral and political views. He took the Presbyterian teachings of social duty seriously and was a firm supporter of liberal humanitarian causes, such as the abolition of slavery and penal reform (Broadie, 2004).

Reid was unambiguous in emphasizing the social aspects of the mind. In the *Essays on the Active Powers*, Reid wrote that humans were 'made for living in society'; our social affections demonstrate our social nature, 'as evidently as that the eye was made for seeing' (1788/1820, p. 439). This involves a very different image of human nature than that found in Locke or Descartes. As Nicholas Wolterstorff has commented, Locke and Descartes depicted 'a solitary individual sitting mute and immobile in a chair, receiving perceptual inputs and reflecting on his own inner life'. By contrast Reid was creating 'an image of the person as a "social being"' (2001, p. 165; see also Haakonssen, 1996).

Not all the principles of common sense reflected the social nature of humans. Animals with perceptual systems need to take the existence of the world for granted – in fact, they do not possess the linguistic facilities for doubting its existence. However, there are certain principles of common sense that are integral to the social character of humans. In a remarkable chapter in the *Essays on the Active Powers*, Reid distinguishes between 'solitary' and 'social' operations of the mind (1788/1820, pp. 432f). Solitary acts are those that can be performed by any person 'in solitude, without intercourse with any other intelligent being' (p. 432). These acts include judging, sensing, hearing, etc. In short, they are the sorts of mental activities explored by Locke and followers such as Condillac and Hartley. Buffier had these activities in mind when he was examining common sense.

Reid argued that such solitary acts are very different from social acts, such as promising, commanding, asking questions and so on. These actions require another person. Reid notes 'a remarkable distinction' between solitary and social operations of the mind. Solitary operations do not require the use of words, whereas social ones do. Of course, people can use words when they see or hear things, but the use of words is 'accidental' to the mental operation: seeing and hearing can take place without the use of words. On the other hand, the social operations cannot be performed without words: 'they cannot exist without being expressed by words or signs, and known to the other party' (p. 433). Thus, it is not possible to make a promise, ask a question and so on, without the use of language. The action in question is performed through language.

Having distinguished between social and solitary operations of the mind, Reid then goes on to make a key theoretical and methodological point: the social operations of the mind cannot be understood in terms of individual ones. He writes that it is common for philosophers to assume that the social operations of the mind are not intrinsically different from the solitary ones and that they are 'only various modifications or compositions of our solitary ones and may be resolved into them' (1788/1820, pp. 433–4). Because previous analysts assumed that the social operations are modifications or compositions of our solitary operations, they concentrated on the solitary operations to the neglect of the social operations.

Reid was, above all, thinking of Locke and his followers, who broke down mental 'operations' into basic units of perception, believing that complex operations are compositions of these basic units. By contrast, Reid was opposing this cognitive atomism. The social operations of the mind could not be reduced into individual cognitive operations. If analysts attempt this, they will miss the irreducibly social nature of human beings. Here was a clear statement that the issues of social psychology cannot be reduced to those of individual psychology.

Since the social operations of the mind depended on language, there was a further implication: human psychology cannot be equated with the psychology of animals that lack language. Thus, the psychology of humans cannot be based on perceptual processing or any other cognitive operation that is common to animals. Something more is required to understand the social mind – the mind of common sense.

As Reid made plain, the most important element in the social operations of the mind is language. Already in *Inquiry*, Reid had argued that the capacity for language separated humans from beasts. Some animals can communicate by means of 'natural' signs. A dog or a horse can recognize when a human voice 'caresses, or when it threatens him', but no animal can have the 'notion of contracts or covenants, or of moral obligation to perform them' (1769, p. 73). Reid repeated the point in *Essays on the Active Powers*. To possess a language, it is necessary to make agreements – namely, that particular sounds should be used in particular ways. Animals, unlike humans, lack the capacity for making such agreements or contracts – these are 'the prerogative of man' and, therefore, so is the ability to create languages (1788/1820, p. 438).

Reid saw the ability to make a promise or contract as being central to the possibility of social life. Social relations would fall apart, unless humans can make agreements. There could be no trade, no social commitments, and no social institutions. All these depend upon shared agreements, as did the possibility of language. In part, Reid was reacting against the view of Hobbes and Locke that society was founded on a social contract, which overcame the pernicious selfishness of the 'state of nature'. Like Shaftesbury, Reid denied that human nature was rampantly individualist. Individuals would not be able to come together to make a social compact, unless they had the ability (and language) to make a contract. The ability to promise, to make pledges, keep contracts and so, must be part of the so-called state of nature. In short, these abilities must be part of human nature.

Principles of Credulity and Veracity

Some of the self-evident principles of common sense, which Reid outlined, relate directly to the social operations of the mind. In particular, Reid identified two such principles: the principle of credulity and the principle of veracity. Reid noted that we do not tend to derive our opinions from individual reasoning, as Locke had tended to assume. Instead most people are influenced by the views of others: 'Their manners, their opinions, their virtues and their vices, are all got by habit, imitation and instruction'. And, he observes tartly, 'reason has little or no share in forming them' (1769, p. 354). We do not arrive at our understanding of the world by judging and assessing individually received sensations: we absorb the common sense of those around us.

This is not a fault in human nature but it is a requirement for a language using creature. We would not be able to imitate others if we were not predisposed to trust them. Therefore, Reid proposed that humans possess a principle of credulity, which is 'implanted in us by the Supreme Being'; this principle is a disposition 'to confide in the veracity of others, and to believe what they tell us' (1769, p. 338). Credulity is, above all, 'unlimited' in children (p. 338). It must be so, given that infants are helpless at birth and have to learn how to speak and act in the social world. They must accept and imitate others before they can learn to challenge and criticize. We could not learn language without this propensity to accept and imitate. When the infant is told the meanings of words, the infant accepts these without distrust. It is only when the infant has become the mature adult that it can set 'bounds to that authority to which (it) was at first entirely subject' (p. 340).

There is a second related principle: this is the principle of veracity which is a 'propensity to speak truth and to use the signs of language, so as to convey our real sentiments' (1769, p. 338). Reid is not so naïve as to suggest that lying is impossible. It is relatively rare, when compared with truth telling. Even the greatest liars, he writes, follow this principle, for 'where they lie once, they speak the truth a hundred times' (p. 336). In general, truth 'is always uppermost, and is the natural issue of the mind' (p. 336). Moreover, this propensity to truth requires no special art or training: it is a 'natural impulse'. Speaking the truth is unlike lying, which does violence 'to our nature' and 'is never practised, even by the worst men, without some temptation' (pp. 336–7). Lying, thus, is only possible against a background of general truthfulness.

These two principles – credulity and veracity – are counterparts to Reid's arguments about general scepticism flying in the face of common sense. Doubting is only possible because we accept some things as certain. We could not accept things for certain if, in most regards, our fellows were not to be trusted. And we could not trust them if they did not predominantly tell the truth. Lying and distrust are only possible because, like doubting, they rest upon their opposites. Accordingly, social life and the practice of language depend upon principles of trust and truth. These principles are not taught to children as the basic principles of learning: they cannot be, for the activity of learning depends upon their intuitive acceptance. Of course, when the child encounters or engages in lying, then the principles will need to be taught explicitly as moral principles. In this way, morality is built into the practices of social life. We could not be social creatures if we were not moral beings. Shaftesbury may have oversimplified the issue by suggesting that we are born with a moral sense. But he was correct in supposing that social life, including the practices of language, requires a sense of morality.

Reid was outlining the psychological preconditions for social life. Interestingly, his principles of veracity and credulity parallel what the philosopher Paul Grice (1975) has termed the 'maxims' of conversation. These are maxims that need to be assumed if conversations are to proceed successfully. We must, for example, assume that the other person is attempting to speak meaningfully. Grice's maxims have been enormously influential in modern linguistics (Kempson, 2003). They include 'the maxim of quality' – namely, the requirement to speak the truth. Recipients of speech should presume that the speaker is following the maxim: in other words, they should presume the speaker's veracity.

Like Reid, Grice is not saying that all speakers follow all the maxims all the time: that would be palpably implausible. However, these maxims constitute the general conditions for conversation. Unless listeners generally assume that speakers are telling the truth, and unless speakers generally assume that listeners are making this assumption, conversations could not get underway. Nor could we cope with those situations in which doubts about truth must be handled. As Wittgenstein – and Reid before him – suggested, we are only able to have doubts within a wider context of trust.

Reid drew broader psychological implications from his principles. Veracity and credulity are inbuilt into our social nature. We could not have a social nature without such principles, for they are the conditions for language and thereby for social life. In arguing thus, Reid was doing more than elaborating the benevolent view of human nature that latitudinarian Protestants shared and that Shaftesbury had argued for. Reid was also developing ideas that come close to those that were apparently re-invented anew by linguistic philosophers in the twentieth century.

Speech Act Theory: Continuities and Rupture

Reid's view on language was very different from Locke's. As was discussed in chapter three, Locke saw language as being rooted in individual cognition. His view was based on the assumption of 'telementation': namely, that the function of language was to transmit ideas, or cognitions, from one person to another. To do this satisfactorily, the categories of language should match the categories of individual cognition. Reid, by contrast, had a pragmatic view of language. He dismissed the concept of inner ideas or cognitions. Language belonged to the social operations of the mind. Socially, we do things with language, such as asking questions, making promises and so on. There was much more to language than merely trying to transmit the inner processes of mind.

In rejecting Locke's cognitive view of language, Reid proposed a social perspective that, it has been claimed, constituted the first proper Speech Act Theory of language (Schumann and Smith, 1990; see also Coady, 1989, 2004; Smith, 1990). The parallels between Reid and twentieth century philosophers such as Austin are intriguing. Not only did Reid defend ordinary sense (and, thus, ordinary language), not only did he question the sense data theory of perception (or 'the way of ideas'), but he also outlined a theory of language that stressed the social actions that language performs. Reid was aware that he was opposing the dominant trends in Western philosophy, just as Austin and Wittgenstein would see themselves doing.

Shortly after the publication of the *Inquiry,* Reid wrote a critical analysis of Aristotle's logic. In a very brief chapter, entitled 'On the Structure of Speech', Reid outlined a pragmatic view of language. He commended Aristotle for distinguishing between those propositions, which can be said to be true or false, and other kinds of speech that are neither true nor false – such as prayers and wishes. Reid said we should also include under the latter category many other forms of speech such as questions, commands, promises, contracts and so on. Aristotle had dismissed these verbal forms as philosophically unimportant, concentrating his attention on propositions that could be true or false. Later philosophers had followed Aristotle, so that the other kinds of speech 'have remained banished from the regions of philosophy to this day' (1774/1822, p. 92). This was, in Reid's view, a profound mistake. These other forms of speech were important, especially for the conduct of social life. It would be useful to analyze them and also 'the operations of the mind which they express' (p. 92).

In essence, this is the position that would be taken by Speech Act Theory which is associated with twentieth century philosophers such as Austin, Wittgenstein and Searle. It is also the position taken by discursive psychologists who have adapted Speech Act Theory into an empirical project for critical psychology. Speech Act Theory asserts that we accomplish social actions with speech, rather than use speech purely to express inner ideas or assert true (or false) propositions. Wittgenstein declared that 'words are deeds' (Wittgenstein, 1992, p. 46). Pointedly, his *Philosophical Investigations* starts by comparing Augustine's view that language comprises words that name things, with an imaginary, simple language used by builders where each word ('block', 'pillar', slab') seems to name an object. When the words are used, however, they are not employed to name objects, but to perform actions. One builder calls out 'slab' and the other brings an object. The meaning of 'slab' is not merely the name of an object but the performance of an action with an object. Wittgenstein's general point was that philosophers get into muddles when they fail to understand how language is ordinarily used.

The general point was to be developed by Austin, particularly in his book *How to do Things with Words* (1962) and in several influential essays published in his posthumous *Philosophical Papers* (Austin, 1979). In these works, Austin discusses the various ways that speaking performs actions. Austin discussed promising. To say 'I promise X' is not to give a report on my mental state, but it is to perform the social action of promising. In this regard, the utterance constitutes the action: it is an 'illocutionary act'. John Searle (1969), in further developing these ideas, stressed how the utterance of a promise counts as a social obligation that is made in the knowledge that the hearer of the utterance will recognize this obligation.

Reid's analysis of promising may have lacked the details given by Austin and Searle, but he was essentially proposing a very similar perspective. Like the Speech Act theorists, Reid was saying that we should pay close attention to the social uses of language. In addition, he brought together two other themes: an anti-cognitivism and a defence of ordinary language (common sense). Speech Act theorists denied that our use of 'psychological' verbs, such as 'know', 'hope', 'see', 'feel', are necessarily reports of inner cognitive states. When we say that we 'see' something, we are not describing inner 'ideas', 'sense data', cognitions, etc. as philosophers have claimed. According to Austin, when I say 'I know something', I am not reporting that 'I have performed a specially striking feat of cognition, superior in the same scale as believing and being sure' (1979, p. 99). Instead, I am telling someone else that they can trust my knowledge on the matter. Ordinary language, he asserted, is so much more reliable than the artificial language used by philosophers.

The basic position of Speech Act Theory was taken up by conversation analysts over thirty years ago and more recently by discursive psychologists. They have retained Speech Act Theory's anti-cognitivism and performative view of language. However, the conversation analysts and discursive psychologists have criticized philosophers such as Austin and Searle for basing their analyses on hypothetical examples, rather than studying everyday interaction as it actually occurs (see, for instance, Hutchby and Wooffitt, 1998; Schegloff, 1996; Wooffitt, 2005). The American sociologist Harvey Sacks, who is often credited with founding Conversation Analysis, claimed that Austin and others really had not studied carefully what speakers are doing with their utterances. Sacks used recorded extracts of actual conversational interactions to show, for example, that speakers use the phrase 'I promise' in subtler ways than suggested by Austin's hypothetical examples (Sacks, 1995, pp. 737f). As Schegloff (1985) noted, 'I promise' is often used in actual conversations, not to perform a promise in the way that Austin or Searle imagined, but to effect a 'unit closure' or to make future arrangements. These sorts of analyses do not undermine Austin's basic point – that utterances are performative – but they provide evidence of the interactional complexity and flexibility of these performances.

Similar points are made by discursive psychologists (for detailed discussions of discursive psychology, see Antaki, 1994; Edwards, 1997; Edwards and Potter, 1993; Harré and Gillett, 1994; Potter, 2006; Potter and Wetherell, 1987; Speer, 2005). According to discursive psychologists, cognitive psychologists have typically looked in the wrong places for the subject matter of psychology. They have sought to study unobservable mental processes, such as cognitions, mental representations, cognitive schemata and so on, treating these as if they were actual existing entities. Instead of considering 'attitudes', 'beliefs', 'feelings', as if they were actual entities, psychologists should be examining what people are doing when they talk about 'attitudes', 'beliefs', 'feelings', etc. This has involved transforming the questions of psychology. Discursive psychologists do not ask, for instance, what constitutes genuine remembering and where memories are stored in the cognitive apparatus; instead, they ask how people make claims to remember and what they are doing when making such claims. The study of 'psychological terminology' in everyday interaction has, in consequence, been a central feature of discursive psychology. In pursuing these matters, discursive psychologists have retained a strong anti-cognitivist position (Antaki, 2006; Billig, 2006; Edwards, 2006; Potter, 2006; te Molder and Potter, 2005).

Again, the theoretical background is not much different from Reid, although the detail of the investigation is. It is not difficult to read backwards (and unhistorically) the spirit of discursive psychology into some of Reid's writings. In the first chapter of *Essays on the Intellectual Powers*, Reid stressed that we should interpret statements using words such as 'conceiving', 'imagining' and 'apprehending' in terms of their social meaning, rather than seeing them as reports of 'ideas'. There may be considerations of 'politeness and good breeding' which lead us to express ourselves with modesty. Instead of expressing an opinion directly, we might say '"I conceive it to be thus, I imagine or apprehend it to be thus"; which is understood as a modest declaration of our judgement' (1785/1854, p. 6).

To use the vocabulary of modern linguists, Reid was noting how indirect speech acts can be used to perform politeness (Brown and Levinson, 1989). In these situations, the recipients of the sort of statements mentioned by Reid do not understand 'I conceive' as the report of an inner cognitive process. It is understood as a way of being polite or, to use Reid's words, not conveying 'the air of dogmaticalness' (1785/1854, p. 6).

Discursive psychologists might not approve of the hypothetical examples that Reid used to illustrate his point. They would prefer that the meaning of any statement should be understood in terms of the sequence of interaction in which it was uttered. Nevertheless, they would be able to see Reid's comments as prefiguring the sort of analysis that has been developed from Speech Act Theory. Certainly, Reid expressed his sympathy in *Inquiry* with understanding the workings of the human mind through close observation. Regarding the social operations of the mind, that would entail the close observation of social acts.

Although an intellectual connection can be made between Reid and Shaftesbury, it would stretch the principle of credulity to claim Shaftesbury as an ancestor of close-detailed, interactional analysis. Methodologically, Conversation Analysis has atomist tendencies. It breaks down sequences of talk to see how specific rhetorical devices operate. Its subject matter can get very detailed and conversation analysts do not then put the details back together into a grand, moral narrative. In *Characteristicks*, Shaftesbury mocked those gentlemen scholars whose enthusiasms turn them into minute examiners of insects or 'the conveniences, habitations and economy of shellfish' (p. 405). A world of professional specialists, who have become expert examiners of micro-pauses and inhalations of breath during conversations, would have been beyond his imagining. One might imagine his scorn. What matters it to me whether I pause here or there? Or whether I said 'um' or 'er'? Does all this minute examining lead me to speak with better manners, more refinement and greater truth?

G.E. Moore and the Forgetting of Reid

Discursive psychologists and conversation analysts rarely, if ever, trace the origins of their perspective beyond Wittgenstein and Austin. They certainly do not go back to Reid. As was discussed in chapter two, the standard accounts, which may be found at the start of research reports of discursive psychology or even in more reflective reviews, tend to be 'shallow' histories. The basic narrative line is simple. The theory of language as interactional action is traced to the philosophy of Wittgenstein and Austin. But philosophy, on its own, does not lead to empirical investigation. The methodological inspiration comes from Sacks who in the 1960s began examining recorded conversations. And the rest is history – or rather it is present discovery. These 'shallow' histories provide no context to show why various themes should have come together in Speech Act Theory. Austin's *How to Do Things with Words* is regularly cited – his *Sense and Sensibilia* rarely so. So, if one was excavating backwards through these conventional histories, the drill would hit bedrock fairly near the surface – in late 1940s to be more precise.

These informal histories imply that Austin and Wittgenstein spun their ideas from their own minds, as they battled against the whole Western tradition of thinking about language and the mind. But, of course, the whole tradition was not against them. Reid had fought similar battles before; and, in so doing, he had been accused of copying an even earlier Jesuit priest. The question is not whether Reid or Buffier influenced these later theorists. There is no reason to think that conversation analysts have generally studied either thinker. The question is about social amnesia, rather than simple influence. One might ask whether the range of similarities between Reid and Speech Act Theory are purely coincidental, or whether there was a moment when a line of continuity might have been maintained, but through an act of academic amnesia it was forgotten? Just as it was possible to identify Cassirer as a forgotten point of continuity between Shaftesbury and Bakhtin, so it is possible to point to G.E. Moore as someone who might have maintained continuity but neglected to do so.

G.E. Moore (1873–1958) was recognized in his lifetime to be one of the most influential figures in British philosophy. Today it is not easy to understand why he was held in such veneration. His writing, to be frank, is stodgy, lacking the wit of Bertrand Russell or the intensity of Wittgenstein. Few but a handful of specialists would now relish reading Moore's *Principia Ethica* from cover to cover. Even the specialists might concede that 'relish' is a bit strong. Nevertheless, it has been claimed that Moore did more than any other single figure to establish the analytic tradition of philosophizing 'which is dominant within the English-speaking world' (Baldwin, 1993, p. vi).

Certainly Austin was a great admirer of Moore. He is reputed to have claimed that Moore influenced him more than any other philosopher. Moore's influence in Austin's work is not difficult to detect. Moore sought to analyze carefully the meaning of philosophical words, pointing out how philosophers were often departing from the ordinary use of language. Although Austin did not always go along with Moore's analyses of meaning, he clearly recognized the importance of what Moore was doing (Austin, 1979, pp. 204ff).

Moore reacted against the idealist movement that dominated late nineteenth century philosophy in Britain. It is easy to see similarities between Moore and Reid. Both saw themselves as battling against predominant philosophical trends that encouraged the belief we can only truly know non-material aspects of the world – namely our ideas of things. In his essay 'The Refutation of Idealism' Moore aimed to refute Berkeley's principle that for any object to exist it must be seen. He claimed that any philosophy which accepted this principle was at variance with the ordinary, common sense view of the world (Moore, 1903/1993). In essence, Moore was following Reid in seeking to refute the way of ideas.

In a late essay, 'In defence of common sense', Moore summarized his basic philosophical position. He explicitly defended the principles of common sense. Like Reid – and also like Buffier – he outlined several basic common sense propositions that he claimed could not be denied sensibly. His list of truisms echoes those that Reid (and Buffier) proposed: that the self exists; that other selves exist and have existed; that I have had many experiences; that the world continues to exist and so on. These were common sense beliefs that were true and that it would be the 'height of absurdity' to deny (Moore, 1959, p. 45). Moore described his philosophical position as that of common sense: 'I am one of those philosophers who have held that the "Common Sense view of the world" is, in certain fundamental features, *wholly* true' (p. 44, emphasis in original). He did not name those other philosophers who had also held this Common Sense view.

Several scholars of Reid's work have commented on the similarities between Moore and Reid and on the fact that Moore rarely quoted Reid by name (e.g., Holt, 1989; Lehrer, 1991; Redekop, 2004). Moore did not cite Reid in either 'Defence of common sense' or 'Refutation of Idealism'. In the latter work, he made the extraordinary claim that, in disputing Berkeley's doctrine, he was investigating a matter 'upon which not Idealists only, but all philosophers and psychologists also, have been in error' (1903/1993, p. 22). In this way, Moore presented himself as the lone battler against an error (namely, that we can only know ideas) that had captured the minds of all other philosophers.

Possibly when Moore wrote his 'Refutation of Idealism' he had not yet read Reid. It is said that after Moore left Cambridge in the early years of the twentieth century he went to live in Edinburgh. There he studied the works of Scottish philosophers including Reid, before returning to Cambridge (Baldwin, 1993). Why he should have to leave Cambridge to study Reid tells us something about the provincialism of the English university. Anyway, two years after 'Refutation of Idealism', Moore was citing Reid. In his essay 'The Nature and Reality of Objects of Perception', Moore criticized Reid because his use of the term 'perception' did not always accord with the common sense view (1905–6/1922, p. 57). Moore's references to Reid tend to be critical. He did not hail Reid as a pioneering forerunner in the battle to defend common sense against the absurdities of philosophy.

The important point is not a moral one. It is not being suggested that Moore directly plagiarized Reid and then sought to hide the fact: there is absolutely no evidence of that. Nor is the important point to suggest that Moore should have cited Reid more frequently and more graciously, although it would be hard to dispute such a judgement. There are two issues, neither of which is directly a moral issue: the first point is about lines of continuity and the second about the conditions of academic practice that encourage amnesia.

The point about continuity can be put simply. Supporters of Speech Act Theory do not generally position their ideas in a line of continuity with Reid. It has taken scholarly excavation to show this continuity (see particularly the work of Schumann and Smith, 1990; Smith, 1990). Moore is pivotal in the story both for what he did and for what he could have done. Had he explicitly linked himself to a tradition of thinking, which went back to Reid, then there would have been little need for the later excavations. Because of Moore's eminence in British philosophy, Reid might then have been incorporated into the standard, shallow self-histories of Speech Act Theory. A generous acknowledgement from Moore would have been likely to have been adopted by Austin. And then the later empirical researchers might have incorporated two more names – Moore and Reid – into their histories, giving them greater depth.

But it did not happen. The Scottish philosopher remained beyond the Cambridge group. The lines of continuity seemed to peter out. In this way, Moore was able to present himself, just as Locke had done, as spinning his ideas from his own mind. The first person singular appears often in Moore's essays. It is not a boastful 'I'. Colleagues and admirers praised Moore's character. One wrote that Moore was dedicated to the pursuit of truth and was a man 'of simple tastes and character, absolutely devoid of all affectation, pose and flummery' (Broad, 1959, p. 12). Similar things were said about Reid. And even about Locke.

Yet, each in their own way seems to have been reluctant to acknowledge forerunners. Reid may have put off reading Buffier, although, having finally done so, he was generous in his acknowledgements. Locke seems to have avoided Gassendi's philosophical works and never acknowledged their similarities with his own ideas. Such similarities were apparent to others. Reid wrote that he did not doubt that Locke's *Essay* 'was mostly spun out of his own thoughts', but 'in many of the notions which we are wont to ascribe to him, others were before him' (1785/1854, p. 328). Reid claimed that it was Gassendi 'from whom Locke borrowed more than from any other author' (p. 10). And then Moore, many years later, seems to have been reluctant to see the similarities between his work and that of Reid.

In each case, there are signs of avoidance. If there is deceit, it is primarily self-deceit, not an intention to deceive the reader. Discipline is needed to keep scholars sitting at their desks. To justify the hours of largely unrewarded self-sacrifice, thinkers such as Locke and Reid must believe in the importance of their mission. In their imaginations, they were venturing where none had gone before. Had Locke thought that his mission was merely to bring Gassendi to the attention of an English audience – or Reid believed that he was doing the same for

Buffier – they would have produced far less. The paradox is that their great works of scholarship required a productive touch of unscholarly amnesia. This is not a defect of character. It is a condition of work. They were labouring in an age which was beginning to mythologize original genius and to encourage lone scholars to imagine that they were autochthonously creating their own ideas.

Concluding Remarks: Psychology in the Age of Discoveries

• • • • • • • • • • • • • • • • •

The basic argument has been a simple one: some of the ideas in today's critical psychology have a longer history than is often supposed. They can be traced back to the early modern period, and, from there, some can be traced even further back to classical stoic philosophy. Neither are the ideas of mainstream cognitive psychology recent creations. They too have historical links with early modernity. John Locke has been justifiably heralded as the father of cognitive psychology. He might have claimed to have invented his own ideas – to have spun them out of his own mind, but a longer lineage can be claimed: through Gassendi and then back to the Epicureans, the historic adversaries of the stoics. In this way, today's arguments between critical and cognitive psychologists have a history. They can be seen to echo arguments in the early modern period; and those arguments echoed even earlier arguments in the classical world.

But what, one might ask, is the implication of tracing this long genealogy? The most obvious implication is that the standard histories of psychology, which typically omit Shaftesbury and skate over Reid, need to be revised. With the development of critical psychology, it was inevitable that there would have to be a re-writing of the histories. Critical psychology proposes different ways of doing psychology and different ways of understanding the nature of thinking. Its ideas have different historical roots than those of mainstream psychology. Locke might justifiably be seen as the parent of cognitive science. But he cannot be the parent of the anti-cognitivism espoused by critical theorists. His foster-son, however, is a forgotten ancestor.

Therefore, Shaftesbury and Reid deserve a more central place in the histories of psychology. However, the development of critical psychology requires more than a revision of psychology's history. It demands a revision of psychology's relation to history. As was seen, Locke claimed that his method of analyzing the mind was 'historic'. In practice this meant excluding history from the study of the mind. Locke considered each mind to be empty at birth and he wished to examine how it became filled with complex ideas during the course of a life. In doing this, he was not concerned with the history of the ideas beyond the individual mind. It was no wonder that Shaftesbury criticized Locke for lacking any deep historical consciousness even of his own ideas. That is why Shaftesbury insisted on seeing his teacher, not as a modern thinker breaking with the past, but as an heir to the Epicureans.

In general terms, Locke's unhistorical method has been adopted by modern cognitive scientists. Their remit is to examine how the individual mind/brain processes information. In doing this, the mind/brain is considered as a self-contained entity, extracted from wider social and historical processes. This extraction is disputed by critical psychologists, who argue that the mental phenomena studied by psychologists belong to historical and social contexts. This means bringing social and historical inquiry back into psychology. The individual mind/brain does not invent its own language, social rituals and structures of interaction. It always exists within, and is determined by, patterns of social life that have their own history. Thus, the study of history is not merely an account of the past, for the processes of social life inevitably bring the past into the present. That is why critical psychology demands a historical consciousness.

It also demands that we be self-reflexive. The self-reflexivity of humans was something that Shaftesbury stressed. Humans do not merely receive sensations from the world and process them cognitively. Unlike other species, we can stand back from the observed world in order to examine ourselves critically. Shaftesbury drew on the teachings of the stoics to argue that reflexive, self-examination was the ultimate task of philosophy. Today, critical psychologists have suggested that psychology needs to be self-reflexive, examining its own ideas critically. The demand for self-reflexivity can be combined with the demand for historical understanding. Together, they suggest that we should enquire about the historical roots of the ideas that we use. That applies to critical psychologists just as much as it does to mainstream psychologists.

Part of this self-reflexive awareness requires tracing lines of historical continuity. Sometimes it is suggested that self-reflexivity belongs to the present age, because we live in peculiarly self-reflexive times. We are constantly questioning ourselves; our governments fund research to examine self-reflexively the effects of their policies; the practices of self-monitoring are very much part of today's world. Anthony Giddens has argued this point. He suggests that one of the distinguishing characteristics of late modernity, separating it from earlier periods, is its 'intrinsic reflexivity' (1991, p. 19). It may be the case that self-reflexivity strongly characterizes today's social practices and ways of thinking. But that does not mean that reflexivity was invented in modern times.

With regard to psychological ideas, we should be cautious against assuming that self-reflexivity is entirely novel. Shaftesbury was very much a self-reflexive thinker and writer. He played with ironic self-criticism in ways that seem in tune with today's post-modern experiments in writing. In Shaftesbury's case, this self-reflexivity was very much connected with his dialogical understanding of the mind, which he traced back to stoic philosophy. To think was to debate with oneself. Self-reflexivity, therefore, arises out of the demand to be self-questioning. This dialogical understanding of the mind seems surprisingly familiar. Again, there are lines of continuity linking central themes in critical psychology to the early period of modernity and then backwards to classical philosophy.

So the present study emphasizes critical psychology's own historical links with ideas that have been excluded from mainstream psychology's history. To date, critical psychologists have tended to accept somewhat shallow histories of their own ideas. Even so, they might not welcome the present suggestions for deepening these histories. Understandably, many would prefer more marginal, downtrodden ancestors than a third Earl, or even a Scottish pastor such as Reid. But, through Shaftesbury, critical genealogists might excavate further to find a link with the great stoic philosopher, Epictetus. A slave, who suffered permanent injury from the beatings of his master, is a more romantic ancestor than an English aristocrat. However, not all the stoics were so low-born. Shaftesbury's other great stoic inspiration, Marcus Aurelius, multi-tasked philosophizing with his day-time job of Roman Emperor.

There is a serious point. Historical consciousness is not a form of consumer choice. We should not imagine ourselves free to wander along the stores of the past, selecting from the shelves any ancestor who will enhance our appearance. More rigour and less self-regard are required. If we only choose the intellectual ancestors who fit the image that we wish to maintain of ourselves, then we run the risk of failing to understand the nature of our ideas. We might wish to convince ourselves that our views are more novel than they are. The result would be a compromised historical consciousness that only offered a partial insight into the ideological origins of our theories.

Accordingly, the present argument offers a cautionary tale for critical psychologists. Do not imagine, so the story warns, that your ideas stand outside the history of the modern era. It is too simple to assert that the age of modernism was the age of individualism and, therefore, any anti-individualist psychology must represent a radical rejection of the modern world. This is why the stories of Shaftesbury and Reid are so important. They tell us that the early modern period was already reacting against the philosophy and psychology of individualism.

The depiction of Shaftesbury as a pre-post-modern figure also disturbs the idea of a simple sequence in the history of ideas. It might be supposed that first there was modern psychology, with its belief in scientific progress and its emphasis on the individual. And then, after modern psychology had failed to deliver on its promises, there was a reaction. So, now we have post-modern psychology, superseding modern psychology and questioning its assumptions. But the example of Shaftesbury illustrates just how many supposedly post-modern psychological ideas can be found in the early days of the modern age. Bakhtin's key themes – the importance of dialogue, heteroglossia and ridicule – are prefigured in Shaftesbury. The reaction against modernity did not have to wait until the modern age was firmly established. It was present right from the start. In this regard, there is justice in Bruno Latour's claim that we were never properly modern (Latour, 1993).

The early modern period was an age of discoveries. Certainly, Locke and his fellow members of the Royal Society thought so. Old prejudices were being thrown aside. The empirical methods of science were revealing how the universe operated. Alexander Pope expressed this sense of discovery in the famous couplet which he hoped would be inscribed as Newton's epitaph in Westminster Abbey:

Nature and nature's laws lay hid in night.
God said, *Let Newton be!* and all was light. (Pope, 2006, p. 242)

However, discoveries do not just happen, as if the miracle of Newton creates light out of darkness; and suddenly astonished onlookers can see what had been hidden. In the arguments between Locke and his critics, we not only see debates about human nature, but also see controversies about what constitutes a psychological discovery.

An age of discoveries requires an ideology of discovery. It has to discover, as it were, what it means by a 'discovery'. The growth of science came with disputes about what constitutes a proper discovery. It is no coincidence that the stories told here involve accusations of unoriginality and even plagiarism. The controversies, which can quickly become personal and vindictive, highlight the issue of discovery in relation to psychology. Locke's dogged critic, Edward Stillingfleet, disputed whether Locke was entitled to claim his 'way of ideas' as a discovery. According to Stillingfleet, other thinkers had previously entertained the same thoughts. Certainly Gassendi, a generation earlier, had proposed similar psychological views to Locke, including a rejection of innate ideas. Locke countered Stillingfleet's accusation by offering a psychological interpretation of discovery. If you formulate ideas yourself, you have discovered them, regardless of what anyone else had previously done. Needless to say, Stillingfleet was not impressed.

The very fact that this debate was possible illustrates that the ideology of discovery was not yet fixed. Today, a scientist, facing a similar charge of unoriginality, is unlikely to use Locke's defence. It would be hardly convincing to say 'I am original because I worked these ideas out for myself; it doesn't matter whether anyone else had previously published these ideas, I am still original'. Failure to know the published work of others is not now a persuasive excuse. A discovery must be historically new, not just psychologically so. It must also be justifiable. Reid disputed whether the great discovery of modern philosophy – the discovery of ideas – was, in fact, a genuine discovery, because he questioned the existence of these internal, psychological entities. You cannot *discover* something that does not exist. It is like claiming to have discovered the North-West passage or the formula for turning tin into gold.

A sympathizer, but not an adversary, might say that this was Reid's great discovery. He saw that Locke's way of arguing conflicted with common sense and he identified the root of the problem. It was Locke's error, shared by Berkeley and Hume, to believe that we do not see things directly but that we experience the world through ideas, cognitions, mental representations or whatever. If this was Reid's discovery, then, just like Locke, he faced the charge of plagiarism and unoriginality. His Gassendi was Claude Buffier. Reid and other Scottish common sense philosophers were accused of stealing from Buffier without acknowledging the Frenchman's priority.

And so it continues. What seems original can be found to have precedents. The Speech Act Theory of ordinary language philosophers can be traced to Reid, even if the lines of continuity have become overgrown through lack of maintenance. Ordinary language philosophers did not acknowledge Reid as their predecessor, and Buffier certainly lay hid in darkness. There was a collective forgetting of the past. A comparable forgetting has accompanied the remarkable rise of Bakhtin to prominence in the last twenty years. He appears, rather like Wittgenstein, as a self-created genius, an autochthonous figure, who disrupts patterns of intellectual continuity. In Bakhtin's case, there is evidence of more than scholarly amnesia. Bakhtin may have actively concealed his direct debts to Cassirer, and thereby his indirect debts to Shaftesbury.

The accusations of plagiarism and unacknowledged borrowing may not be edifying but they signify something important. An age of discoveries values intellectual originality. This unites today's academic world with the early modern period. The cult of originality persists. In today's social sciences there is a multiplicity of new theories, frameworks, approaches, each jostling for attention and each advertising its own originality. 'Breakthroughs' are regularly proclaimed; funding agencies back 'leading-edge' research. There is, of course, rivalry. One scholar's self-proclaimed 'cutting edge' discovery is a competitor's unoriginal repetition of earlier work. Nowadays, the language is typically more restrained than that employed by Reid's anonymous accuser. But the conditions for discovery and denial are similar.

Shaftesbury, however, positioned himself outside the culture of discovery. He did not belong to the circles around the Royal Society. And he never attended university. Moreover, he questioned the very concept of discoveries. In the early letter which he wrote to Locke about his philosophical studies, he wrote disparagingly about the followers of Descartes and Hobbes who announced their 'discoveries' to the world. There were few worthwhile discoveries to be made about human nature. Indeed, a so-called discovery could be 'worse than nothing', if it resulted in a deterioration of our thoughts or actions (Beer, 1979, p. 153).

Shaftesbury's view on discoveries indicated a very different perspective than that of Locke or even Reid. It is no coincidence that of the three major figures discussed in this work, Shaftesbury is the one against whom no major charges of plagiarism were levelled. Unlike Locke, Shaftesbury was not claiming to be spinning out his ideas from his own mind. He did not imagine himself to be breaking with past ways of thinking. Quite the contrary, he sought to justify his ideas by claiming the authority of the past. Shaftesbury argued, as Reid was to do, that common sense was superior to the speculations of modern philosophy. His concept of common sense included the notion that humans are born with a sense of community. Shaftesbury did not claim this to be a new, exciting, cutting-edge breakthrough in the psychology of common sense. Nor did he cite new discoveries to back up his claim. Instead, he justified his theoretical move by citing the authority of Juvenal, who, Shaftesbury suggested, had used the phrase *sensus communis* in a similar manner.

There could be no accusation that Shaftesbury was plagiarizing Juvenal, since he was openly citing him. Nor could Shaftesbury be charged with claiming an unwarranted originality, for he was not putting forward his interpretation of Juvenal as if it were new: in fact, he cited classical scholars in his support. If a charge is to be made, it would have to be a very different one – indeed, the reverse of plagiarism. Shaftesbury might to be accused of putting forward new ideas under the guise of an ancient ancestry. The critic might argue that Shaftesbury had not spun his ideas out of the ancient texts, but was passing off his own discoveries as if they had a venerable history.

In today's academic world, that would seem a curious accusation. But that is the point. The contemporary climate encourages a shallow historical perspective. Discoveries and breakthroughs can be the more easily proclaimed if academics are not looking for deeper continuities with the past. In this regard, the conditions of academic life match wider conditions of life. As Richard Sennett (1999) has argued, today's way of life magnifies a sense of the present, creating insecurities and corroding character. This is one more reason why a critical perspective needs historical awareness.

Shaftesbury imagined a glorious past in the ancient Athens of Socrates, using this image to criticize the triviality and selfishness of his own times. The idea of a past golden age lends itself most naturally to conservatism. If only we could turn the clock backwards and return to past times, the conservative sighs. However, in an era in which the present is obliterating a sense of the past, a fantasy of past possibilities need not be the sole property of the conservative. In the twentieth century, Walter Benjamin realized this. He suggested that reclaiming the past – taking it seriously – could be an act of radical critique against the present. It would rub against the grain of a present that is simultaneously disavowing the past and abandoning dreams for the future (Benjamin, 1973). Certainly, Shaftesbury, for all the parallels with the themes of post-modern psychology, still rubs against the grain of the present.

There are good theoretical reasons for remembering the writings of Shaftesbury – and those of Reid. The demand for a historical and self-reflexive consciousness means that we must resist becoming pre-occupied only with present times and with the recent past. But, beyond the issues of theory and critique, there is a simpler message. The story of Shaftesbury and his relations with his foster-father Locke reaches out across time. Philosophy is mixed with the complex psychology of love, sensitivity and human fallibility. This would not be possible were the people of the past completely distant from ourselves. There is a continuity of humanity. Like all good stories, this one does not contain a single or a simple moral. Beyond the demands of theory, the tale deserves to be retold for its own sake. Were this story ever to become completely forgotten, then something irreplaceable would have been lost.

Chronological Table

Ancient World

469–399 BCE	Life of Socrates
429–347	Life of Plato
341–271	Life of Epicurus, founder of Epicurean school of philosophy
55–135 CE	Approximate dates of life of Epictetus, great stoic philosopher
161	Marcus Aurelius, stoic philosopher, becomes Emperor of Rome
180	Death of Marcus Aurelius

Early Modern Period

1588	Birth of Thomas Hobbes
1592	Birth of Pierre Gassendi
1632	Birth of John Locke
1642	English Civil War begins
1649	Execution of Charles I; start of Commonwealth and rule of Cromwell
1651	Thomas Hobbes's *Leviathan* published
1655	Posthumous publication of Gassendi's *Syntagma Philosophicum*
1660	Collapse of Commonwealth and Charles II restored as king; foundation of Royal Society
1666	Locke meets Ashley Cooper, later first Earl of Shaftesbury
1671	Birth of third Earl of Shaftesbury
1683	Locke flees to Holland
1687	Publication of Newton's *Principia*
1688	Glorious Revolution: James II deposed
1689	Locke returns to England; William III and Mary II appointed joint monarchs

1690	Publication of Locke's *Essay Concerning Human Understanding*, *Two Treatises of Government*, and *Letter Concerning Toleration*
1696	Start of Locke's controversy with Stillingfleet, Bishop of Worcester
1699	Unofficial publication of Shaftesbury's *An Inquiry Concerning Virtue*
1702	Death of William III, accession of Queen Anne
1704	Death of John Locke
1705	Publication of Damaris Masham's *Occasional Thoughts in Reference to a Virtuous or Christian Life*
1710	Birth of Thomas Reid
1711	First edition of Shaftesbury's *Characteristicks*; Shaftesbury moves to Naples
1713	Death of Shaftesbury
1717	Publication of Claude Buffier's *Traité des premières vérités*
1737	Reid ordained minister at New Machar, Aberdeenshire
1739–1740	Hume's *Treatise on Human Nature* published
1745	Publication of Dennis Diderot's *Principes de la philosophie morale*, a loose translation of Shaftesbury's *Inquiry*
1746	Publication of Condillac's *Essai sur l'origine des connaissances humaines*
1751	Reid appointed at King's College Aberdeen
1764	Reid succeeds Adam Smith as Professor of Moral Philosophy at Glasgow University; publication of Reid's *Inquiry into the Human Mind*
1780	Anonymous English translation of Buffier's *Traité*, accusing Reid of plagiarism
1785	Publication of Reid's *Essays on the Intellectual Powers of Man*
1788	Publication of Reid's *Essays on the Active Powers of Man*
1789	French Revolution
1796	Death of Thomas Reid

Modern Period

1889	Birth of Ludwig Wittgenstein in Vienna
1895	Birth of Mikhail Bakhtin in Orel, Russia
1903	G.E. Moore publishes 'Refutation of idealism'
1911	Wittgenstein comes to Cambridge
1917	Russian Revolution
1924	Stalin takes power in Soviet Union

1929   Bakhtin exiled to Kazakhstan for six years
1932   Original publication of Cassirer's *Platonic Renaissance in England*
1933   Nazis take power in Germany; Cassirer flees
1940   Bakhtin submits his dissertation on Rabelais, but it is not published until 1965
1951   Death of Wittgenstein
1953   First edition of Wittgenstein's *Philosophical Investigations*
1962   Posthumous publication of J.L. Austin's *Sense and Sensibilia*, based on lectures delivered in 1947
1975   Death of Bakhtin; publication in Moscow of work which would be translated in English as *The Dialogic Imagination*

References

Aarsleff, H. (1994). Locke's influence. In V. Chappell (ed.), *Cambridge Companion to Locke*. Cambridge: Cambridge University Press.

Adorno, T.W., Frenkel-Brunswik, E., Levinson, D.J. and Sanford, R.N. (1950). *The Authoritarian Personality*. New York: Harper.

Altemeyer, B. (1981). *Right-Wing Authoritarianism*. Winnipeg: University of Manitoba Press.

Altemeyer, B. (1988). *Enemies of Freedom: Understanding Right-Wing Authoritarianism*. San Francisco: Jossey Bass.

Altmann, A. (1973). *Moses Mendelssohn: A Biographical Study*. Philadelphia: Jewish Publication Society of America.

Anderson, B. (1983). *Imagined Communities*. London: Verso.

Antaki, C. (1994). *Explaining and Arguing*. London: Sage.

Antaki, C. (2006). Producing a 'cognition'. *Discourse Studies*, 8, 9–16.

Arendt, H. (1959). *The Human Condition*. New York: Anchor.

Arendt, H. (1963). *Eichmann in Jerusalem*. New York: Viking Press.

Aristotle (1987). *De Anima*. Harmondsworth: Penguin.

Ash, M.G. (1998). *Gestalt Psychology in German Culture, 1890–1967*. Cambridge: Cambridge University Press.

Ashcraft, R. (1990). John Locke's library: portrait of an intellectual. In J.S. Yolton (ed.), *A Locke Miscellany*. Bristol: Thoemmes.

Ashmore, M. (1989). *The Reflexive Thesis*. Chicago: Chicago University Press.

Ashmore, M., Myers, G. and Potter, J. (1995). Discourse, rhetoric and reflexivity: seven days in the library. In S. Jasanoff et al. (eds), *Handbook of Science, Technology and Society*. London: Sage.

Austin, J.L. (1962). *How to Do Things with Words*. Oxford: Clarendon Press.

Austin, J.L. (1964). *Sense and Sensibilia*. Oxford: Oxford University Press.

Austin, J.L. (1979). *Philosophical Papers*. Oxford: Clarendon Press.

Axtell, J.L. (1991). Locke, Newton and the 'elements of natural philosophy'. In R. Ashcroft (ed.), *John Locke: Critical Assessments*, vol. IV. London: Routledge.

Ayers, M. (1991). Locke's logical atomism. In R. Ashcroft (ed.), *John Locke: Critical Assessments*, vol. IV. London: Routledge.

Ayers, M.R. (1994). The foundation of knowledge and the logic of substance: the structure of Locke's general philosophy. In G.A.J. Rogers (ed.), *Locke's Philosophy*. Oxford: Oxford University Press.

Bakhtin, M.M. (1981). *The Dialogic Imagination*. Austin: University of Texas Press.

Bakhtin, M.M. (1984). *Rabelais and His World*. Bloomington: Indiana University Press.

Bakhtin, M.M. (1986). *Speech Genres and Other Late Essays*. Austin: University of Texas Press.

Baldwin, J.M. (1897). *Social and Ethical Interpretations in Mental Development: A Study in Social Psychology*. London: Macmillan.

Baldwin, T. (1993). Introduction. In T. Baldwin (ed.), *G.E. Moore: Selected Writings*. London: Routledge.

Bartlett, F. (1932). *Remembering*. Cambridge: Cambridge University Press.

Beattie, J. (1790). *Elements of Moral Science*. Edinburgh: T. Cadell and W. Creech.

Beattie, J. (1804). *An Essay into the Nature and Immutability of Truth*. Edinburgh: Denham and Dick.

Beer, E.S. de (ed.) (1976). *The Correspondence of John Locke*, vol. II. Oxford: Clarendon Press.

Beer, E.S. de (ed.) (1978). *The Correspondence of John Locke*, vol. III. Oxford: Clarendon Press.

Beer, E.S. de (ed.) (1979). *The Correspondence of John Locke*, vol. V. Oxford: Clarendon Press.

Bellegarde, Abbé de (1707). *Reflexions on Ridicule and the Means to Avoid It*. London: Thomas Newborough.

Benjamin, L.T. (2007). *A Brief History of Modern Psychology*. Oxford: Blackwell.

Benjamin, W. (1973). *Illuminations*. London: Fontana.

Bennett, M.R. and Hacker, P.M.S. (2003). *Philosophical Foundations of Neuroscience*. Oxford: Blackwell.

Bergson, H. (1911). *Laughter*. London: Macmillan and Co.

Berkeley, G. (1710). *A Treatise Concerning the Principles of Human Knowledge: Part I*. Dublin: James Pepyat.

Bernier F. (1784). *Abregé de la philosophie de Gassendi*. Lyon: Anisson, Posuel and Rigaud.

Billig, M. (1995). *Banal Nationalism*. London: Sage.

Billig, M. (1996). *Arguing and Thinking*, second edition. Cambridge: Cambridge University Press.

Billig, M. (2003). Critical discourse analysis and the rhetoric of critique. In G. Weiss and R. Wodak (eds), *Critical Discourse Analysis*. London: Palgrave.

Billig, M. (2005). *Laughter and Ridicule: Towards a Social Critique of Humour*. London: Sage.

Billig, M. (2006). A psychoanalytic discursive psychology: from consciousness to unconsciousness. *Discourse Studies*, 8, 17–24.

Blair, H. (1793). *Lectures on Rhetoric and Belles Letters*. Philadelphia: Mathew Carey.

Boring, E.G. (1929). *History of Experimental Psychology*. New York: Appleton-Century.

Boring, E.G. (1950). *History of Experimental Psychology*, revised edition. New York: Appleton-Century-Crofts.

Boswell, J. (1906). *The Life of Samuel Johnson*. London: J.M. Dent.

Bouillier, F. (1846). Introduction. In F. Bouillier (ed.), *Oeuvres Philosophiques de Père Buffier*. Paris: Adolphe Delahays.

Boyer, E. (2003). Schliemacher, Shaftesbury and the German Enlightenment. *Harvard Theological Review*, 96, 181–205.

Boyle, R. (1686). *A Free Inquiry into the Vulgarly Received Notion of Nature*. London: John Taylor.

Brandist, C. (1997). Bakhtin, Cassirer and symbolic forms. *Radical Philosophy*, 85, 7–20.

Branquinho, J. (2001). Introduction. In J. Branquinho (ed.), *The Foundations of Cognitive Science*. Oxford: Oxford University Press.

Brennan, T. (2005). *The Stoic Life*. Oxford: Clarendon Press.

Broad, C.D. (1959). G.E. Moore. In G.E. Moore, *Philosophical Papers*. London: George Allen and Unwin.

Broadie, A. (2004). Reid in context. In T. Cuneo and R. van Woudenberg (eds), *The Cambridge Companion to Thomas Reid*. Cambridge: Cambridge University Press.

Brown, J. (1752). *Essays on the Characteristics*. London: C. Davis.

Brown, P. and Levinson, S.C. (1989). *Politeness*. Cambridge: Cambridge University Press.

Bruner, J. (1987). Prologue to the English edition. In R.W. Rieber and A.S. Carlton (eds), *The Collected Works of L.S. Vygotsky*. New York: Plenum Press.

Buchan, J. (2004). *Crowded with Genius: The Scottish Enlightenment – Edinburgh's Moment of the Mind*. New York: HarperCollins.

Buffier, C. (1717/1846). Traité des premières vérités. In F. Bouillier (ed.), *Oeuvres Philosophiques de Père Buffier*. Paris: Adolphe Delahays.

Buffier, C. (1724/1846). Éléments de métaphysique. In F. Bouillier (ed.), *Oeuvres Philosophiques de Père Buffier*. Paris: Adolphe Delahays.

Buffier, C. (1780). *First Truths and the Origins of our Opinions Explained*. London: J. Johnson.

Burke, P. (1993). *The Art of Conversation*. Ithaca: Cornell University Press.

Burman, E. (1996). Continuities and discontinuities in interpretive and textual approaches to developmental psychology. *Human Development*, 39, 330–345.

Campbell, G. (1776/1856). *The Philosophy of Rhetoric*. New York: Harper and Brothers.

Carey, D. (2000). Hutcheson's moral sense and the problem of innateness. *Journal of the History of Philosophy*, 38, 103–111.

Carey, D. (2006). *Locke, Shaftesbury, and Hutcheson: Contesting Diversity in the Enlightenment and Beyond*. Cambridge: Cambridge University Press.

Carey, S. (2001). The representation of number in natural language syntax and in the evolution of thought: a case study of the evolution and development of representation resources. In J. Branquinho (ed.), *The Foundations of Cognitive Science*. Oxford: Oxford University Press.

Cassirer, E. (1951). *The Philosophy of the Enlightenment*. Princeton, NJ: Princeton University Press.

Cassirer, E. (1953). *The Platonic Renaissance in England*. London: Nelson.

Charleton, W. (1654). *Physiologia Epicuro-Gassendo-Charltonia*. London: Thomas Heath.

Charleton, W. (1670). *Epicurus's Morals*. London: Simon Miller.

Chomsky, N. (1957). *Syntactic Structures*. The Hague: Mouton.

Chomsky, N. (1964). *Aspects of the Theory of Syntax*. Cambridge, Mass: MIT Press.

Chomsky, N. (1966). *Cartesian Linguistics*. New York: Harper and Row.

Chomsky, N. (2000). *New Horizons in the Study of Language and Mind*. Cambridge: Cambridge University Press.

Chouliaraki, L. and Fairclough, N. (1999). *Discourse in Late Modernity*. Edinburgh: Edinburgh University Press.

Churchland, P.A. (2001). Towards a neurobiology of the moral virtues. In J. Branquinho (ed.), *The Foundations of Cognitive Science*. Oxford: Oxford University Press.

Clark, K. and Holquist, M. (1984). *Mikhail Bakhtin*. Cambridge, Mass: Harvard University Press.

Clifford, J. and Marcus, G.E. (eds) (1986). *Writing Culture*. Berkeley: University of California Press.

Coady, C.A.J. (1989). Reid on testimony. In M. Dalgarno and E. Matthews (eds), *The Philosophy of Thomas Reid*. Dordrecht: Kluwer.

Coady, C.A.J. (2004). Reid and the social operations of the mind. In T. Cuneo and R. van Woudenberg (eds), *The Cambridge Companion to Thomas Reid*. Cambridge: Cambridge University Press.

Coates, R. (1999). *Christianity in Bakhtin: God and the Exiled Author*. Cambridge: Cambridge University Press.

Cohen-Cole, J. (2005). The reflexivity of cognitive science: the scientist as model of human nature. *History of Human Sciences*, 18(4), 107–139.

Coleridge, S.T. (1990). John Locke. In J.S. Yolton (ed.), *A Locke Miscellany*. Bristol: Thoemmes.

Collier, M. (2005). Hume and cognitive science: the current status of the controversy over abstract ideas. *Phenomenology and the Cognitive Sciences*, 4, 197–207.

Condillac, E. (1746). *Essai sur l'origine des connoissances humaines*. Amsterdam.

Condillac, E. (1754/1798). *Traité des Sensations*. Paris: Batilliot Frères.

Condillac, E. (1756). *An Essay on the Origin of Human Knowledge, Being a Supplement to Mr Locke's Essay on Human Understanding*, translated by T. Nugent. London: J. Nourse.

Condor, S. (2003). 'The least doubtful promise for the future?' The short history of Tajfel's 'sociopsychological' approach to laboratory experimentation. In J. Lázló and W. Wagner (eds), *Theories and Controversies in Societal Psychology*. Budapest: New Mandate.

Cousin, V. (1834). *Fragments philosophiques*, vol. 1 (third edition). Paris: Ladrange.

Cousin, V. (1834/1871). *Elements of Psychology*. New York: Ivison, Blakeman, Taylor and Co.

Cousin, V. (1864). *Philosophie Écossaise*. Paris: Michel Lévy.

Cranston, M. (1985). *John Locke: A biography*. Oxford: Oxford University Press.

Cudworth, R. (1678). *The True System of the Universe*. London: Richard Royston.

Cudworth, R. (1731/1996). *A Treatise Concerning Eternal and Immutable Morality*. Cambridge: Cambridge University Press.

Cuneo, T. and van Woudenberg, R. (2004). Introduction. In T. Cuneo and R. van Woudenberg (eds), *The Cambridge Companion to Thomas Reid*. Cambridge: Cambridge University Press.

Curzon, H. (1712). *The Universal Library, or Compleat Summary of Science*. London: T. Warner.

Daniels, N. (1989). *Thomas Reid's 'Inquiry': The Geometry of Visibles and the Case for Realism*. Stanford: Stanford University Press.

Danziger, K. (1990). *Constructing the Subject: Historical Origins of Psychological Research*. Cambridge: Cambridge University Press.

Danziger, K. (1994). Does the history of psychology have a future? *Theory and Psychology*, 4, 467–484.

Danziger, K. (1997). *Naming the Mind: How Psychology Found Its Language*. London: Sage.

Danziger, K. (2001). Whither the golden oldies of the ESHHS: the historiography of psychological objects. Address given to 20th annual meeting of European Society for the History of the Human Sciences, Amsterdam.

Darwin, C. (1877). A biographical sketch of an infant. *Mind*, 2, 285–294.

de Barry, P. (2002). *Thomas Reid and Scepticism*. London: Routledge.

Denby, D. (2005). Herder: culture, anthropology and the enlightenment. *History of the Human Sciences*, 18, 55–76.

Dennett, D. (1991). *Consciousness Explained*. Harmondsworth: Penguin.

Dennett, D. (1995). *Darwin's Dangerous Idea*. Harmondsworth: Penguin.

Derrida, J. (1982). *Margins of Philosophy*. Chicago: University of Chicago Press.

Derrida, J. (2002). The animal that therefore I am (more to follow). *Critical Inquiry*, 28, 369–418.

Destutt de Tracy, A.L.C. (1803–1815). *Élémens d'idéologie*. Paris: Courcier.

Diderot, D. (1745/1876). Principes de philosophie morale. In *Oeuvres Complètes*, vol. 1. Paris: Garnier.

Diener, E. (1979). Deindividuation, self-awareness and disinhibition. *Journal of Personality and Social Psychology*, 37, 1160–1171.

Dixon, T. (2003). *From Passions to Emotions: The Creation of a Secular Psychological Category*. Cambridge: Cambridge University Press.

Dore, J. (1986). The emergence of language from dialogue. In A. Mandelker (ed.), *Bakhtin in Contexts*. Evanston: Northwestern University Press.

Downes, D.M. (2005). *Interactive Realism*. Montreal: McGill-Queen's University Press.

Draaisma, D. (2000). *Metaphors of Memory: A History of Ideas about the Mind*. Cambridge: Cambridge University Press.

Duckitt, J. (2003). Prejudice and intergroup hostility. In D.O. Sears, L. Huddy and R. Jervis (eds), *Oxford Handbook of Political Psychology*. Oxford: Oxford University Press.

Eagleton, T. (1990). *Ideology of the Aesthetic*. Oxford: Blackwell.

Edwards, D. (1997). *Discourse and Cognition*. London: Sage.

Edwards, D. (2006). Discourse, cognition and social practices: the rich surface of language and social interaction. *Discourse Studies*, 8, 41–50.

Edwards, D. and Potter, J. (1993). *Discursive Psychology*. London: Sage.

Emerson, C. (1996). The outer world and inner speech: Bakhtin, Vygotsky and the internalization of language. In H. Daniels (ed.), *An Introduction to Vygotsky*. London: Routledge.

Emerson, C. (2000). *The First Hundred Years of Mikhail Bakhtin*. Princeton: Princeton University Press.

Epictetus (1910). *The Moral Discourses*. London: J.M. Dent.

Fairclough, N. (1992). *Discourse and Social Change*. Cambridge: Polity.

Fairclough, N. (1995). *Critical Discourse Analysis*. London: Longman.

Farah, M.J. (2000). *The Cognitive Neuroscience of Vision*. Oxford: Blackwell.

Farah, M.J., Rabinowitz, C., Quinn, G.E. and Liu, G.T. (2000). Early commitment of neural substrates for face recognition. *Cognitive Neuropsychology*, 17, 117–123.

Farr, R.M. (1996). *The Roots of Modern Social Psychology*. Oxford: Blackwell.

Fisher, S. (2000). Atomism. In W. Applebaum (ed.), *The Scientific Revolution*. New York: Garland Science.

Fitch, W.T., Hauser, M.D. and Chomsky, N. (2005). The evolution of the language faculty: clarification and implications. *Cognition*, 97, 179–210.

Fodor, J.A. (2003). *Hume Variations*. Oxford: Clarendon Press.

Fodor, J.A. and Lepore, E. (2002). *The Compositionality Papers*. Oxford: Oxford University Press.

Forbes, W. (1824). *An Account of the Life and Writings of James Beattie, LL.D.* London: William Baynes.

Force, P. (2003). *Self-Interest before Adam Smith*. Cambridge: Cambridge University Press.

Fowler, T. (1882). *Shaftesbury and Hutcheson*. London: Sampson Low, Marston, Searle and Rivington.

Fox, D. and Prilleltensky, I. (eds) (1997). *Critical Psychology: An Introduction*. London: Sage.

Fraser, A.C. (1856). *Essays in Philosophy*. Edinburgh: W.P. Kennedy.

Fraser, A.C. (1898). *Thomas Reid*. Edinburgh: Oliphant Anderson and Ferrier.

Freedheim, D.K. (ed.) (2003). *Handbook of Psychology: Volume One, History of Psychology*. Hoboken, NJ: John Wiley.

Freud, S. (1921/1985). Group psychology and the analysis of the ego. In S. Freud, *Civilization, Society and Religion*, Penguin Freud Library, Vol. 12. Harmondsworth: Penguin.

Freud, S. and Breuer, J. (1895/1991). *Studies on Hysteria*. Harmondsworth: Penguin.

Fromm, E. (1971). *The Crisis of Psychoanalysis*. London: Jonathan Cape.

Fuchs, A.H. and Milar, K.S. (2003). Psychology as a science. In D.K. Freedheim (ed.), *Handbook of Psychology: Volume One, History of Psychology*. Hoboken, NJ: John Wiley.

Fuster, J. (2003). *Cortex and Mind*. Oxford: Oxford University Press.

Gallie, R.D. (1989). *Thomas Reid and 'The Way of Ideas'*. Dordrecht: Kluwer.

Gardiner, M. and Bell, M.M. (1998). Bakhtin and the human sciences: a brief introduction. In M.M. Bell and M. Gardiner (eds), *Bakhtin and the Human Sciences*. London: Sage.

Gauthier, I., Behrman, M. and Tarr, J. (1999). Can face recognition really be dissociated from object recognition? *Journal of Cognitive Neuroscience*, 11, 349–370.

Gellner, E. (1983). *Nations and Nationalism*. Oxford: Basil Blackwell.

Gergen, K.J. (1973). Social psychology as history. *Journal of Personality and Social Psychology*, 26, 309–320.

Gergen, K.J. (1985). The social constructionist movement in modern psychology. *American Psychologist*, 40, 266–275.

Gergen, K.J. (1992). Toward a postmodern psychology. In S. Kvale (ed.), *Psychology and Postmodernism*. London: Sage.

Gergen, K.J. (1994). *Toward Transformation in Social Knowledge*, second edition. London: Sage.

Gergen, K.J. (1997). Social psychology as social construction: the emerging vision. In C. McGarty and S.A. Haslam (eds), *The Message of Social Psychology*. Oxford: Blackwell.

Gergen, K.J. (1999). *An Invitation to Social Construction*. London: Sage.

Gergen, K.J. (2001a). *Social Construction in Context*. London: Sage.

Gergen, K.J. (2001b). Psychological science in a postmodern context. *American Psychologist*, 56, 803–813.

Gergen, K.J. and Graumann, C.F. (1996). Psychological discourse in historical context: an introduction. In C.F. Graumann and K.J. Gergen (eds), *Historical Dimensions of Psychological Discourse*. Cambridge: Cambridge University Press.

Giddens, A. (1991). *Modernity and Self-Identity*. Cambridge: Polity Press.

Gigerenzer, G. (1996). From tools to theories: discovery in cognitive psychology. In C.F. Graumann and K.J. Gergen (eds), *Historical Dimensions of Psychological Discourse*. Cambridge: Cambridge University Press.

Gilligan, C. (1982). *In a Different Voice*. Cambridge, Mass: Harvard University Press.

Glasersfeld, E. (1984). An introduction to radical constructivism. In P. Watzlawick (ed.), *The Invented Reality*. New York: Norton.

Goldie, M. (ed.) (1997). *Locke: Political Essays*. Cambridge: Cambridge University Press.

Goodale, M.A. (2003). *Sight Unseen: An Exploration of Conscious and Unconscious Vision*. Oxford: Oxford University Press.

Goodwin, J.C. (1999). *A History of Modern Psychology*. New Jersey: John Wiley.

Gough, B. and McFadden, M. (2001). *Critical Social Psychology: An Introduction*. London: Palgrave.

Grean, S. (1967). *Shaftesbury's Philosophy of Religion and Ethics*. Ohio: Ohio University Press.

Gribbin, J. (2006). *The Fellowship: The Story of a Revolution*. Harmondsworth: Penguin.

Grice, H.P. (1975). Logic and conversation. In P. Cole and J. Morgan (eds), *Syntax and Semantics*, vol. 3. New York: Academic Press.

Haakonssen, K. (1996). *Natural Law and Moral Philosophy: From Grotius to the Scottish Enlightenment*. Cambridge: Cambridge University Press.

Habermas, J. (1987). *The Theory of Communicative Action*. Oxford: Polity Press.

Habermas, J. (1989). *The Structural Transformation of the Public Sphere*. Cambridge, Mass: MIT Press.

Hall, M.B. (2002). *Henry Oldenberg: Shaping the Royal Society*. Oxford: Oxford University Press.

Harnish, R.M. (2001). *Minds, Brains, Computers: The Foundations of Cognitive Science*. Oxford: Blackwell.

Harré, R. (1979). *Social Being*. Oxford: Blackwell.

Harré, R. (2002). *Cognitive Science: A Philosophical Introduction*. London: Sage.

Harré, R. and Gillett, G. (1994). *The Discursive Mind.* London: Sage.

Harris, I. (1998). *The Mind of John Locke: A Study of Political Theory in its Intellectual Setting.* Cambridge: Cambridge University Press.

Harris, J. (1744). *Three Treatises.* London: J. Nourse and P. Vaillant.

Harris, R. (1997). *Landmarks in Linguistic Thought.* London: Routledge.

Harris, R. (2002). The rise of the language myth. In R. Harris (ed.), *The Language Myth in Western Culture.* Richmond: Curzon Press.

Harris, R. (2004). Integrationism, language, mind and world. *Language Sciences*, 26, 727–739.

Hartley, D. (1748/1834). *Observations on Man, His Frame, His Duty, His Expectations.* London: Thomas Tegg.

Hauser, M.D., Chomsky, N. and Fitch, W.T. (2002). The language faculty: what is it, who has it and how did it evolve? *Science*, 298, 1569–1579.

Hayward, W.G. and Tarr, M.J. (2005). Visual perception II: high level vision. In K. Lamberts and R.L. Goldstone (eds), *Handbook of Cognition.* London: Sage.

Hepburn, A. (2003). *An Introduction to Critical Social Psychology.* London: Sage.

Hergenhahn, B.R. (2001). *An Introduction to the History of Psychology.* Belmont, Calif: Wadsworth Thomson.

Herman, A. (2002). *The Scottish Enlightenment: The Scots' Invention of the Modern World.* London: Fourth Estate.

Hermans, H.J.M. and Dimaggio, G. (2007). Self, identity, and globalisation in times of uncertainty: a dialogical analysis. *Review of General Psychology*, 11, 31–61.

Hirschkop, K. (2001). Bakhtin in the sober light of day. In K. Hirschkop and D. Shepherd (eds), *Bakhtin and Cultural Theory.* Manchester: Manchester University Press.

Hobbes, T. (1650/1999). *Human Nature and De Corpore Politico.* Oxford: Oxford University Press.

Hobbes, T. (1651). *Leviathan.* London: Andrew Crooke.

Hobsbawm, E.J. (1992). *Nations and Nationalism since 1780.* Cambridge: Cambridge University Press.

Holquist, M. (2002). *Dialogism: Bakhtin and his World.* London: Routledge.

Holt, D.C. (1989). The defence of common sense in Reid and Moore. In M. Dalgarno and E. Matthews (eds), *The Philosophy of Thomas Reid.* Dordrecht: Kluwer.

Hume, D. (1740/1964). *A Treatise of Human Nature*, vol. 2. London: Dent.

Hutchby, I. and Wooffitt, R. (1998). *Conversation Analysis.* Cambridge: Polity Press.

Hutcheson, F. (1726). *Inquiry into the Original of Our Ideas of Beauty and Virtue.* London: J. Darby.

Hutcheson, F. (1728). *Essay on the Nature and Conduct of the Passions.* London.

Hutton, S. (1996). Lord Herbert of Cherbury and the Cambridge Platonists. In S. Brown (ed.), *British Philosophy and the Age of Enlightenment.* London: Routledge.

Hutton, S. (2002). The Cambridge Platonists. In S. Nadler (ed.), *A Companion to Early Modern Philosophy.* Oxford: Blackwell.

Ibáñez, T. and Iñinguez, L. (eds) (1997). *Critical Social Psychology.* London: Sage.

Jackendoff, R. and Pinker, S. (2005). The nature of the language faculty and its implications for evolution of language (reply to Fitch, Hauser and Chomsky), *Cognition*, 97, 211–225.

James, W. (1890). *The Principles of Psychology*. London: Macmillan.

Jansz, J. (2003). Psychology and society: an overview. In J. Jansz and P. van Drunen (eds), *A Social History of Psychology*. Oxford: Blackwell.

Jay, M. (1984). *Marxism and Totality*. Cambridge: Polity Press.

Johnson, M.H. (2000). Cortical mechanisms of cognitive development. In M. Gazzaniga (ed.) *Cognitive Neuroscience*. Oxford: Blackwell.

Jolly, N. (1999). *Locke: His Philosophical Thought*. Oxford: Oxford University Press.

Jones, D. and Elcock, J. (2001). *History and Theories of Psychology: A Critical Perspective*. London: Arnold.

Joy, L.S. (2000). *Gassendi the Atomist*. Cambridge: Cambridge University Press.

Kames, H.H. (1774). *Sketches of the History of Man*, vol. 1. Edinburgh.

Keane, B.P. and Pylyshyn, Z.W. (2005). Is motion extrapolation employed in multiple object tracking? Tracking as a low-level, non-predictive function. *Cognitive Science*, 52, 346–368.

Kellogg, R.T. (2003). *Cognitive Psychology*. Thousand Oaks: Sage.

Kempson, R. (2003). Pragmatics: language and communication. In M. Aronoff and J. Rees-Miller (eds), *The Handbook of Linguistics*. Oxford: Blackwell.

Kivy, P. (2003). *The Seventh Sense: Francis Hutcheson and Eighteenth Century British Aesthetics*. Oxford: Oxford University Press.

Klein, L.E. (1994). *Shaftesbury and the Culture of Politeness: Moral Discourse and Cultural Politics in Early Eighteenth Century England*. Cambridge: Cambridge University Press.

Klein, L.E. (1999). Introduction. In L.E. Klein (ed.), Shaftesbury, *Characteristics of Men, Manners, Opinions, Times*. Cambridge: Cambridge University Press.

Klein, L.E. (2005). Cooper, Anthony Ashley, third earl of Shaftesbury (1671–1713). In *Dictionary of National Biography*. Oxford: Oxford University Press.

Koffka, K. (1922). Perception: an introduction to *Gestalt-theorie*. *Psychological Bulletin*, 19, 531–585.

Koffka, K. (1928). *The Growth of the Mind*. New York: Harcourt, Brace and Co.

Kohlberg, L. (1969). Stage and sequence: the cognitive-developmental approach to socialization. In D.A. Goslin (ed.), *Handbook of Socialization Theory and Research*. Chicago: Rand McNally.

Köhler, W. (1929). *Gestalt Psychology*. New York: Horace Liveright.

Kristic, K. (1964). Marko Marulic: the author of the term 'psychology'. *Acta Instituti Psychologici Universitatis Zagrabiensis*, 36, 7–13.

Kroll, R.W.F. (1991). The question of Locke's relation to Gassendi. In R. Ashcroft (ed.), *John Locke: Critical Assessments*, vol. IV. London: Routledge.

Kuehn, M. (1987). *Scottish Common Sense in Germany, 1768–1800*. Kingston and Montreal: McGill-Queen's University Press.

Kulick, D. (2006). Theory in furs: masochistic anthropology. *Contemporary Anthropology*, 47, 933–952.

Kvale, S. (1992a). Postmodern psychology: a contradiction in terms? In S. Kvale (ed.), *Psychology and Postmodernism*. London: Sage.

Kvale, S. (ed.) (1992b). *Psychology and Postmodernism*. London: Sage.

Laslett, P. (1990). John Locke as founder of the Board of Trade. In J.S. Yolton (ed.), *A Locke Miscellany*. Bristol: Thoemmes.

Latour, B. (1993). *We Have Never Been Modern*. London: Longman.

Le Bon, G. (1896). *The Crowd*. London: T. Fisher Unwin.

Leahey, T.H. (1987). *A History of Psychology*, second edition. Englewood Cliffs: Prentice-Hall.

Leahey, T.H. (2003). Cognition and learning. In D.K. Freedheim (ed.), *Handbook of Psychology: Volume One, History of Psychology*. Hoboken, NJ: John Wiley.

Lehrer, K. (1991). *Thomas Reid*. London: Routledge.

Locke, J. (1690). *A Letter Concerning Toleration*. London: Awnsham Churchill.

Locke, J. (1690/1768). *An Essay Concerning Human Understanding*. London: H. Woodfall *et al.*

Locke, J. (1690/1977). *Two Treatises of Government*. London: Dent.

Locke, J. (1697a). *Letter to the Bishop of Worcester*. London: A. & J. Churchill.

Locke, J. (1697b). *Reply to the Bishop of Worcester's Answer to His Letter*. London: A. & J. Churchill.

Locke, J. (1699). *Reply to the Right Reverend the Lord Bishop of Worcester's Answer to his Second Letter*. London: A. & J. Churchill.

Locke, J. (1721). *Some Thoughts Concerning Education*. London: A. Churchill.

Locke, J. (1990). P.H. Nidditch and G.A.J. Rogers (eds), *Drafts for the 'Essay Concerning Human Understanding' and Other Philosophical Writings*, Oxford: Clarendon Press.

Long, A.A. (1999). Stoic psychology. In K. Algra (ed.), *The Cambridge History of Hellenic Philosophy*. Cambridge: Cambridge University Press.

Long, A.A. (2002). *Epictetus: A Stoic and Socratic Guide to Life*. Oxford: Clarendon Press.

Long, A.A. and Sedley, D.N. (1987). *The Hellenistic Philosophers: Volume 1, Translations of the Principal Sources, with Philosophical Commentary*. Cambridge: Cambridge University Press.

Lyotard, J. (1984). *The Post-Modern Condition*. Minneapolis: University of Minnesota Press.

Mably, l'Abbé de (1765). *Observations sur l'histoire de la France*. Geneva: La Compagnie des Libraires.

Mably, l'Abbé de (1766). *De la législation ou principes des lois*. Amsterdam.

Mably, l'Abbé de (1767). *Entretiens de Phocion sur le rapport de la morale avec la politique*. Amsterdam.

Macintosh, J.J. (2005). Robert Boyle on Epicurean atheism and atomism. In M.J. Osler (ed.), *Atoms, Pneuma and Tranquility: Epicurean and Stoic Themes in European Thought*. Cambridge: Cambridge University Press.

Macnamara, J. (1999). *Through the Rearview Mirror: Historical Reflections on Psychology*. Cambridge, Mass: MIT Press.

Mandler, G. (1985). *Cognitive Psychology: An Essay in Cognitive Science*. Hillsdale: Lawrence Erlbaum.

Marcil-Lacoste, L. (1982). *Claude Buffier and Thomas Reid: Two Common Sense Philosophers*. Kingston: McGill-Queen's University Press.

Marcus Aurelius (1701). *The Emperor Marcus Antoninus, His Conversation with Himself* (trans. J. Collier). London: Richard Sare.

Marcus Aurelius (1742). *The Meditations of the Emperor Marcus Aurelius Antoninus: With Notes and an Account of His Life*. Glasgow: Robert Foulis.

Marcuse, H. (1968). *One Dimensional Man.* London: Sphere Books.

Markova, I. (2003). *Dialogicality and Social Representations: The Dynamics of Mind.* Cambridge: Cambridge University Press.

Martin, R. and Barresi, J. (2000). *Naturalization of the Soul.* London: Routledge.

Marx, K. (1844/1973). *Economic and Philosophic Manuscripts.* London: Lawrence and Wishart.

Marx, K. and Engels, F. (1846/1970). *The German Ideology.* London: Lawrence and Wishart.

Masham, D. Cudworth (1990). The life and character of Mr John Locke. In J.S. Yolton (ed.), *A Locke Miscellany.* Bristol: Thoemmes.

Masham, D. Cudworth (1705). *Occasional Thoughts in Reference to a Vertuous or Christian Life.* London: J. Churchill.

McCosh, J. (1875). *Scottish Philosophy: Biographical, Expository, Critical.* London: Macmillan.

McGuire, J.E. and Tamny, M. (2003). *Certain Philosophical Questions: Newton's Trinity Notebook.* Cambridge: Cambridge University Press.

McNaughton, D. (1996). British moralists of the eighteenth century: Shaftesbury, Butler and Price. In S. Brown (ed.), *British Philosophy and the Age of Enlightenment.* London: Routledge.

Michaud, Y. (1989). Reid's attack on the theory of ideas: from a reconsideration of Reid's argument to a reassessment of the theory of ideas. In M. Dalgarno and E. Matthews (eds), *The Philosophy of Thomas Reid.* Dordrecht: Kluwer.

Middleton, D. and Brown, S.D. (2005). *The Social Psychology of Experience.* London: Sage.

Milgram, S. (1974). *Obedience to Authority.* London: Methuen.

Mill, J.S. (1838/1962). Bentham. In M. Warnock (ed.), *Utilitarianism: John Stuart Mill.* London: Fontana.

Milton, J.R. (1994). Locke's life and times. In V. Chappell (ed.), *Cambridge Companion to Locke.* Cambridge: Cambridge University Press.

Milton, J.R. (2000). Locke and Gassendi: a reappraisal. In M.A. Stewart (ed.), *English Philosophy in the Age of Locke.* Oxford: Oxford University Press.

Moore, G.E. (1903/1993). The refutation of idealism. In T. Baldwin (ed.), *G.E. Moore: Selected Writings.* London: Routledge.

Moore, G.E. (1905–6/1922). The nature and reality of objects of perception. In G.E. Moore (ed.), *Philosophical Studies.* London: Routledge and Kegan Paul.

Moore, G.E. (1959). *Philosophical Papers.* London: George Allen and Unwin.

Morawski, J. (2005). Reflexivity and the psychologist. *History of the Human Sciences,* 18, 77–105.

Morson, G.S. and Emerson, C. (1989). Introduction. In G.S. Morson and C. Emerson (eds), *Rethinking Bakhtin.* Evanston: Northwestern University Press.

Moscovici, S. (1985). *The Age of the Crowd.* Cambridge: Cambridge University Press.

Mulkay, M. (1991). *Sociology of Science.* Milton Keynes: Open University Press.

Murray, D.J. (1995). *Gestalt Psychology and the Cognitive Revolution.* New York: Harvester/Wheatsheaf.

Neisser, U. (1967). *Cognitive Psychology.* New York: Appleton-Century-Crofts.

Neisser, U. (2002). Wolfgang Köhler, 1887–1967. In *Biographical Memoirs, National Academy of the Sciences*, Vol. 81. Washington, DC: National Academy Press.

Nelson, A.A. (2000). The development and neural basis for face recognition. *Infant and Child Development*, 10, 3–18.

Osler, M.J. (1994). *Divine Will and the Mechanical Philosophy: Gassendi and Descartes on Contingency and Necessity in the Created World*. Cambridge: Cambridge University Press.

Osler, M.J. (2000). Epicureanism. In W. Applebaum (ed.), *The Scientific Revolution*. New York: Garland Science.

Osler, M.J. (2002). Pierre Gassendi. In S. Nadler (ed.), *A Companion to Early Modern Philosophy*. Oxford: Blackwell.

Osler, W. (1990). John Locke as a physician. In J.S. Yolton (ed.), *A Locke Miscellany*. Bristol: Thoemmes.

Oswald, J. (1766). *An Appeal to Common Sense in Behalf of Religion*. Edinburgh: Kincaid and Bell.

Parker, I. (1999). Critical psychology: critical links. *Annual Review of Critical Psychology*, 1, 3–18.

Parker, I. (2002). *Critical Discursive Psychology*. London: Palgrave Macmillan.

Pettersson, B. (2004). Exploring the common ground: *sensus communis*, humour and the interpretation of comic poetry. *Journal of Literary Semantics*, 33, 155–167.

Piaget, J. (1959). *The Language and Thought of the Child*. London: Routledge.

Piaget, J. (1968). *The Moral Judgement of the Child*. London: Routledge.

Pinch, T. and Pinch, T. (1988). Reservations about reflexivity and new literary forms: or why let the devil have all the good tunes. In S. Woolgar (ed.), *Knowledge and Reflexivity*. Chicago: Chicago University Press.

Pinker, S. (1994). *The Language Instinct*. Harmondsworth: Penguin.

Pinker, S. (1997). *How the Mind Works*. Harmondsworth: Penguin.

Plunkett, K., McCleod, P. and Rolls, E.T. (1998). *Introduction to Connectionist Modeling of Cognitive Processes*. Oxford: Oxford University Press.

Poole, B. (2001). From phenomenology to dialogue: Max Scheler's phenomenological tradition and Mikhail Bakhtin's development from 'Toward a philosophy of the act' to his study of Dostoevsky. In K. Hirschkop and D. Shepherd (eds), *Bakhtin and Cultural Theory*, second edition. Manchester: Manchester University Press.

Poole, B. (2002). Bakhtin and Cassirer: the philosophical origins of Bakhtin's carnival messianism. In M.E. Gardiner (ed.), *Mikhail Bakhtin*, vol. one. London: Sage.

Pope, A. (2006). *Major Works*. Oxford: Oxford University Press.

Potter, J. (2001). Wittgenstein and Austin. In M. Wetherell, S. Taylor and S.J. Yates (eds), *Discourse Theory and Practice*. London: Sage.

Potter, J. (2006). Cognition and conversation. *Discourse Studies*, 8, 131–140.

Potter, J. and Wetherell, M. (1987). *Discourse and Social Psychology*. London: Sage.

Preyer, W. (1889). *The Development of the Intellect*. New York: D. Appleton and Company.

Prince, M. (1996). *Philosophical Dialogue in the British Enlightenment: Theology, Aesthetics and the Novel*. Cambridge: Cambridge University Press.

Prince, M. (2004). Editing Shaftesbury's *Characteristicks*. *Essays in Criticism*, 54, 38–59.

Pylyshyn, Z.W. (2001). Connecting vision with the world: tracking the visual link. In J. Branquinho (ed.), *The Foundations of Cognitive Science*. Oxford: Oxford University Press.

Pylyshyn, Z.W. (2004). *Seeing and Visualising*. Cambridge, Mass: MIT Press.

Rand, B. (ed.) (1900). *The Life, Unpublished Letters and Philosophical Regimen of Anthony, Earl of Shaftesbury*. London: Swan Sonnenschein.

Redekop, B.W. (2004). Reid's influence in Britain, Germany, France, and America. In T. Cuneo and R. van Woudenberg (eds), *The Cambridge Companion to Thomas Reid*. Cambridge: Cambridge University Press.

Reid, T. (1769). *An Inquiry into the Human Mind on the Principles of Common Sense*. London: T. Cadell.

Reid, T. (1774/1822). A brief account of Aristotle's logic with remarks. In *The Works of Thomas Reid, volume 1*. New York: Duyckinck, Collins and Hannay, and R. and W.A. Bartow.

Reid, T. (1785/1854). *Essays on the Intellectual Powers of Mind*. London and Glasgow: Richard Griffin.

Reid, T. (1788/1820). *Essays on the Active Powers of Mind*. Edinburgh: Ogle, Allardice and Thomson.

Reid, T. (1793). *Essays on the Intellectual and Active Powers of Man*. Philadelphia: William Young.

Richards, G. (1992). *Mental Machinery, the Orignis and Consequences of Psychological Ideas*. London: Athlone.

Richards, G. (2002a). *Putting Psychology in its Place: A Critical Historical Overview*. London: Routledge.

Richards, G. (2002b). The psychology of psychology. *Theory and Psychology*, 12, 7–36.

Richards, G. (2004). Noah Porter's problem and the origin of American psychology. *Journal of the History of the Behavioural Sciences*, 40, 353–374.

Rivers, I. (1991). *Reason, Grace and Sentiment*, volume 1. Cambridge: Cambridge University Press.

Robinson, D.N. (1986). *An Intellectual History of Psychology*. Madison: University of Wisconsin Press.

Rogers, G.A.J. (1996). Science and British philosophy: Boyle and Newton. In S. Brown (ed.), *British Philosophy and the Age of the Enlightenment*. London: Routledge.

Rogoff, B. (1990). *Apprenticeship in Thinking*. New York: Cambridge University Press.

Rogoff, B. and Lave, J. (eds)(1999). *Everyday Cognition*. Cambridge, Mass: Harvard University Press.

Rosch, E. (2000). Reclaiming categories. In R. Núñez and W.J. Freeman (eds), *Reclaiming Cognition*. Thorverton: Imprint Academic.

Rose, N. (1985). *The Psychological Complex: Psychology, Politics and Society in England, 1869–1939*. London: Routledge and Kegan Paul.

Rose, N. (1996). Power and subjectivity: critical history and subjectivity. In C.F. Graumann and K.J. Gergen (eds), *Historical Dimensions of Psychological Discourse*. Cambridge: Cambridge University Press.

Russell, B. (1927/1999). *An Outline of Philosophy*. London: Routledge.

Ryle, G. (1963). *The Concept of Mind*. Harmondsworth: Penguin.

Sacks, H. (1995). *Lectures on Conversation*. Oxford: Blackwell.

Sacks, M. (2000). *Objectivity and Insight*. Oxford: Oxford University Press.

Sampson, E.E. (1977). Psychology and the American ideal. *Journal of Personality and Social Psychology*, 35, 767–782.

Sampson, E.E. (1981). Cognitive psychology as ideology. *American Psychology*, 36, 730–743.

Sampson, E.E. (1993). *Celebrating the Other*. New York: Harvester Wheatsheaf.

Sampson, E.E. (2000). Of rainbows and differences. In T. Sloan (ed.), *Critical Psychology: Voices for Change*. London: Macmillan.

Santayana, G. (1933). *Some Turns of Thought in Modern Philosophy*. Cambridge: Cambridge University Press.

Sarasohn, L.T. (1996). *Gassendi's Ethics: Freedom in a Mechanist Universe*. Ithaca, NY: Cornell University.

Sayers, J. (1994). *Mothers of Psychoanalysis*. New York: W.W. Norton.

Schaeffer, J.D. (1990). *Sensus Communis: Vico, Rhetoric and the Limits of Relativism*. Durham, NC: Duke University Press.

Schegloff, E.A. (1985). On some questions and ambiguities in conversation. In J.M. Atkinson and J. Heritage (eds), *Structures of Social Action*. Cambridge: Cambridge University Press.

Schegloff, E.A. (1996). Confirming allusions: toward an empirical account of action. *American Journal of Sociology*, 102, 161–216.

Scholl, B.J. and Leslie, A.M. (1999). Explaining the infant's object concept: beyond the perception/cognition dichotomy. In E. Lepore and Z. Pylyshyn (eds), *What Is Cognitive Science?* Oxford: Blackwell.

Schumann, K. and Smith, B. (1990). Elements of speech act theory in the work of Thomas Reid. *History of Philosophy Quarterly*, 7, 47–66.

Searle, J.R. (1969). *Speech Acts*. Cambridge: Cambridge University Press.

Seigel, J. (2005). *The Idea of the Self*. Cambridge: Cambridge University Press.

Selby, J.M. and Bradley, B.S. (2003). Infants in groups: a paradigm for the study of early social experience. *Human Development*, 46, 197–221.

Sennett, R. (1999). *The Corrosion of Character: Personal Consequence of Work in the new capitalism*. New York: W.W. Norton.

Shaftesbury, Anthony Ashley Cooper, Third Earl of 1698. Preface. In *Select Sermons of Dr Whichcot*. London: Awnsham and John Churchill.

Shaftesbury, Anthony Ashley Cooper, Third Earl of 1711/1999. In L.E. Klein (ed.), *Characteristics of Men, Manners, Opinions, Times*. Cambridge: Cambridge University Press.

Shaftesbury, Anthony Ashley Cooper, Third Earl of 1746. *The Letters of the Earl of Shaftesbury, Collected into One Volume*. No publisher given, but probably R. Foulis of Glasgow.

Shaftesbury, Anthony Ashley Cooper, Third Earl of 1900a. The Philosophical Regimen. In B. Rand (ed.), *The Life, Unpublished Letters and Philosophical Regimen of Anthony, Earl of Shaftesbury*. London: Swan Sonnenschein.

Shaftesbury, Anthony Ashley Cooper, Fourth Earl of 1900b. A sketch of the life of the Third Earl of Shaftesbury. In B. Rand (ed.), *The Life, Unpublished Letters and Philosophical Regimen of Anthony, Earl of Shaftesbury*. London: Swan Sonnenschein.

Sher, R.B. (1991). Professors of virtue: the social history of the Edinburgh moral philosophy chair in the eighteenth century. In M.A. Stewart (ed.), *Studies in the Philosophy of the Scottish Enlightenment*. Oxford: Clarendon Press.

Shinn, M.W. (1900). *The Biography of a Baby*. Boston: Houghton Mifflin.

Shotter, J. (1986). A sense of place: Vico and the social production of identities. *British Journal of Psychology*, 25, 199–211.

Shotter, J. (1991). Bakhtin and Billig: monological versus dialogical practices. *American Behavioural Scientist*, 36, 8–21.

Shotter, J. (1993a). *Conversational Realities*. London: Sage.

Shotter, J. (1993b). *Cultural Politics of Everyday Life*. Milton Keynes: Open University Press.

Shotter, J. (1993c). Harré, Vygotsky, Bakhtin, Vico, Wittgenstein: academic discourse and conversational realities. *Journal for the Theory of Social Behaviour*, 23, 459–482.

Shotter, J. and Billig, M. (1998). A Bakhtinian psychology: from out of the heads of individuals and into the dialogues between them. In M.M. Bell and M. Gardiner (eds), *Bakhtin and the Human Sciences*. London: Sage.

Sloan, T. (ed) (2000). *Critical Psychology: Voices for Change*. London: Macmillan.

Smith, A. (1759/1976). *The Theory of Moral Sentiments*. Indianapolis: Liberty Fund.

Smith, B. (1990). Towards a history of speech act theory. In A. Burkhardt (ed.), *Speech Acts, Meanings and Intentions: Critical Approaches to the Philosophy of John R. Searle*. New York: de Gruyter.

Speer, S. (2005). *Gender Talk: Feminism, Discourse and Conversation Analysis*. London: Routledge.

Spellman, W.M. (1997). *John Locke*. Basingstoke: Macmillan.

Spencer, H. (1864). *First Principles of a New System of Philosophy*. New York: D. Appleton.

Sperber, D. (2000). Introduction. In D. Sperber (ed.), *Metarepresentations: a Multidisciplinary Perspective*. Oxford: Oxford University Press.

Stanley, T. (1687/1743). *A History of Philosophy*. London: A. Millar.

Steinglass, M. (1988). Intellectual man of mystery: the battle over Mikhail Bakhtin. *Lingua Franca*, 8(3).

Stewart, D. (1822). The life and writings of Thomas Reid. In *The Works of Thomas Reid*, vol. 1. New York: Duyckinck, Collins and Hannah, and R. and W.A. Bartow.

Stewart, M.A. (1991a). The stoic legacy in the early Scottish Enlightenment. In M.J. Osler (ed.), *Atoms, Pneuma and Tranquility*. Cambridge: Cambridge University Press.

Stewart, M.A. (1991b). The Scottish Enlightenment. In S. Brown (ed.), *British Philosophy and the Age of Enlightenment*. London: Routledge.

Stillingfleet, E. (1697a). *A Discourse in Vindication of the Doctrine of the Trinity*. London: Henry Mortlock.

Stillingfleet, E. (1697b). *Answer to Mr Locke's Letter Concerning Some Passages Relating to his Essay of Humane Understanding*. London: Henry Mortlock.

Sully, J. (1895). *Studies of Childhood*. London: Longmans, Green and Co.

Swift, J. (1704/1909). Battle of the books. In *Essays and Belles Lettres*. London: Dent.

Swift, J. (1709/1909). Hints towards an essay on conversation. In *Essays and Belles Lettres*. London: Dent.

Szakolczai, A. (1998). *Max Weber and Michel Foucault*. London: Routledge.

Szakolczai, A. (2000a). *Reflexive Historical Sociology*. London: Routledge.

Szakolczai, A. (2000b). Norbert Elias and Franz Borkenau: intertwined life-worlds. *Theory, Culture and Society*, 17(2), 45–69.

Tajfel, H. (1972). Experiments in a vacuum. In J. Israel and H. Tajfel (eds), *The Context of Social Psychology*. London: Academic Press.

Tajfel, H. (1981). *Human Groups and Social Categories*. Cambridge: Cambridge University Press.

Te Molder, H. and Potter, J. (eds) (2005). *Conversation and Cognition*. Cambridge: Cambridge University Press.

Teo, T. (1998). Klaus Holzkamp and the rise and decline of German critical psychology. *History of Psychology*, 1, 235–253.

Teo, T. (2005). *The Critique of Psychology*. New York: Springer-Verlag.

Toland, J. (1696). *Christianity Not Mysterious*. London: Sam Buckley.

Tolman, C.W. (1994). *Psychology, Society and Subjectivity: An Introduction to German Critical Psychology*. London: Routledge.

Tolman, C.W. and Maiers, W. (eds) (1991). *Critical Psychology*. Cambridge: Cambridge University Press.

Toolen, M. (1998). A few words on telementation. In R. Harris and G. Wolf (eds), *An Integrational Linguistics*. Oxford: Elsevier.

Trevarthen, C. (1977). Descriptive analyses of infant communicative behaviour. In H.R. Schaffer (ed.), *Studies in Mother-Infant Interaction*. London: Academic Press.

Trevarthen, C., Aitken, K., Papoudi, D. and Robarts, J. (1996). *Children with Autism*. London: Jessica Kingsley.

Tuffin, K. (2005). *Understanding Critical Social Psychology*. London: Sage.

Turnbull, J. (1740/2005). *The Principles of Moral and Christian Philosophy*, vol. 1. Indianapolis: Liberty Fund.

Turnbull, J. (1742/2003). *Observations on Liberal Education in All Its Branches*. Indianapolis: Liberty Fund.

Ussher, J. (2000). Critical psychology in the mainstream: a struggle for survival. In T. Sloan (ed.), *Critical Psychology: Voices for Change*. London: Macmillan.

van Dijk, T.A. (1993). Principles of critical discourse analysis. *Discourse & Society*, 4, 249–283.

van Ginneken, J. (1992). *Crowds, Psychology and Politics, 1871–1899*. Cambridge: Cambridge University Press.

Vico, G. (1975). *The Autobiography of Giambattista Vico*. Ithaca: Cornell University Press.

Voitle, R. (1984). *The Third Earl of Shaftesbury*. Baton Rouge: Louisiana State University Press.

Volosinov, V.N. (1973). *Marxism and the Philosophy of Language*. Cambridge, Mass: Harvard University Press.

Voltaire. (1756/2006). Préface: poème sur le désastre de Lisbonne. In Voltaire, *Pièces en Vers, Oeuvres Complètes*. Naintre: L'Association 'Voltaire Intégral'.

Vygotsky, L. (1987). *Thought and Language*. Cambridge, Mass: MIT Press.

Walker, W. (1994). *Locke, Literary Criticism and Philosophy*. Cambridge: Cambridge University Press.

Walkerdine, V. (2000). *Critical Psychology*. London: Lawrence and Wishart.
Weiss, E. and Wodak, K. (eds) (2003). *Critical Discourse Analysis*. Besingstoke: Palgrave.
Wertheimer, M. (1981). *A Brief History of Psychology*. Fort Worth: Harcourt Brace Jovanovich.
Wertsch, J.V. (1991). *Voices of the Mind*. London: Harvester/Wheatsheaf.
Whichcote, B. (1698). *Select Sermons*. London: Awnsham and John Churchill.
Wilkinson, S. (ed.) (1986). *Feminist Social Psychology*. Milton Keynes: Open University Press.
Wittgenstein, L. (1968). *Philosophical Investigations*. Oxford: Basil Blackwell.
Wittgenstein, L. (1975). *On Certainty*. Oxford: Basil Blackwell.
Wittgenstein, L. (1981). *Zettel*. Oxford: Basil Blackwell.
Wittgenstein, L. (1992). *Culture and Value*. Oxford: Blackwell.
Wittgenstein, L. (1993). *Philosophical Occasions*. Indianapolis: Hackett Publishing.
Wolin, S. (2003). *Toqueville Between Two Worlds*. Princeton: Princeton University Press.
Wollaston, W. (1738). *The Religion of Nature Delineated*. London: John and Paul Knapton.
Wolterstorff, N. (2001). *Thomas Reid and the Story of Epistemology*. Cambridge: Cambridge University Press.
Wolterstorff, N. (2004). Reid on common sense. In T. Cuneo and R. van Woudenberg (eds), *The Cambridge Companion to Thomas Reid*. Cambridge: Cambridge University Press.
Wood, P. (1991). Science and the pursuit of virtue in the Aberdeen enlightenment. In M.A. Stewart (ed.), *Studies in the Philosophy of the Scottish Enlightenment*. Oxford: Clarendon Press.
Wood, P. (2004). Thomas Reid (1710–1796). In *Oxford Dictionary of National Biography*. Oxford: Oxford University Press.
Wooffitt, R. (2005). *Conversation Analysis and Discourse Analysis*. London: Sage.
Woolhouse, R. (1994). Locke's theory of knowledge. In V. Chappell (ed.), *Cambridge Companion to Locke*. Cambridge: Cambridge University Press.
Wundt, W. (1907). *Outlines of Psychology*. London: Williams and Norgate.
Xu, F, Carey, S. and Quint, N. (2004). The emergence of kind-based object individuation in infancy. *Cognitive Psychology*, 49, 155–190.
Yaffe, G. (2002). Earl of Shaftesbury. In S. Nadler (ed.), *A Companion to Early Modern Philosophy*. Oxford: Blackwell.
Yolton, J.W. (1985). *Locke: An Introduction*. Oxford: Basil Blackwell.
Young, R.M. (1990). Herbert Spencer and inevitable progress. In G. Marsden (ed.), *Victorian Values*. London: Longman.
Zappen, J.P. (2000). Mikhail Bakhtin (1895–1975). In M.G. Moran and M. Ballif (eds), *Twentieth Century Rhetoric and Rhetoricians*. Westport: Greenwood Press.
Zimbardo, P. (1969). The human choice: individuation, reason and order versus deindividuation, impulse and chaos. *Nebraska Symposium on Motivation*, 17, 237–307.

Name Index

Aarsleff, H., 42
Addison, Joseph, 145, 146
Adorno, T.W., 136
Altemeyer, B., 136
Altmann, A., 143
Anderson, B., 25, 108
Anne II, Queen, 34, 85
Antaki, C., 22, 178
Arendt, H., 12, 13, 129
Aristotle, 32, 63, 64, 128, 162, 176
Arnold, Thomas, 118
Ash, M.G., 114
Ashcraft, R., 70
Ashmore, M., 147
Austin, J.L., 22, 39, 151, 161, 163,
    164, 176, 177, 179, 180, 182
Axtell, J.L., 53
Ayers, M., 65, 67

Bakhtin, M.M., 4, 5, 22, 123, 127, 131,
    132, 133, 135, 136, 138, 139, 140,
    145, 147–151, 180, 187, 188
Baldwin, J.M., 40
Baldwin, T., 180, 181
Barresi, J., 117
Bartlett, F., 116
Beattie, James, 152, 155, 158, 164,
    168, 169
Beer, E.S. de, 53, 59, 87, 89, 189
Bell, M.M., 123
Bellegarde, Abbé de, 127, 128
Benjamin, L.T., 29
Benjamin, W., 190
Bennett, M.R., 29
Bentham, Jeremy, 111
Bergson, Henri, 144
Berkeley, Bishop George, 154, 155,
    162, 163, 180, 181, 188
Bernier François, 63, 66, 70, 71

Billig, M., 18, 22, 25, 76, 108, 138,
    144, 178
Blair, Hugh, 90, 156
Boring, E.G., 14
Boswell, James, 154
Bouillier, F., 169
Boyer, E., 108
Boyle, Robert, 7, 52, 53, 65, 67, 70,
    71, 88
Bradley, B.S., 107
Brandist, C., 148
Branquinho, J., 39
Brennan, T., 115
Breuer, J., 70
Broad, C.D., 182
Broadie, A., 152, 171
Brown, John, 76, 111
Brown, P., 178
Brown, S.D., 22
Bruner, J., 140
Buchan, J., 153
Buffier, Father Claude, 167–172,
    180–183, 188
Burke, P., 127
Burman, E., 19
Butler, Joseph, 171
Butler, Judith, 23

Campbell, George, 152, 169
Carey, D., 157, 158
Carey, S., 48
Carter, Elizabeth, 8
Cassirer, E., 56, 83, 108, 148, 149,
    151, 180, 188
Charles II, King, 33, 34, 66
Charleton, Walter, 66, 67, 70, 100
Chomsky, N., 47, 48, 57
Chouliaraki, L., 18
Churchland, P.A., 112

Subject Index